Praise for Hari Ziyad

"Hari Ziyad is one of those writers who transports you into the moments, the minutes, and the seconds of Black life in subtle and gentle ways that are rarely possible. Every word drips with a deep love and commitment to telling true and just stories about our nuanced Black queer lives. *Black Boy Out of Time* is so moving, so alive, so real. This book is a reclamation and celebration of Black childhood and coming-of-age in all its hidden beauty and pain. We need this memoir, and I'm so grateful Ziyad is here to write it."

—Jenn Jackson, Syracuse University professor and *Teen Vogue* columnist

"Hari Ziyad consistently creates work that centers the voices and lives of the most marginalized members in our society. Not only is their work brilliant and insightful, but they challenge readers to examine themselves in a way very few writers can do. Alice Walker once wrote, 'Those who love us never leave us alone with our grief. At the moment they show us our wound, they reveal they have the medicine.' Ziyad's words cut deep, but they also provide healing."

—Shanita Hubbard, author of *Miseducation: A Woman's Guide to Hip-Hop*

"Hari Ziyad is committed to recovering the unrecoverable—the seconds, the minutes, the hours of things shed and discarded as if there were no value to be found in what we were, even though it leads us to what we are. Ziyad is surgical in this pursuit, attempting to be as careful but incisive as possible so that memory does more than remember: it testifies. Like all of their previous writings, *Black Boy Out of Time* is tribute to and examination of the necessary, the overlooked, the irreconcilable, and the witnessing the world would much rather not do. Ziyad is both lightning rod and lightning bolt."

—Robert Jones Jr., author of *The Prophets* and creator of Son of Baldwin

"Every generation has its defining writers, and Hari Ziyad is one of ours. Their writings force you to interrogate and challenge everything you thought you knew and to look at the wound you pretended wasn't there, but they never leave you without the cure to finally heal the pain."

—George M. Johnson, bestselling author of *All Boys Aren't Blue* and *We Are Not Broken*

"Black 'boys' who never come of age, who are always already someone or some*thing* else, are at the heart of Hari Ziyad's work. Ziyad writes with clarity, passion, care, and a deep love for all Black people—especially those of us who are constantly moving through and around gender. *Black Boy Out of Time* is a necessary read for Black queer boys and nonbinary people who can relate to finding themselves in a world designed to keep them lost."

—Da'Shaun Harrison, author of *Belly of the Beast: The Politics of Anti-Fatness as Anti-Blackness*

"I often think about cultural work as before Hari Ziyad and after Hari Ziyad. I don't know that there is another writer and cultural worker who has done more to make us intellectually, imaginatively, and bodily engage with the ways that traditional conceptions of gender, sexuality, Blackness, class, childhood, empire, and power necessarily mangle our relationships to each other. Hari's work goes far beyond bombastic pull quotes or titillating essay titles. In their hands, we see language being cared for, carved up, and absolutely dismantled. More than anything, Hari's art insists that we ask not simply the hard questions, but the unintelligible questions we've convinced ourselves have no answers. In their work, I understand that pointed questions rooted in a love of Black queer folk must be part of our liberation. They have changed the way people write, think, and love one another on and off the internet."

—Kiese Laymon, author of *Heavy*, *Long Division*, and *How to Slowly Kill Yourself and Others in America*

"Hari Ziyad's incisive writing is a rare mix of balladry, criticism, and reportage. They write of the times with clarity and courage. They appeal to truth and beauty. And in so doing offer us Black-loving art that is both shotgun and balm."

—Darnell L. Moore, author of *No Ashes in the Fire: Coming of Age Black and Free in America*

"Hari Ziyad's work is the cohesion of all their interests in the so-called marginalized into a single force that illuminates just how central to freedom communities that are abused and underestimated by this society truly are. If the margins are said to be the dwelling place of Ziyad's subjectivity, then they see their job as showing how the ones in the margins are also the ones who ensure Earth keeps spinning. Through their eyes, the disfigured, the queer, and the riotous are given life, a stage, a platform, and an embrace."

—Phillip B. Williams, author of *Thief in the Interior*, winner of the 2017 Whiting Award, Kate Tufts Award, and Lambda Literary Award

"Alongside James Baldwin and Audre Lorde, Darnell L. Moore and Danez Smith, Hari Ziyad's work fits in as an exciting new entry in the canon of queer Black American literature. At the same time, Ziyad's writing stands out as a stunningly original voice, and they tackle race and gender in ways writers of all races seem to find too hot to touch. Yet as challenging as Ziyad's ideas are, they are not inaccessible. Though Ziyad writes explicitly as a Black writer with Black readers in mind (and Black children at the heart of their work), white people are always asking me about their provocative stories. Ziyad stirs impassioned debates and strong reactions from both those people I know who have been following their work for years and those who are encountering it for the first time."

—Steven W. Thrasher, Northwestern University professor and author of *The Viral Underclass: How Racism, Ableism, and Capitalism Plague Humans on the Margins*

"Hari Ziyad is a new and important voice narrating for readers both the trauma experienced by Black people and their struggle for liberation. Throughout this text, Ziyad pulls back the curtain and interrogates how anti-Black racism manifests not only in the structures Black people encounter but also in our interactions between each other. Beyond providing texture to the hurt that, too often, animates Blackness, Ziyad's book details for the reader the possibilities and directions of Black freedom and healing today, and it explores how we must protect Black children from a perpetual cycle of trauma. Ziyad's book will add nuance and depth to current renderings of what it is to be Black and queer and what type of personal/political liberation is possible."

—Cathy J. Cohen, author of *The Boundaries of Blackness: AIDS and the Breakdown of Black Politics and Democracy Remixed: Black Youth and the Future of American Politics*

BLACK BOY OUT OF TIME

BLACK

BOY

OUT OF

TIME

a memoir

HARI ZIYAD

Little

a

Published by Little A, New York

www.apub.com

Amazon, the Amazon logo, and Little A are trademarks of Amazon.com,
Inc., or its affiliates.

ISBN-13: 9781542091329 (hardcover)
ISBN-10: 1542091322 (hardcover)

ISBN-13: 9781542091312 (paperback)
ISBN-10: 1542091314 (paperback)

Cover design by Faceout Studio, Lindy Martin

Cover illustration by David Cooper

All photos courtesy of the author.

Printed in the United States of America

First edition

To Mata: The kinds of lessons you left always swim in the blood. This is my promise to remember that next time . . .
And to Toshani, Malani, and Aja: Here is also my vow to ensure you never forget.

Contents

AUTHOR'S NOTE

Memories, always being shaded by subjectivity and biases both conscious and unconscious, are much more temperamental than I sometimes realize, but I have tried to re-create events, locations, and conversations with honesty. In some instances, I have purposefully changed identifying characteristics and the names of individuals and places in order to maintain privacy, or combined a minimum amount of characters and events for readability. My greatest fear in writing this memoir was that I might encroach upon a story that is someone else's to tell or distort narratives in a harmful way, and perhaps that is on some level unavoidable when you are exploring the deep intricacies of a life that is connected to so many others, but I hope you can sense the care for this story's subjects in these pages.

MISAFROPEDIA

I used to resent the fly who has the whole world to buzz around but stays circling my head anyway. I learned only recently that insects orbit our bodies because they are attracted to our decaying skin. They sense the parts of us that are dying, that we would never otherwise notice. Perhaps, in the single month they have to live, they are just trying to share in this terrifying experience together—just saying, "I am dying, too"—but all I ever heard was a nuisance.

My grandmother Mother Bhūmi lived with my family in Cleveland Heights, Ohio, for the last four years of her life. Whenever I came home during a break from college, she would single me out to go on walks with her, no matter who else was around or capable. I still don't know why she picked me. I used to believe she was simply testing my patience. Now I wonder if, like the fly, she was being drawn to the parts of me that I had begun to lose over the years: pieces of my childhood that reflected so much of the life she would soon lose, too.

When my grandmother converted to Vaishnavism, she was given the name Bhūmata, which is also what Hindus call the earth goddess. My mother was called Kṛṣṇanandini, though she raised me to call her Mata—the Sanskrit word for *mother*. They both found faith in Kṛṣṇa, the central god of their Hindu denomination, but Mother Bhūmi, who struggled with bipolar disorder my whole life, lost pieces of herself along the way. She died in 2014—"of natural causes," the medical report said, but that's a lie. When Black folks die, it is never so simple.[1] When Black folks die, it can always be traced to the myriad ways the state has perfected killing us over the last five centuries of colonization.

The other day, I had a nightmare in which Mata was chanting. Her long fingers lurched around furiously inside the cloth bag that she carries with her everywhere to hold her sacred chanting beads. The bag is stitched with a figure of Kṛṣṇa, who is described in Hindu scriptures as being so black he appears blue. The figure on the bag is rendered blue, as Kṛṣṇa usually is, but with no trace of the black he's supposed to be.

After Mata was initiated into Vaishnavism, she made a vow to repeat the mantra from which the sect gets its nickname—27,648 names of Kṛṣṇa or the names of his energies—on her beads daily. I regularly witnessed this process take up hours of her day, and so it wasn't the chanting that turned the dream into a nightmare. It was the way the words spilled off her tongue like blood, like a plea, like, *What more can I fucking lose to this world to stop it from trying to kill me?* It was that I didn't remember how to speak without my tongue being forced by the brutality of this world, so I could not form words to offer her protection from brutality. I just sat there, grasping for sentences to comfort my mother like they were the last few pockets of air in a slowly submerging room of a capsized ship.

I woke up to my sweat turning adhesive between the sheets and my skin, and Mata's repeated prayers seared into my mind: *Hare Kṛṣṇa Hare Kṛṣṇa, Kṛṣṇa Kṛṣṇa Hare Hare, Hare Rāma Hare Rāma, Rāma Rāma Hare Hare.*

For her sixty-sixth birthday, she had asked all ten of her children for the same thing she requested the previous year, and the year before that: "I just want you to commit to chanting one round a day." One round—1,728 names.

"Okay, but what do you *really* want?" I responded with an eye roll. She knew I wasn't the praying type.

"Money would be nice," she relented. And so I sent her money.

I still think that if Mata could wish for any one thing in the world, it would be that each of her children, who now range in age from twenty-one to fifty, take the religion of her mother more seriously. But only a few of us were chanting regularly before the disease.

She told me about her uterine cancer diagnosis just the day after that sixty-sixth birthday, at the beginning of 2018.

It was spreading.

"I don't want you to freak out," she said over the phone in that pliant voice of hers, as warm and sweet as a mug of hot chocolate. My heart skipped as she stirred in the words "rare and aggressive." I could tell that my mother had practiced this call numerous times, and I assumed she had delivered the news to my older siblings already. But as meticulously as she'd phrased it, underneath her carefulness I still heard, "I don't want you to be a child." The unuttered words mocked me through the filter I'd built policing myself, trying to get away from the little boy I had been conditioned to want to leave behind.

Almost immediately after I hung up, I finally began chanting like Mata had always asked. Praying, pleading, too. We all did—the ten of us who were brought into this world through her now deadly womb. Or her womb was always deadly, I suppose. It was always Black, and its likelihood of carrying a fatal cancer was always higher because of it—just one of many such racial health disparities that the United States has not eradicated, despite medical advances.[2] (Research by my sister Ganga, an epidemiologist who studies chronic stress across social groups, illustrates this.[3]) Other disparities—that Black women in this country are three times more likely to die from pregnancy-related issues than white women, for example—exist for the same reason, too.[4] And when researchers say people with underlying health conditions are the most vulnerable to public health crises, as doctors are forced to choose whom to let die once health-care systems become overwhelmed, they are talking about people with bodies like Mata's. They are talking about how her body is always more expendable in an anti-Black system that devalues her existence. They are talking about Mata's Black womb.

This same womb created us, her children, each a promise to be the steadfastly religious Hare Kṛṣṇa devotee into which she worked so hard to chisel us. Each a promise that would not be fulfilled until she was already dying, until it was too late.

Faithless promises. Broken promises.

All of us Black promises who still can't figure out how to pray to a god in a way that would have them save us from harm—both that others inflict and that we do. Promises who've twisted ourselves like pretzels to fit into a society that will never have space for us.

Who can really protect Black children in an anti-Black world?

I have filled this book with the unanticipated prayers discovered in this experiment of finding new faith, or at least one that was new to me. A faith that truly honors all that Black people lose in trying to persist through structural and systemic anti-Blackness, and returns us to those things in the spirit of Sankofa, that Akan symbol of reclamation that became a significant emblem to so many in the African diaspora as they sought out their roots. A faith for us Black, queer people who have survived the anti-Black, anti-queer, organized religions that have been thrust upon us in place of the healing spiritual practices of our ancestors. Faith that my mother might come out the other end of this horrible health crisis whole, when she was barely surviving before.

I imagine that a search for this type of faith is the same reason Mata ultimately turned to chanting Hare Kṛṣṇa. I would argue that she was seeking something she could believe in to save her and her family from the violence she faced as a poor Black woman in America, even though she'd never say this expressly. I believe she was searching for something to protect her from having to provide refuge for another seventeen-year-old shot six times in the back by the police just for being Black, like she and her mother were forced to do with my oldest uncle, Jasper. She was looking for something to protect her from having to call the life he lived afterward "making it," though he carried the last, inoperable bullet in his body until he died. She was seeking to reclaim an ancestral healing practice, too, trying to hold on to the puzzle pieces of our lineage that were chipped away by colonization and a state unwilling to meet my Black grandmother's bipolar disorder with care.

But Mata would probably deny the past is what she is searching for. "This material world," she always says, "is full of suffering."

There is nothing in it to salvage, not even among the jigsaw shards Mother Bhūmi, the riddle who gave birth to her, left behind. There is only chanting Kṛṣṇa's names.

When Mata and Mother Bhūmi renounced the "material world" in 1972 to join the Hare Kṛṣṇa religion, they were twenty and forty, respectively. Both of them had already waded through various denominations of Christianity and Islam, and had even spent some time in the Church of Jesus Christ of Latter day Saints. It made sense that Mata, as the oldest daughter of an often-single mother and as essentially a coparent to her six younger siblings, would journey together with Mother Bhūmi through faith. But this interdependent exploration probably also contributed to their fiercely volatile relationship—especially as Mother Bhūmi's disease progressed and went untreated.

When I was younger, I only ever saw Mother Bhūmi with her mental health at its worst. By the time I was born, her illness had spiraled in the absence of a proper diagnosis, and we weren't around her much. When I did see her, it was often because of some emergency. She lived many of these years without the health care, basic financial necessities, or supportive community to keep her illness from consuming her.

I don't remember much about Mother Bhūmi from that time other than the terrifying altercations between her and Mata. I once even witnessed my grandmother spit at Mata, an image still seared into my memory in vivid color. I saw so many such horrors that I would cry myself to sleep sometimes, wondering whether I ever fully knew my own grandmother's love, and whether the answer to that meant I never *could* fully know it. But then she designated me her walking partner.

I could usually anticipate Mother Bhūmi's request. Her bright eyes would shrink between bulbous cheekbones and unruly eyebrows as she pressed her lips together in a toothless smile, flaring her nostrils mischievously. "Would you walk your grandmother around the block?" she would ask in third person at random intervals during the weeks I was home for break. Her voice was an earthquake, still powerful despite its tremors. Her frame still felt towering to me, though it clocked in at no more than five feet three, even before accounting for the inches she lost with old age and the large, colorful head wraps she always wore.

By this point, she was managing her bipolar disorder and taking her medicine, and my parents cared for most of her fundamental necessities after moving her in. I had learned to cope with most of her idiosyncrasies. By "around the block," I knew she meant five or six streets over. It could take more than an hour strolling at the leisurely pace her weathered bones required.

One particular day I had something to do, some party to attend thrown by friends from high school with whom being young was the only thing I had in common, but I couldn't bring myself to say no to her. It might have been just a grandchild's instinct to avoid disappointing their grandmother, an instinct that grew as I began to understand just how much she had been disappointed already. Or maybe it was the part of me I thought I had lost, the part of me that caused her to keep buzzing around, asking me to accompany her on these strolls. Maybe that part of me knew this would be our last walk together in this life.

"Sure," I said, preparing myself for another overwhelming religious sermon sprinkled with conversations we'd already had multiple times but she'd forgotten having. On our walks, Mother Bhūmi would sometimes tell me about all the occasions on which she had been attacked by police as she fought for the rights of Black people as an activist in her community. She told me about being attacked by men who were supposed to love her. About being attacked as a Black Hindu woman worshipping in Hare Kṛṣṇa temples, which, in this country, are overwhelmingly white. She always came back to how nothing stopped her from loving Kṛṣṇa and her guru, though the abuses that white supremacists and men and so-called religious leaders had rained upon her did separate her from her tenderest aspects in critical ways.

I was busy contorting myself to become the man I thought I had to be—severing myself from my own tenderest aspects to make myself palatable to a cruelly normative world—and it hadn't occurred to me to consider what it meant if we had both been separated from our tenderness. It hadn't occurred to me to consider whether this separation, on each of our parts, had shaped my ability to love and be loved by my grandmother. If the distance between us wasn't all on her.

I had been blaming Mother Bhūmi's bipolar disorder, which clearly had been exacerbated by the attacks she described, for the many times I'd seen her brutalized by the police officers who came to address the "disturbances" she instigated during her breakdowns—as if to be mentally ill in a society that fuels mental illness is reason enough for the state to punish a person. My walks with my grandmother were beginning to illuminate how unfair I had been.

Strolling at her side, I was increasingly faced with the idea that carceral logics—beliefs rooted in policing, punishing, and incarcerating the socially undesirable and in locking up those who don't fit neatly into this society's binary definitions of selfhood—were at the root of everything that had been unfair to our entire family. Because the only solution they offer is punishment, adhering to carceral logics prevents us from recognizing our role in each other's pain, sometimes even as a coping mechanism developed in an understandable attempt to avoid the cruel and constant hand of punishment ourselves.

I was beginning to understand all the ways I'd also adopted carceral logics in my unsuccessful pursuit of fitting neatly into society's definitions of manhood—definitions I was told I had to achieve in order to find protection. Unfeeling, violent definitions of manhood that didn't make room to heal my own traumas, let alone make room to heal my grandmother's. This time, I walked beside Mother Bhūmi as she paced much more quietly down the manicured street, until we reached the first main corner.

Cleveland Heights, which is now about half-Black, can be understood along the familiar trajectory of many of Cleveland's "diverse" suburbs: to live here, Black, middle-class families had to fight redlining (and, in some cases, white-supremacist mob violence) to make space for themselves, only to be subject to predatory lending practices and increased policing, which to this day contribute to a constant decline in their wealth and safety.[5] Still, Cleveland Heights is mostly populated by households with more money than residents have in the poorer, Blacker city of neighboring Cleveland proper, where I was born. This is reflected in its sizable yards and their characteristic foliage, which were now aging brown and yellow and red with the coming autumn. Mother Bhūmi's unmistakable grittiness seemed out of place here, but her thin body, wrapped delicately in a vibrant sari, progressively relaxed with each step, appearing to welcome the idyllic calm on the street. Rare wordless minutes passed before she finally broke the silence with that Alabama drawl she'd lugged with her when she'd moved to Ohio as a teenager.

"Do you have a girlfriend?"

I instinctively let loose the kind of humorless laugh that pulls air out of one's head rather than the lungs, compelling a spell of dizziness. There was a sixty-year gap between us—her at eighty-one, me at twenty-one—and we were both only a half year away from our shared birthday month. And yet so much of the life she and I should have shared was already lost and too far gone.

"No," I replied aloud. *I have a boyfriend,* I told her in my head, a small part of me hoping the pieces of her that had been passed down in the blood now rapidly carrying oxygen out of my brain might overhear.

I would never tell Mother Bhūmi I was queer aloud. By then, I had imagined that she was sealed off by her own carceral ways of thinking—punitive ideas she heeded that encouraged harming those who did not fit this society's norms around gender, even if they were family. It wasn't that she couldn't understand my queerness or love me if she knew, but I believed that the parts of her that *would* understand and love me were buried so deep beneath her own pain that they would take years to excavate. Years I knew she didn't have. Years that had been stolen from her, just like my childhood had been pried away from me.

How much could I blame her for what she replaced them with? How much could I blame myself for internalizing self-hatred while trying to find what about me was worth saving in an anti-Black, anti-queer world that hated me, too? How much could I blame Mata? And how much should I hold accountable the world that separated us from our childhoods in the first place and told us that blaming each other was all we could ever do about it? Was it my, my mother's, or my grandmother's fault that we were too fractured ourselves to hold every aspect of one another, or did the problem stem from an anti-Black society that wouldn't allow any of us to exist as fully whole people within it?

Sometimes on our walks, Mother Bhūmi would recite to me "pastimes," the word used for religious parables in the Hare Kṛṣṇa tradition. One in particular still resonates with me: the pastime of Prince Dhruva Mahārāja.

When Dhruva was only five years old, his stepmother—jealous of his status as heir to the throne at the expense of her own younger son—forced him from his father's lap during an otherwise unimportant father-son moment. Because she was the king's favorite wife, Dhruva's father permitted her to stop the prince from sitting on his lap without protest. When Dhruva complained, his stepmother told him that no one but god would be able to grant him the privilege of his father's lap again.

The five-year-old took his stepmother's irreverent challenge to heart and went to the forest to suffer through religious austerities so severe they are said to have shaken the foundations of heaven and earth, in hopes of compelling divine intervention. In order to appease the child before his profound sacrifice destroyed the universe, Viṣṇu—an incarnation of Kṛṣṇa—finally appeared and offered to grant Dhruva whatever benediction he desired. Even though the prince responded that witnessing such divinity was enough for him, he was still rewarded with a kingdom even larger than his father's. Many Hindus regard Dhruva as one of the utmost examples of devotion, and for his faith he was afforded the status of a star.

For most of my life, I had tried desperately to find myself in Dhruva, in all of Mother Bhūmi's and Mata's stories of faith and devotion, but Dhruva never could have been a Black boy in this world. I say this not simply because his story is rooted in Indian folklore. I say this because Dhruva's god's sanctity was propagated throughout this country with white people in mind and not us. When Dhruva was invoked in my and my siblings' Black lives, Black suffering for the sake of pious ideals never proved to be enough for divine intervention—for any kind of deliverance from the carceral structures that haunted us. Sacrificing a tenderer relationship to gender—childhood's relationship of openness, gentleness, and vulnerability—and beating myself up trying and failing at perfectly masculine performances, under the direction of my parents and their gods, never brought me salvation. Renouncing these "impious" parts of themselves and their bodies never results in kingdoms for Black children.

In a colonized world, the gods before whom Black children are told to humble themselves require them to toil without ever being seen in the images of these gods, leaving them with only the false promise of being saved. This was true on the plantation, where Black children were designated as capital much the same as their parents, and thus any attempts to live as free as the model white child were met with beatings or worse. And that is true in America today, as exemplified by the persistent wealth, health, and criminalization gaps that Black children still face at every level of assimilation into the country's culture.[6]

Too often, the gods Black children are presented with demand they conform to respectability politics, with morals rooted in what white society sets as the standards for behavior—standards that were designed specifically to exclude them.[7] In this colonized world, there will never be a god who appears for Black children just because they believe and suffer and are careful enough. Any god who might save them requires a new world entirely.

Because Black freedom requires a new world, writing about it sometimes necessitates new language. Just as often, if not more, it requires refamiliarizing ourselves with the old languages we may have forgotten. Ancestor veneration allowed me to really see my grandmother—and, by extension, all my complicated relationships—in a new light and to have the necessary conversations I once thought were impossible, and following root workers and medicine people who are knowledgeable about indigenous anti-colonial practices and methods has led me to much of what is described in these pages.[8] But I also needed to wrestle with these ancient concepts in novel ways to apply them to my modern life.

In 2008, Black feminist scholars Moya Bailey and Trudy of *Gradient Lair*, facing a dearth of shared language for the intersection of misogyny and Blackness, coined the term "misogynoir" to describe "the anti-Black racist misogyny that Black women experience."[9]

Similarly, "misopedia" is a word meaning the hatred or disdain of children, but there is no commonly understood word in this language for the specific way this hatred manifests in the lives of Black children. There is no commonly shared word to describe why our children are so uniquely harmed by everything from health-care inequity to lack of access to education. Why our children are so constantly gunned down in the streets by police. And so, in a related vein to "misogynoir," and in the hopes of illuminating this specific expression of misopedia, I offer "mis*afro*pedia" to mean the anti-Black disdain for children and child-hood that Black youth experience.

As a term, "misafropedia" helps me to describe the systematic oppression of and disdain for Black children—a disdain that culminates in discarding Black children's existence. Their existence is discarded literally in the abuse and incarceration of Black children within systems such as the school-to-prison pipeline—as when police handcuffed six-year-old Kaia Rolle and held her in a detention center for throwing a tantrum in class in 2019.[10] And it is discarded figuratively in how the state attempts to indoctrinate Black people into abusing and disregard-ing our own childhood natures to pursue idealized, binary concepts of manhood or womanhood.

My hope is that with access to a more robust lexicon to describe our experiences, coupled with an appreciation for the imaginative work of those communities who don't rely on colonization for understanding, we will also be able to better manifest the experiences we wish to have. I want to offer colonized Black people—and myself in particular—a type of road map for reclaiming the childhoods we sacrificed or that were forsaken for us because of misafropedia. I want this book to help dis-abuse me—and perhaps many of us—of the hatred for Black children that underlies the belief that they should perpetually suffer like Dhruva, without any of his rewards.

I must have been around five the first time Mata shared with me Dhruva's pastime. That also happened to be the year I had another unforgettable nightmare, this time about Mata and my father dying, which was followed by me crashing headlong into my first panic attack.

Maybe Dhruva's story had prompted me to think about my own father's lap dissolving underneath my body, of forests in which I would perform never-ending sacrifices to get him back, and the panic attack was just my inability to make sense of why I woke up before any god appeared.

Maybe the anxiety was simply me trying to make sense of the fact that, even then, I knew there were no unimportant father-son moments—not when the death and encaging of Black fathers is a birthright. A drive down the wrong road, selling the wrong cigarette without a license, driving *with* a license and reaching for it at the wrong time when asked for identification—any moment could have been my father's last with me, so every moment with him counted. But the world kept pushing me to look for god in the same direction as Dhruva had gone to suffer and sacrifice, even when I knew in my bones that there must have been more places to seek salvation.

In my search for other prayers, I had to conceive of other pastimes—other parables out of the stories that offered me the space to imagine Black childhoods differently than I had been able to when I was determined to twist myself apart to fit ideals that weren't designed for me.

On August 1, 2016, five-year-old Kodi Gaines was shot by police officers who had forced their way into his mother's home, claiming they were attempting to serve her a warrant for a traffic violation. Kodi's own mata, Korryn Gaines, had experienced many previous violent encounters with the police, a few of which she recorded and uploaded to Facebook and Instagram. In many of these videos, Gaines identified the carceral state's policing for what it is: an irredeemable, anti-Black practice. She marked it as another system of enslavement, masked by the same mutation that sonically blends the word "overseer" with "officer" in "Sound of da Police" by KRS-One (whose stage name, coincidentally, was inspired by his own exploration of the Hare Kṛṣṇa religion). Then she called for the carceral state's abolition.

Korryn had attempted to record what would later become the moment of her death as well. However, before killing her, law enforcement contacted Facebook to have them suspend her account while she was broadcasting the altercation live. The site complied with little hesitation. The only witness to Korryn's murder was her son, who would go on to explain in a later video recorded by Korryn's sister: "My mother said back off . . . so the police said, 'We is back up.' So then they started shooting. Then she went on the couch. And then the police just took me. She died. The end."

Korryn's end came just as the Movement for Black Lives began accelerating. Given that, one might have expected her death to be a cause du jour, considering it was prompted by something so egregiously minor as a traffic violation, a child was injured, and the state so brashly flexed its awful power to limit the witnesses of its abuse. Popular media and those who sought its favor had so far built the visible parts of this movement around victims who died with their hands up. But Korryn epitomized the refuser, the enslaved who jumps overboard, the grandmother who fights back against a state that criminalizes her mental illness, the child who disappears rather than becoming an adult intent on rending themselves into pieces.

In one of the videos Korryn posted to Instagram of an earlier run-in with police, she detailed how embracing this type of refusal pushes beyond the colonial concept of a linear existence that ends with death, pushes beyond this colonized world I was stolen away from my childhood into, where death is an inextricable feature of Black life, exclaiming, "I'll live on forever, my nigga!"

Kodi called his mother's death "the end." But she left with him the wondrous possibility that this could also be the beginning of the story—the same story my mother has always told of how this material world, with its devastating health crises and its unwillingness to answer them, is "filled with suffering," even when she didn't quite know how to escape it. A repeating pastime that shows us over and over again that this world has been built upon the premise that Black people must endlessly grow up to be punished, until we refuse this world entirely, like Korryn did.

In refusing state policing under carceral logics, Korryn presented a parable about how liberating it could be to abolish all cycles of policing Black children and the adults they should be allowed to grow into:

how we speak, love, and live until we are broken. Until we are in prison. Until we are dead. Until we kill the children inside us. And in the story of Kodi, the baby boy to whom she gifted this lesson, I might finally find myself, if I can mind the message she left him, too.

~

Mother Bhūmi told me that she was tired and ready to head home much earlier than I expected. She looked physically fine to walk a little bit longer, but I don't believe she was talking about the fatigue of moving her legs. Her body was still relaxed, but something inside her seemed to be swaying, barely holding up in the wind. "I'm tired," she repeated, this just another type of chanting.

Immediately after the hysterectomy she underwent to treat the cancer, Mata looked just like her mother did in that moment. Like an ailing tree. If they were both dying trees, then abolishing the oppressive cycles of separation that this carceral world forces Black people into—separation from oneself, from one's childhood, and from each other—was always Mata's and Mother Bhūmi's roots, my roots, the roots, the answer, the full story, the reason to be tired of living and to *live on forever, my nigga* at the same time.

If Mother Bhūmi was a tree, autumn had only just broken. The end of a season, the beginning of another, tangled up like a bundle of twigs. Most streets in Cleveland Heights, including Beechwood Avenue, where we lived, are not only lined with trees but named after them, and my grandmother was finally not out of place. And as we headed back in the direction we came, the leaves were just beginning to fall.

CANTO I

Black

CHAPTER ONE

CARCERAL DISSONANCE

"Everything seems normal," the doctor said, shuffling the papers inked with my results in front of her as if they were cards in a game of spades and she had no interest in learning the rules.

"Are you sure?" I asked, barely registering the pain of the hairs on my finger as they got caught in the engagement ring I anxiously twisted in circles. For the longest time, I didn't know if I loved the odd tresses sprouting from every area of my body other than my head, which has been balding since I was twenty, or if they made me look animal. In this moment, I felt profoundly beast-like.

The doctor plastered on a preprogrammed smile as she looked out from under her purple ombré pixie cut, which perfectly encapsulated the *young! hip! edgy!* demographic targeted by the health insurance company running this medical center. I'd learned recently that Josh Kushner, Ivanka Trump's brother-in-law, was a part owner of the company. This did make me question why I was still paying for its services, but not enough to go through the hassle of trying to find an alternative in New York State's utterly confusing health-care marketplace, which was supposed to be the solution to the country's underinsured problem. It was not.

"Well, let's wait for the blood tests, but the EKG results are fine," the doctor said, crossing her ripped-jeaned legs.

"Okay . . ."

This was the second time in the past three years I'd found myself in front of a doctor with concerns about my heart. The last time, I'd wound up in an ambulance after having palpitations that wouldn't stop in the office of my former job.

"You need to go!" the office manager had advised.

"Are you sure?" I asked then, too, once again requiring someone else's validation of my well-being. The palpitations *seemed* urgent, given that nothing like that had happened to me before, but going to the doctor had never been my first option for solving problems with my body. Not until I'd at least tried what I now understand to be largely untested home remedies with which my mother had met all sorts of maladies I'd sustained as a child—like swallowing a dollop of Vicks or applying shea butter topically, which Mata insists improves even internal bodily functions when rubbed in thoroughly. Untested or not, you can't tell me that shit didn't work at least sometimes.

"Go!" the office manager urged again. She was an older Black woman who reminded me of my mother, which meant I mythologized her to know more about my body than I did. Plus, I had health insurance for the first time since college, so I assumed that would prevent any financial burden. I thought money had been the primary reason the doctor was a last resort—reserved for after we'd plodded through my mother's list of deviceful, quick fixes—when I was growing up. That assumption is, of course, belied by the fact that Mata is currently undergoing a traditional Ayurvedic medicine treatment in India after passing on trying chemo, immunotherapy, and hormone therapy to fight the cancer. My siblings and I would have eagerly paid whatever her insurance didn't for the standard treatments, but we have collectively agreed to be as supportive of this untested remedy she has decided on as we can. It doesn't seem like we have any other option.

"You're fine," the nurse had announced after running that first EKG.

A $2,000 bill for a ten-block emergency vehicle ride and three years later, here I was again. But I had learned my lesson. I walked to the medical center this time.

"What was it that you started mentioning earlier?" the purple-haired doctor said, setting aside the papers that told her I was fine and giving me that smile white people give when they are sure they're helping you. *You don't get it,* I wanted to say instead of answering her question. *I wake up every day feeling like Kano has pulled my heart from my chest in a* Mortal Kombat *fatality.*

"I forget," I replied honestly, looking forward to getting home and impulse buying a video game I would play only on one quiet afternoon to manage my stress. When the doctor first had walked into the room, I'd tried to tell her that I had a medical concern, and she cut me off before I even got all the words out. "We have a set amount of time, so we need to jump right into the physical you scheduled. If there's extra time at the end, you can ask any other questions," she'd said, offering up that robotic smile again.

The truth was I already knew what was wrong with my heart. I had diagnosed myself with social anxiety a long time ago. I fit all the symptoms, and my anxiety had spiked in recent months with a decline in Mata's health and an uptick in public engagements. I'd had two panic attacks over the previous year. I feel the anxiety most in my chest. For the past several months, there had been a constant tightening there, as though my heart were cratering in on itself more and more for every wall I didn't punch but wanted to—my body recognizing that something must be smashed even as I policed it into pacifism.

I knew what was wrong, but I had refused to start psychotherapy or obtain an official diagnosis. Sure, this refusal might have been pathological, but not in the sense that Black people all have some disabling stigma around getting help for our mental health issues. Some of us do stigmatize therapy, thinking that it indicates a person is weak. This stigma seems less pervasive in recent generations, but I'm certain that it has infested my own thinking at times. I'm also sure there was more to my initial reluctance than an irrational disdain for therapy. After five hundred years of the atrocities of colonialism and no repair, there must be more to Black folks' struggles than our own failures. How could talking with one person heal the wound of systemic and generational oppression that affects almost everyone I love?

There's the very real history of medical malpractice. There's a legacy full of Tuskegee experiments and forced sterilization of Black women by doctors who lied to them. This was what North Carolina's state-run eugenics program did to fourteen-year-old Elaine Riddick in 1968, after she gave birth to a child conceived when a neighbor raped her. Riddick has spoken publicly about how she didn't find out she couldn't have any more children until five years later, after she was married.[11] When the state isn't mining Black wombs for labor, it is policing them with the same brute force it uses against the Black children they birth.

There are also the $2,000 ambulance bills and doctors who are hip enough to dress like young Black folks but not hip enough to make time for our questions. There's growing up never having seen a doctor because of a lack of access and no one to bring you gently into familiarity. There are doctors who disregard what we know about our bodies because they have anti-Black biases about what these bodies can do, deduce, and withstand. All of this is real—most of it I've experienced firsthand—and it leads to a logical aversion to medical professionals, particularly those whose effectiveness relies on how much they get to know you . . . which means it also relies on how vulnerable you allow yourself to be.

My reticence toward therapy extended beyond the far-too-often-overlooked fact that medical professionals have not been safe for us historically, however. I don't think I'm much more averse to therapists than I am to other medical doctors, and I made my way to Purple Pixie

Cut's office just fine (albeit after first attempting some of my mother's inventive home remedies). I went to therapy willingly in college, and it was helpful. I encouraged it for other people all the time. But I had come to embrace the reality that much of the fuel that fed the fire of my anxiety was inexhaustible, or at least it was something I did not want to exhaust. I am still afraid of anyone policing my emotions and my body in the name of looking out for me, because doing the same thing to myself was what made it so difficult to recognize and deal with my anxiety in the first place.

I am a Black person who has seen Black friends die, Black family members stuffed in cages, my Black grandmother beaten, and my Black body raped. I am a Black person who has seen these atrocities replay themselves over and over again on the news, on the internet when I turn off the TV, and on the walk home through my rapidly gentrifying neighborhood when I shut off my phone.

I am a Black person from a lineage of Black people who, for centuries, have never stopped seeing these cruelties. And in the dreams that I often could not access because my anxiety kept me awake, I couldn't stop seeing these cruelties either. This anxiety was just my mind being colonized in the same ways that my external world has been. I was forced to see atrocities against my people everywhere, and even if I could screen them from my view, how then could I ever know where to move to get out of the way of them devouring me?

This society has conditioned me to believe that healing is just the muting of one's rage. I have been taught that healing looks like celebrating the forgiveness offered by the relatives of Charleston's Emanuel African Methodist Episcopal Church members to the white supremacist who killed their loved ones during a prayer meeting, without demanding he or the state that emboldened him take any accountability. But I couldn't survive muting my rage much longer. I couldn't survive uncritically forgiving a world that would not stop harming me, and so I had accepted that I just would not heal. At least not in that way, and I didn't yet know any other.

I left the doctor's office with the lump still clogged in my chest like a clump of nappy hair in a drain, and only then, after a ragged breath through an oddly inflamed throat, did I finally remember that I'd meant to ask her about a suspected allergy that had been making getting through my days miserable. I scuttled down into the train station feeling defeated and Blacker than I'd ever been. There, I was immediately confronted with a teenager being held by two cops, each twice his size, for questioning on the platform, just to the other side of the turnstile. The boy was Black, too.

I heard the words "fare evasion" and "I just needed to get home to my mom." The city was ramping up police presence in the subway to crack down on turnstile hopping, claiming that everyone needs to be punished for not paying for services to make sure "our trains run smoothly." Watching the scene unfold, I thought about who was included in this "our": Who owns these trains. Who profits most from them.

In 2019, the city announced that it planned to spend $249 million over the next four years on increased transit police presence, partially financed by the mere $200 million it expects these measures to save on fare evasion.[12] Those expectations are dubious on their own, but it's also important to note that despite increased policing that year, subway fare evasion actually rose from 3.9 percent of riders in June to 4.7 percent in August. (Bus fare evasion dropped from 24 percent to 22 percent during the same time.[13]) The MTA also announced plans to spend $5.1 billion to install elevators in subway stations citywide, at a cost of about $81 million per station. Almost no comparable country has spent more than $25 million to add elevators to a transit station.[14] (For the sake of comparison, Lyon, France, added one elevator for $4 million.) These scandalous price tags fall in a long history of MTA backroom dealing and wasteful spending that a 2017 New York Times investigation blamed on "excessive staffing, little competition, [and] generous contracts."[15] Who was benefiting from making sure "our trains run smoothly" in this way?

Certainly not twenty-two-year-old Malaysia Goodson, a Black mother who, in January 2019, fell while trying to carry her stroller and baby down the subway stairs because there was no working elevator at her station and died (her official cause of death listed cardiac hypertrophy, which can lead to sudden death after physical stress, and hyperthyroidism as factors[16]). She might still be alive if such misguided spending hadn't prevented cheaper, quicker elevator installation. Certainly not the disabled community, who have been rallying for more transit accessibility for years, and who still struggle to find consistently working elevators that might exist in abundance if the government spent $4 million instead of $80 million on them (and if this government weren't committed to oppressing the disabled). Not the many homeless people who are harassed by police for sleeping in the subways, nor the shelters and other public services they rely on that could desperately use the funding from these hypothetical savings.

As I watched the Black boy being detained, the cop watcher in me awakened. I decided to stay and observe the situation a little longer to make sure shit didn't go left. Or any more left, rather. My chest tightened further as I pondered how, if this teenager didn't pay this ticket, he could go to jail, and it was reasonable to think he may have been unable to pay. Obscene costs are relative, which New York City had to know if it was waging a war on fare evasion that looked to cost more than it returned. It took me two years to pay off that $2,000 ambulance bill. I thought back to having those heart palpitations, and how all I could consider then was that I just needed to get home to my mom, too. All I could consider now was how my mother just needed to make it through treatment, and the teenager had the same expression I did when I wanted to punch a wall. And right when the cop asked for his ID, the boy booked it. Ran. Fled to freedom. I never did that anymore.

My chest loosened for just a moment. I couldn't help flashing a smile at the kid's audacity and courage, and my dilemma gained some clarity, a mirror in a steamy room when the door suddenly swings open and it begins to defog. In just a split second, my understanding of healing and rage began to feel incredibly unconsidered. There must have been a way to heal without surrendering to policing myself, but somewhere along the line, I'd lost the necessary bravery to go that path. I gave up on resisting the confines of this world and the state that keeps them in place.

I looked down at the hair on my fingers and wondered why I cared so much about looking like an animal. When had I stopped using these hands to punch walls that need breaking down?

A few weeks prior, my friend Cloud had sent me the contact information for their therapist.

"Thanks, I'll look into it," I said, intending this to be a polite little lie.

"You should," they insisted, flashing that bright smile of theirs and struggling commendably to walk the line between nagging and stern encouragement.

"I said I will!" I repeated, punching them playfully—but dismissively—on the shoulder.

"I know you feel ambivalent about it, though," they persisted, rubbing their shoulder, "and I just want to make sure you know that I hear you. But he's really good. He's Black. He's queer. It's not about fixing you; it's about managing how you deal with the issues, and that's how he approaches it."

I still didn't think much of it. Cloud is white. They didn't get it. Even now, I don't think they do, or ever will. But in that moment on the platform, looking at the cops stumbling over themselves in pursuit of this boy in the subway, I was forced to consider a different perspective of how I was dealing with this anxiety that I had come to proudly own. I knew I wanted to deal more like this boy who had escaped from unjust captors, and I knew it was possible because he had accomplished it.

But I still didn't know how.

I still didn't know how to manage the anxiety of being Black in America without policing everything that comes with it. I had set up an altar and had begun to chant again, which felt like a start, but I was afraid of fully committing to even these proven spiritual models for fear of being overwhelmed by religiosity again. I wanted more than anything to gain a better understanding of ways to embrace the fire and not be subsumed by it, and so I decided to at least give therapy a try as I continued these other practices, and sent an email to the therapist Cloud had suggested when I got home.

~

I understand that talk therapy isn't viable for everyone. Even if it were, those who need it most don't always have the means to fund what can be painfully expensive sessions. Just today, I found out I can't even book an appointment with my primary care doctor until two months down the road, and securing an appointment with a specialist or therapist can take even longer. Only telling folks to "go to therapy" often isn't a realistic solution to the reality of their lives; nor is it an answer to the systemic issues they face.

Therapy is not a substitute for communal healing practices or a community that cares for you, but it can help you better recognize what that community looks like or aid you in becoming a member of a caring community for somebody else—and for yourself— when done with that goal in mind. It is a resource. And for folks who experience marginalization, it can be especially helpful if your therapist shares a marginalized experience with you. They are then less likely to question whether your experience is valid. I'm not sure we would have gotten very far if my therapist weren't Black and queer, or if he didn't encourage me to continue exploring healing practices taught to me by root workers at the same time.

"What are you here for?" he asked in our first session, sitting across from me in a small room that smelled like lavender and brass, unblinking.

"My mother is dying. I'm probably depressed about that. I know I've been struggling with anxiety. And just in general the world's a messed-up place, which kinda sucks."

I laughed. He asked me to slow down, take my problems one at a time, take them seriously, parse them out. He blinked just when I needed proof of his humanity, that he wasn't the robot Purple Pixie Cut had been. We started with my mother.

"I just feel like we just got on a path back to something good," I offered, clutching a throw pillow to my stomach to try to force it to settle.

"Back?"

"Yeah. Like how things were when I was younger. When I didn't question her love for me, and my queerness wasn't a problem. We lost something and we'd just started getting it back. And now it's too late."

"What exactly did you lose?"

I went through the list: my rock, my confidence, my safe space, my home, my family, my religion, my—

"Self. You feel as though you lost yourself," he summarized.

"In a way, yeah."

I told him that I was getting married the following year. How I never assumed my mother wouldn't be at the wedding, but there was this need to let her know how much it meant that she planned on coming after all we'd been through. How much it meant particularly after her traumatizing reaction to learning of my queerness. I felt this need to let her know that I recognized the growth she'd made. That I knew she still had fears and concerns that she wouldn't address, concerns about celebrating my love for someone who wasn't a woman.

I told my therapist that I was struggling because I felt like I never got a chance to say any of that to her. And I knew I still had time to tell her; even if the cancer meant she wouldn't make it to the wedding, it wouldn't take away that she still intended to. But it didn't *feel* like I had time. Because the part of me that could express all this the way it needed to be expressed was lost somewhere, punching at walls in my chest cavity, while I was laughing it all off to keep from crying.

"Have you heard of inner-child work?" my therapist asked at the end of our session.

I pictured myself speaking to a baby doll in a baby voice about the things that had hurt me when I was young, hoping to mend childhood wounds, or some other pop-psychology drivel, and chuckled some more, gripping the pillow even tighter. "In passing."

"I think it could really help with getting back in connection with what you lost, which I think is a first step to healing this relationship that is obviously very important to you. Would you be open to trying that in here?"

Now I was picturing the teenager running away from the police through the subway, and my knees went weak. Then I pictured the boy with my face, me with his knees. It felt like something to believe in . . .

"I'm open to trying anything, I guess," I replied, explaining that I'd also taken chanting back up, and recently had begun trying to communicate with my deceased grandmother per the guidance of a Hoodoo priestess friend in the same search for wholeness. A brief flash of surprise crossed his face and I gulped, afraid he might dismiss these exercises as pseudoscientific. But he only nodded encouragingly, suggesting *Inner Bonding: Becoming a Loving Adult to Your Inner Child* by Margaret Paul, PhD, if I wanted to read more about the practice of inner-child work.

"You might find it helps supplement what you're already doing," he said, making a note to email me the link to order the book.

"Inner Bonding is a process of connecting our Adult thoughts with our instinctual gut feelings, the feelings of our 'Inner Child,'" Paul writes, "so that we can live free of conflict within ourselves." Getting back in touch with your Inner Child is not about romanticizing childhood, she explains, but recognizing that our essential nature isn't the negative feelings that may have been prompted by childhood trauma, and reclaiming that nature.

The work, Paul argues, is "to question and to resolve, as much as we possibly can, the false, generally shame-based, self-limiting beliefs we have lived by up to now." To challenge the self-policing that prevents us from loving ourselves. We take up this challenge by bringing our Inner Child back into our lives through recognizing when they are showing up in our thoughts and actions, and parenting that nature when it reacts from trauma with a care the child may have not received from anyone else.

Paul utilizes all the pop-psychology jargon I imagined, with a writing style that would not be out of place in a Goop advertisement, but still I found myself pulled into the process. I heard the younger me being told that their queerness isn't enough, their Blackness is too much, and the voice telling the younger me these things was almost as much my voice as anyone's.

I heard myself policing the younger version of me into silence even when they tried to rebuke being stifled, and I knew that this was not sustainable. I found myself wanting to believe what the work Paul describes could do for me, wanting to go on this journey to help heal from my anxieties, and frustrated that she didn't quite bring me there—and not just because of her New Age approach.

"She gets it, but she doesn't *really* get it," I told my therapist a few sessions later, after I had finally finished the book.

"What do you mean?"

"The shame that our Inner Child internalizes—she writes about it as if it's all about your individual experiences and interpersonal interactions. All based on what our parents did or didn't do to us, with no real accounting for the systemic problems entrenched in society—no real accounting of anti-Blackness or anti-queerness—and not enough concern for community healing. It feels like a very individualistic kind of self-help." What I didn't say was that I still feared therapy in general might have the same limitations.

"I see."

"The policing I do to shame my Inner Child, I'm encouraged to do that every day by the whole nation-state of America. I'm encouraged to mute my anger at injustice, never to speak my mind about the state harming me or the oppression I feel and experience by law, and that doesn't just affect me. That affects everyone in my community."

I told him about all the times I had been encouraged to think that demanding more than a two-party system or any radically different form of governance was asking for too much and being unrealistic, even though I knew that folks in my community needed something radically different. I told him about all the times I'd been encouraged to be respectable in the way I spoke, the way I looked, and where I went, and if I didn't meet respectability standards that were incompatible with who I really was, then it became my fault. I told him how I believed this encouragement came from the state on down, that there are laws and crimes regulating all these things, and how I was sure my parents had learned to encourage me to live this way from the state, too. I was sure because I am constantly learning to encourage those around me the same way.

I caught myself heating up and immediately apologized. I hadn't planned to dive into critical race theory in these sessions.

"I don't want to sound preachy," I said.

This was self-policing, too, he offered. In order to heal, which was what these sessions should help me do, he reminded me that I had to be free to talk about how I thought I'd learned to police myself, even if I thought something that seemed "out there." Even if I thought that I ultimately learned to police myself from a carceral system built on the ashes of a global slave trade, from a world that punishes and encages us simply for being Black.

I envisioned child me, little Hari-Gaura, a Black boy struggling to wear their given name in a world that made it so hard to do so, listening to my therapist's reassurance and finding some relief. It seemed so clear then: *If I am ever to stop policing my Inner Child, I have to be free to explore how I was policed out of my childhood, and how that was influenced by the state's dependence on all Black people being policed.*

"I guess what I'm trying to say is that the dissonance I have with my Inner Child is carceral. It's based on living in an anti-Black, prison-based society. Paul doesn't reckon with *that*," I explained, still a bit reluctantly—still expecting my therapist not to fully get it, to think I sounded ridiculous.

"What would reckoning with that look like?"

"I don't know," I said, thinking about my grandmother and the crude altar set up to her in my room.

Over the next few sessions, we talked about how the disconnect a Black person has from their Inner Child could be an extension of what W. E. B. Du Bois called "double consciousness," the experience of "always looking at one's self through the eyes" of an anti-Black society. Though Du Bois's theory is over- and misused in some academic circles, I was again relieved that my therapist encouraged this thought experiment. Bringing the reality of Blackness into inner-child work was the only way this frame could possibly be healing for me.

I was relieved to tell him more about my grandmother—about my belief that we are all born whole, with our childlike joys and our intergenerational traumas, our instincts and our rationality, our vulnerabilities and our strengths, but Mother Bhūmi would know better than most how the state is relentless in its attempts to tear Black people in two.

Mother Bhūmi was proof that this country has perfected using criminalization to rupture everything that makes us complete, to rupture our families and our lineage in order to better ensure our continued commodification after centuries of slavery. This is exemplified by how the carceral system today overwhelmingly provides wells of slave labor, money, and voting power to white communities in the form of prisons.[17] I explained to my therapist how I thought this commodification was directly linked to what writer and scholar Saidiya Hartman refers to as "fungibility," or the process of "exploiting the vulnerability of the captive body as a vessel for the uses, thoughts, and feelings of others," in her book *Scenes of Subjection*.[18]

I offered that a particular and criminalizing expression of double consciousness exists that causes an irreconcilable fissure between a Black person and their childhood nature, in order to ensure their fungibility and lack of wholeness. The rupturing of Black people from our Inner Children serves to repurpose that childlike space inside us for the uses, thoughts, and feelings of the state. It replaces our openness to new ideas, feelings, and experiences with a learned willingness to criminalize ourselves and each other for refusing to conform to normalized tropes, propping up an entire prison-industrial complex along the way. And it is an extension of the same carceral logics that tried to take my grandmother from me.

"For Black people, this separation from our childhoods is a carceral dissonance."

The words almost spilled out of me. I frowned at the throw pillow, disappointed in its protracted betrayal as it became more and more useless at holding things down inside.

"And when did this carceral dissonance begin for you?"

"I don't know. Whenever I started accepting the pressures to conform to the world, whenever I started to adopt respectability in an attempt to survive it."

"So your carceral dissonance can only end when you undo those beginnings."

It was not a question.

"What would undoing it look like?" I asked.

"Maybe that's something you have to figure out with your Inner Child," my therapist said.

I paused, trying to imagine it. "I don't know where to start."

"Ask him."

I laughed, but he was dead serious.

"You said you were willing to try anything."

"I did, didn't I?"

CHAPTER TWO

A PRAYER FOR MY FATHER

Hari-Gaura,

I should start off by apologizing. If we still have this in common, you really don't appreciate being thrust into a deep-ass conversation you didn't plan for. This is a bit like showing up at somebody's house unannounced. I haven't talked to you in ages. I haven't braced you for this. That's on me.

If I'm being honest, trying to start a conversation with you, my "Inner Child," feels just as uncomfortable as when I began praying again after Mata's diagnosis, or when I set up an altar and started talking to Mother Bhūmi after she passed. Maybe all these things are the same, in a manner. But as uncomfortable as praying and giving offerings to pictures of our grandmother were at first, they made a whole lot of what I was struggling with on my own better in ways I couldn't have even imagined. They made me feel like I wasn't alone. *Know* I wasn't.

I'm here writing to you because my therapist swayed me to try. Because I've listened and learned from my elders in this craft—including James Baldwin and Toni Morrison and Kiese Laymon— who have demonstrated the immense depths a relationship might reach when one has difficult dialogues directly with another on the page. But really I'm here because there are so many things that I know you never heard, that you needed to hear, and I want you to finally hear them. If it's not too late.

I think that ultimately what I've been struggling with is the fact that no one ever made you understand that you are valuable and worthy enough to stay—to be carried inside me and protected. What I've been seeking healing from, through prayer and therapy and ancestor communication, is the fact that I will always be lonely without you. The thing is, I still don't know how to express that fully yet. I hope you'll bear with me as I figure this out.

Oddly enough, Daddy has been a critical guide along this journey. As you know, the man has always loved a terrible joke. By now, you might think people would have stopped responding facetiously, "Eighteen?! Do you even know all of their names?" when they find out how many siblings I have. But nope. They still do it. And every time I can just picture Daddy roaring with laughter as he tilts back his head, a leathery, bald island surrounded by waves of white-water hair.

There's never been much logic to the question—most people know the names of

thousands of people, so why would it be difficult to remember fewer than two dozen of those
closest to you? But Daddy wouldn't mind. For
him, a bad joke always hides something more
interesting underneath. And against my teenage
self's wishes, I'm becoming more like him, finding
myself laughing at this question more often these
days. Rediscovering my own hidden gem by recall-
ing Daddy's fascination with his children's names
when it happens. They say time moves in only one
direction, but it seems to keep bringing me back
to the people and things that came before me
when I least expect it, how I least expect it, as
long as I let it.

I think that's the first thing you should know:
how you see the past will change in the future.
You'll see our grandmother differently, yourself differently, our parents differently than you do now.
But what I'm still learning is that you can also have
a say in *how* you see those things. A person's history is not just a static fable that must be accepted
in whatever form it is given to them; history is
something that we are all constantly shaping with
our current perspectives. History is, at least in part,
what we interpret it to be. For a long time, my
interpretation of history was one indoctrinated
into me by the same people who tell us that slavery
has no reverberations and we should just get over
it—a deathly limiting perspective that didn't allow
me to truly reckon with how I have been influenced
by what came before me any more than it allowed
me to reckon with how I can influence it.

In exploring how to truly witness how I have been affected by our past, I am compelled to acknowledge that reshaping how I understand it affects what came before me, too. It affects how the past shows up in my life, in the stories I tell about it, and thus it affects what the past is to whomever I tell these stories. And I guess that's really why I was so open to this Inner Child thing: I realized that maybe I can still affect you, too. Protect you, the way you deserved to be protected.

Hari-Gaura, I've been thinking a lot recently about how Daddy didn't spare you talk of dying despite how young you were. It was as if he knew your youth wouldn't spare you from experiences with death any more than it did for Kodi Gaines or any other Black child in this world, and he addressed it accordingly.

"When I'm on my deathbed," Daddy would say, his long limbs swinging lankly around in the air to emphasize his point, "what's the last thing I would want to tell you?" (He still asks me the same thing almost whenever I see him, and by now I know instinctively what he'd make his last words.)

"Live your name," he says to each of his children every time, as if it's the most profound lesson to ever leave his lips, and maybe it is. "You were named this for a reason."

I've grown on our full name, Hari-Gaura Bilal Das Ziyad, and have gained a new appreciation for it as a combination of Arabic and Sanskrit monikers and a linguistic coming together of

Mata's and Daddy's adopted religions. Mata says an angel gave her the idea for "Hari-Gaura" in a dream while she was pregnant. Hari, which is how most people know me today, is a name of Kṛṣṇa, meaning "one who replaces bad things with good ones," and Gaura means "golden." Traditionally, the name is reversed—Gaura-Hari—but the angel wanted to emphasize our contrarianism, I suppose.

Given that she hadn't screened for sex and the name is generally gendered male, Mata says the dream was how she knew she would have a boy. I want to tell her that this interpretation of her dream is how *I* know the ways society determines gender are bullshit—based on arbitrary rules that don't have the capacity to hold the fullness of our existence. But I don't.

We were named Bilal after an enslaved African Muslim whose master tried to crush him by rolling a boulder over his chest for practicing Islam, and who later became the prophet Muhammad's first official caller of prayer. Sometimes, when I'm struck by anxiety, I think about how even the chest pains are ancestral. This helps the panic to ease and (or because) it makes me laugh like our father again.

Das is a common Hindu surname meaning "servant of," usually given because it would otherwise be blasphemous to go by a name of god. And Ziyad means "extra" or "abundance."

Daddy wants us to either always remember to have the courage of Bilal to pray to and serve a golden god who takes away bad things and replaces them with an abundance of good ones, or pray to a god who replaces bad things with a regular amount of good ones, and just be extra about it. Without further clarity, of course we were going to do the latter, but our father still acts shocked to witness my queerness.

I was twenty-six and Daddy had just told another terrible joke, cackling a siren sound as he drove me through downtown Cleveland to our parents' house from the airport. The contrast between the metropolis veneer of the structures and the scarcity of pedestrians in this city has always struck me as oddly dystopian, but ongoing gentrification had brought the amount of activity more into alignment with how the place looked this time around. A sermon from Wallace D. Muhammad II played on low volume in the background, though I couldn't pick up on what he was lecturing about.

Daddy and Mata had just gotten a new vehicle, a silvery-green Honda CR-V that all the siblings had chipped in to help buy. But it was mostly funded by our oldest sister, Rani, who—as the first of us to reach even modest financial means—has always been so inspiringly generous with her money. This fact complicates my relationship to childhood poverty in a way that makes it all the more important to be clear that I don't speak for all Black people who grew up poor, but I don't always remember that. I have way more memories of the old, beat-up Toyota minivan our parents owned for most of our life, which had picked up one too many yellow marks from us children swiping against the stumps on the side of the porch in the months and years after we first received our licenses.

"Honda makes really good cars," Daddy advised when he stopped laughing, as if I'd ever shown any interest in the facts of automobiles. He straightened out his eyeglasses, a lens nearly falling out because of a missing screw. I reminded myself to buy him a new pair the next time I got paid, imagining myself Rani.

"It might not be fancy, but a bird in the hand is worth two in the bush," Daddy continued in his odd little language of idioms. "And don't ever buy American."

He swore he was just talking about the quality of manufacturing overseas, though I couldn't help but hear a *fuck you* to the prescribed patriotism of the anti-Black country he had lived in for seventy-eight long years.

"Thanks for the advice," I teased.

"You're welcome," he said, with such sincerity that I felt guilty about the sarcasm.

I was on a last-minute trip back to Cleveland from New York. I lived in Brooklyn, but I had just found out I might have to move to LA to work on a television show. This had always been my dream. I wanted to be excited, but Mata was recovering from her hysterectomy, and because of my possible move, I knew this might be the last time I saw her for a while. I knew this might be the last time I saw her. It's almost impossible to feel excitement about anything when the threat of fatal disease is lurking around the corner.

Daddy wasn't late to the airport like he usually is, but I wasn't surprised. Mata's cancer had declared so many things different. Something made him think to ask me again to recite what he would want me to remember when he dies, and I think the thing that made him ask was Mata. I think he was also asking what *she* would want me to remember.

I made my joke more obvious this time, responding that he would remind me on his deathbed that if my queerness is too much, if I am extra, it's his fault. But again he didn't laugh. The light skin he passed down to us turned unnaturally pale about his knuckles as he gripped the steering wheel of the Honda a little tighter, and the man calling for prayer that day began softly singing out the Adhān on the radio. I was surprised to still remember the words. And in that moment, I felt more like our father than he was.

He's still uncomfortable with the truth, with the fact that I am queer, but by now he has to know that I'm right about my queerness being bound to him. He named us this and told us to embrace all our extraness—told each of his children to embrace what he chose to call us. I'm still figuring out how, exactly, to do that, but I think I'm getting closer. I think so because now when people ask me, "Do you even know all of your siblings' names?" I hear our father, and I understand that "live your name" has become just as much my living words as our father's dying ones.

In high school, I wanted to legally change my name from Hari-Gaura to just Hari because it seemed more acceptable to white people who don't like to pronounce long names unless it's something like Tsiolkovsky, and I thought I needed to be accepted by them to find safety. Thank god I am past that. Now I better understand that our father's naming process—which changed from biblical to Qur'anic as he moved through these two religions—was a way for us to be born with the lessons he learned along this pilgrimage, instead of having to learn them on our own. As someone who had changed his own name from David to Tariq, it wasn't that he wanted us to be forever tied to some destiny he'd bestowed upon us against our will; he just wanted us to remember that the destiny he bestowed and the ones we choose for ourselves would always be connected, even if we choose differently from him.

When I hear the joke about our siblings' names today, I laugh at how Daddy was extra successful at ensuring I would never forget this command. How he was a Ziyad before both of us. How, if I can just replace the bad things in our parents' lessons with good ones and hold on to the rest, the best of them will never die. And you might know that you are valuable and worthy enough to come back, too.

CHAPTER THREE

NOWALATERS

My father and mother had their first children in their late teens and early twenties and their last at fifty-nine and forty-seven, respectively. The kids my father had before he married Mata mostly lived with their own biological mothers growing up, and I still don't see them as much as I should.

My oldest brother on Mata's side, Syamasundara—Syama, as we call him—lived at our house when I was born, along with the four siblings who were born between us: Kṛṣṇa-Kumari, Mohan, Ganga, and Ghanasyam. My two oldest sisters, Bhakti and Rani, were already well into adulthood and no longer living at home. By the time Syama moved out, there were two younger siblings, Kṛṣṇa-Jivani and Visnu, to fill the space. Occasionally, my brother and sister from my father's earlier marriage, David and Tauheedah, would stay with us, too. There never seemed to be enough room, but in our little house with its chipping yellow paint on Cleveland's East Side, we somehow made it work.

My little sister Kṛṣṇa-Jivani—whom we call Kiss—still swears this was the best house we ever lived in, even though it was easily when our poorness was most apparent. The front yard was a dandelion bed, with thorny rosebushes twisted through the rusty fence enclosing it. I know now that dandelions are considered weeds, but back then I thought they were more beautiful than the roses that decorated the corroding fence. Maybe they still are to Kiss, who was only five when we moved away but who has remained as good as any child at seeing things others might overlook. I want to believe this means she's been trying to repair the fracture caused by her carceral dissonance, too.

But maybe she just misses the cluttered corner store where we'd travel on early summer days after a season of collecting coins from odd jobs and aunties. And what's not to miss? We'd come back home armed with piles of treats that could last us many months, even as several pieces dropped through the nets we made with our tiny fingers and into the cracks of the sidewalks, where they melted and smoothed the ground the way the city government refused to: Frooties penny candies (which you could buy for actual pennies), Lemonheads, Chick-O-Sticks, and my favorite, Nowalaters—as we called them in our Black midwestern drawl.

There's something particularly joyful about the roundness Black folks give to words with the accent we inherited only partially from the various dialects of our southern foreparents, many of whom moved to Cleveland during the Great Migration in search of factory jobs. I don't think I realized the real name of the taffy was "Now and Later" until I was grown—that it wasn't just one word that magically merged both the present and the future in the sweetest, tartest treat on a bright summer day. It was sugar *and* it was Black language puckered in our mouths. In the midst of the poverty that had enveloped the city with the decline of the manufacturing industry and the anti-Black barriers many people faced when trying to find work in other fields, there was plenty of magic to find in our hood—but I wouldn't always believe in it.

Mata says that up until she gave birth to me, she was finishing her bachelor's in education at Cleveland State University and student-teaching at a school for "at-risk" girls downtown.[19]

"I was supposed to have co-teachers, but they left me to care for the girls alone that semester," she tells me. "Their excuse was that I was a good enough teacher to handle it by myself—even though I was pregnant!" Her voice betrays the exhaustion she's carried for years. Even now I hear it, but still forget to ask her how she managed, how she felt, how tired she must have been. Of course she was capable of overcoming. She is a Black woman, after all—held hostage by a myth of limitless strength that allows her meager rest.

The little yellow house with the always chipping paint wasn't exceptional for East 128th Street, except for being one of a few with a fenced-off lawn. I wonder whether my parents chose it for this added layer of protection, however inadequate it might have been, against the dangers outside. I know they chose my home birth at that house for this reason, entrusting my passage into this life to a Black midwife, who became one of my many godmothers. In our early years, it seemed that whatever small modicum of agency over our well-being Mata found she could steal back from the world for her children, she almost always would. This same thievery was at work in her decisions to raise us primarily in Hare Kṛṣṇa communities and to homeschool nearly all her children until she thought we were ready to face the outside world on our own, or as ready as we could be.

I would grow to resent homeschooling, begging Mata and my father every other day during junior high to enroll me in a public school. But when I was younger, I loved spending the school days with just my siblings. Mata never gave us too excessive an amount of homework, there was no real delineation between the school year and summer break, and I honestly wouldn't have had it any other way.

Once she instilled a passion for reading, outside of a daily scripture class on the Śrīmad-Bhāgavatam, Mata mostly just ensured books were available and left us to our own devices (unless we needed something requiring her to demonstrate specific examples). She trusted the knowledge we would pick up in our own natural curiosities between our excursions making battle weapons out of sticks and duct tape in the backyard, mimicking the knights we learned about in the old, browning encyclopedias she kept stacked in the basement we otherwise avoided because of a persistent mildew problem and the asbestos bursting from the walls.

But I didn't lack for community when I was homeschooled. Even with all the peculiar Hare Kṛṣṇa chanting and the constant smog of incense filling our house, the neighborhood kids were drawn to our home in ways that rejected the characterization of Black children as violently resistant to nonconformity, a popular narrative among white people and those who seek proximity to them.

The way Mata's evangelism manifested—keeping the door open for anyone to eat with us because prasādam, or food first offered to Kṛṣṇa, is considered purifying—might have had something to do with how well we got along with the neighborhood children. It was also a very Black manifestation. State-designed poverty forced many of the neighborhood kids to skip meals—sometimes we had to do the same—but that has never seemed to stop the Black people I've known from sharing with one another.

During our family's last few summers on East 128th, my older siblings Ganga and Ghanasyam would lead the building of a yearly "clubhouse" in the backyard. We organized our friends to gather materials for it from the local demolition sites and scrapyards that seemed to line every other block. Most of them didn't blink an eye when asked to contribute corner-store treats or money or to help build the frame for the clubhouse—our requirements for joining.

But Roberto was different. This might have been a story about the most carefree, joyful, fellowship-filled time of my life, if I didn't have to account for my perception of him.

In the way I've told this story before—a way I only recently began to question, having not thought deeply about it for some time—I would speak of Roberto as a physically imposing, overly aggressive, and unpredictable figure, the villain in an otherwise perfect tale of childhood community. I placed him in the role of the antagonist who ruined everything for us that year, tormenting me and my siblings at every turn. Roberto was much bigger than Ghanasyam—who at ten was around the same age, three years older than me—and I interpreted this fact as proof that he used his weight to get his way and as evidence of how terrifying he was. I remember him having a few heated arguments with Ganga, who was twelve at the time, about the decisions she made as clubhouse leader, and I used this to paint him as always seeking fights because of some innate hostility. He didn't have the same regard for the clubhouse we'd built, and I used this to craft a tale about how jealous he was of what we had. Even though we were both poor, he was a different type of poor from me.

In this version of the story, other poor Black children were always a different type of poor from me.

It was easy for me to use the facts of Roberto's body and his very typical youthful conflicts and his poorness to fabricate him as a hulking, envious saboteur with a penchant for cruelty, which became the explanation for why we disinvited him from the clubhouse the last summer we lived at that house. And that was the first story that came to mind when I tried to find the root of my carceral dissonance: the story of this large Black boy who didn't know how to be in a community. There must have been a reason my childhood was threatened, I told myself, and Roberto was the easy target. He could be a morality tale about how you shouldn't treat other people. I could use my memories to create a history that the facts couldn't fully support on their own. And I did exactly that, all the way up until I started to write about the last time we built the clubhouse and how it felt like my childhood was lost with it, as I tried to trace the beginning of that loss.

But my memories don't tell the full story. When I sat to write, I found myself blanking on the details. What was the "way" that Roberto was trying to get? What were Roberto and my sister arguing about, and why did I assume he had sought out those arguments? What exactly were his plans to sabotage the clubhouse? Did I actually remember anything about him beyond his Blackness, his poorness, his ordinary childhood disputes? Why was I so committed to telling this story when I had nothing else to back it up, and what other possible stories were there? What story would the childhood version of me who actually experienced this have told, their perception not yet fully tainted by the biases and misafropedia that I've come to hold?

Looking back on it, my conflicts with Roberto were, in fact, fairly mundane. But the figure he grew into in my mind—a figure that solidified over years of refusing to interrogate the way I told this story—was anything but. Misafropedia creates monsters out of Black children simply for being children, and I had internalized this concept by virtue of not actively working against it. It's wild how there didn't have to be a specific, spectacularly terrible thing a Black child did in order for me to villainize and criminalize them spectacularly and almost automatically—how an ordinary story about ordinary childhood things can stick with you by anti-Black adhesive for so long if you aren't critical of the ideas and beliefs you take for granted.

On our walks, Mother Bhūmi showed herself to be a complicated but caring grandmother who was suffering through countless traumas at a time when I'd fashioned her a raving monster who caused only suffering. She was demonstrating that there are many different versions of the past, that each is affected by the perception of the person telling the story. Why did I cling to this specific narrative of Roberto being a villain and this belief that my childhood would have been perfect without him? What systems of power affect the meaning I give to this story? Why have I believed for so long that there can be only this one version and this one meaning?

One could argue that there are indisputable historical facts, but what we do with those facts, and our acknowledgment of some facts and not others when describing our past, means that there is no way to perceive the past objectively. We are subjective beings. It is necessary to reimagine one's past narratives without clinging to a false sense of objectivity, and to always question our biases and where they might come from. Without doing so, it's no coincidence that I used the details I can access today to imagine Roberto in the same way Mike Brown was described by the police officer who murdered him. "I felt like a five-year-old holding on to Hulk Hogan," said Officer Darren Wilson, trying to justify shooting the eighteen-year-old on the side of the road in Ferguson, Missouri, in 2014. "He looked up at me, and had the most intense, aggressive face. The only way I can describe it—it looks like a demon."[20]

To hear this white police officer tell his account of Brown's murder, the young man was angry for no discernible reason, just as Roberto seemed to me in my recollections. Angry without cause. Beast, not boy. Bloodthirsty and devious. His violence was constructed as inevitable, regardless of whether it actually occurs. His violence was manufactured as perpetual, even when a pattern can't be established. Because if you construct the story like that, then a Black child deserves whatever comes to them. Both Wilson and I were raised in the same America. The America that demonizes all Black children—and the Blackest of them will always be caught in the gun's scope when you don't question where you are pressured to point it.

Like me, both Brown and Roberto were Black boys from what are still some of the Blackest neighborhoods in this country. It doesn't just so happen that both Wilson and I could uncritically imagine them as flat caricatures any more than it just so happens that those neighborhoods are today home to some of the Black communities most criminalized and incarcerated by the state. It was as easy for me to refuse to recognize the complexity of the Black children like Roberto in my past as it would be to refuse to recognize the complexity of the places we called home.

When I was growing up, Cleveland was almost always listed as one of the ten poorest cities in America according to census data, and it usually made it into the top two.[21] (It is listed as the second-poorest city today.) There were system-wide anti-Black practices in housing and water distribution that led to more than a quarter of kindergarten students screened in the city having a history of lead exposure at or above the level considered dangerous.[22] And just as this demonstrates that Flint, Michigan, wasn't the first Black city to suffer through a lead water crisis, mine wasn't the only house in Cleveland lined with exposed asbestos. We live in a world of unresolved Black traumas and a society where our response to trauma is punitive violence rooted in inflexible perspectives about the people who experience them, and those inflexible perspectives can never make room for our children to exist freely.

This is a culture where state vengeance is lauded as the solution to any problem, where we so regularly send to prison the Black and poor people whom capitalism excludes from accessing resources, punishing them for trying to survive inside a state-designed and anti-Black scarcity model. A culture where any conflict or interpersonal discord that arises from the simple fact that different people are living among each other in the same place is made indistinguishable from oppressive violence. Poor kids fighting over poor-kid things is met with the same punitive gaze and disinterest in accountability as adults fighting to exploit and capitalize on each other's labor and bodies. On the few, but still too frequent, occasions that I came home to that little yellow house to see one of my older siblings crying because one of his Black friends had been killed, I was always already armed with a plethora of reasons for why and how they might have deserved it by the time I reached my door. If I chose to bear those arms, I was also choosing to live in a specific version of the present defined by the state. I often did.

I don't recall many other details about Roberto beyond his large body and our ordinary childhood conflicts. But my refusal to see Black children outside of the worst stories the state writes about them was more a matter of not giving room to a Black child's full context than it was of not having access to that context. Misafropedia is a choice—a refusal to recognize the many rich stories that make up the whole of

Black childhood, even when those stories have been told to us. It is important to make different choices, to make space for Black children's stories, not because theirs are always perfect but because Black children demonstrate how to exist in a world where no one has to have a perfect story. Because Black children hold perspectives with the necessary flexibility to account for living in community with other people. I spent so long refusing to recognize and protect Black children, refusing to reject the state's inflexible story about them, that I could not write a story that gave room to other narratives even if given all the tools to do so.

~

By the time I was twelve, in the thick of begging to be sent to a "real" school, I had again made friends with most of the kids on my new street. It was one of the Blacker streets in a suburb that is still far more segregated than it likes to put on, although many of the middle-class Black folks who lived there clutched tightly to whatever superiority they could hold over those of us from Cleveland proper. Tierra and Titi (two neighbor girls I pretended to have a crush on because my best friend next door, Miguel, did) lived across the street from us in a small but dainty orange house that somehow managed to always have its grass cut the same length.

"She's so fine," Miguel said, waving goodbye to Tierra after we'd run her tiny Chihuahua back to the orange house following its escape, having just saved it from the jaws of Miguel's German shepherd, who was chained up in his backyard. We did not tell Tierra how close to death her excitable pup had been when we handed it back to her, its eyes bulging and bony body shaking wildly.

"Thank you," she'd said, blinking her long lashes at us.

Tierra was a year older than me and Miguel, and glided around with that video-girl look: shorts always mad short, hair always just done, baby hairs greased nice. Some of the parents on our street called her and her sister, Titi, who was my age, "fast" because of how grown these parents regarded them both to be—although, at the time, I still knew to question why that wasn't a problem on the part of the people doing the regarding.

"She is fine." I nodded in agreement as Miguel and I walked back across the street toward his house to finish our workout, trying to convince myself I was attracted to Tierra, too. I certainly thought her pretty, but if you were to ask me then about a girl I'd want to spend time with, it would have been her next-door neighbor Sarah. Sarah had always been kind to me and loved a lot of the nerdy shit I was into, too. Spending time with her, however, always meant spending time with her sister, Marissa, as the two were inseparable.

At first, Miguel and I got along with both sets of sisters, but they despised each other. If the story on our street was that Tierra and Titi were fast and bougie, it was also that Sarah and Marissa, who were hardly concerned with looking like anyone's video girls, were envious, with their less manicured lawn and older clothes. This story, of the haughty versus the envious, was the one told to explain their constant clashing, but Miguel and I had learned from both sets of sisters that the actual story was much more real. Much more childlike and tender. Much more complex.

Titi and Marissa had been best friends a long time ago, but Marissa felt that Titi had betrayed her trust. Titi had never apologized, thinking her action—something small enough that all of them had forgotten the details—should be forgiven by a person who claimed to love her. The hurt became an avalanche. And Sarah and Tierra got involved to defend their little sisters.

"Aw shit, here the fuck they go again," Miguel said, shaking his freckled face and throwing his hands dramatically into the air.

"Bitch, what did you say?!" Tierra screamed at Marissa, who had been sitting on her porch, talking on the phone.

"Why, god, why?!" Miguel pleaded into the sky as I laughed, turning around to witness a sight we'd both seen so many times before.

"Everything isn't about your nasty ass!"

"Who you calling nasty, dirty bopper?!"

Tierra and Marissa hurled obscenities back and forth for only seconds before Titi came out of her house, face coated thick with Vaseline, putting her hair up in a bun. I grabbed Miguel's arm when Tierra took out her earrings, and he sighed reluctantly as we headed toward them. By the time Tierra and Titi had made it down to their lawn, Sarah had come out to back up her sister, too. Within minutes, all four girls were tumbling around the grass, hair being pulled, faces being scratched. The jaws of Miguel's German shepherd suddenly seemed welcoming as we reached down to pull our friends apart.

When we finally succeeded in wrenching the four girls off one another, they yelled at each other for a few more moments, then finally stormed back inside their homes.

"Jesus," Miguel said, nursing a scratch he'd caught on his cheek in the fray.

"She's fine," I agreed again, "but ghetto."

For the first time, I summed up their feud the way some adults on our street did. Over the next few years, I came to act toward them like those adults did, too, avoiding my friends for their problems and ignoring them when they tried to tell us what their fights were really about. Ignoring them instead of helping them end their fights the way we knew everyone involved deserved to have them ended.

Whatever stories those adults on our street looked down their noses to tell about Tierra, Titi, Sarah, and Marissa, they all had the same ending: these girls were *ghetto*. And as beautiful as Miguel found Tierra, as warm and compellingly quirky as I found Sarah, as understandable as we found each of their stories about why they were angry with each other, *ghetto* meant I would learn to keep my distance from them more and more as I got older. I would have to if I wanted to find my place in a society that has always been violent toward the ghetto, lest I continue to be dismissed as just a ghetto kid from Cleveland proper, too.

Even in high school, when their fighting had completely subsided, I kept my distance from Sarah because of the way her struggles with her sister's former best friend had been reduced. I had seen it not as just the ordinary conflict that it was but as a representation of a kind of Black—too loud, too assertive, too poor—that the world was teaching me to reject in both myself and others. Sarah and I remained friendly, but we would never be as close as we could have been. As I wanted to be, even after I understood my attraction to her was not romantic.

"I was just trying to protect my sister," Sarah repeated at track practice one day during her senior year, my junior, after a classmate brought up the well-known story of her constant fights in order to dismiss her in an argument. I began to walk away, even as Sarah turned to me and said it again, so clear, heartfelt, and intelligible: "I just have to always protect my sister."

It's a beautiful thing to me now, how, without question, as young girls they would almost teleport to each other's side when one felt threatened. At the root of their fighting, at the root of all our "ghetto," was always love, a love that first drove two families apart, then drove sisters closer together. And though you could argue whether there are healthier expressions of this love, whether every urge to protect the people you love has to end with shedding blood, you could not deny that the love was there. You could, though, ignore it. And I did.

Struggling against the limitations of my current perspective of Roberto and recognizing that my younger self might have had a different understanding of him and his motivations than the previous, clearly harmful one I held on to without much basis for so long has also helped me to realize that I owe Sarah an apology. If my love for Black people is real, acknowledging that I hold and have held anti-Black views means being accountable for them, and that requires me to apologize for the way I flattened Sarah and her story throughout our brief friendship and to make amends.

It's not that my younger self would have had some objective view of her or Roberto. But my younger self might have told a different story, and that possibility inherently challenges the narrative I'd used to define my past, a narrative I *mistook* as objective. Because I can't ever truly know my younger self's perspective fully, working to reclaim my childhood opens up vast possibilities for other perspectives and allows many narratives to exist at once, with some given more appropriate validity and others given more appropriate criticism and reflection. It allows me to acknowledge that I once reduced Sarah and Roberto to anti-Black caricatures of themselves and that the history of my doing so will always be a part of me and something I must reckon with, even as I explore more affirming perspectives that might stop me from ever reducing Black children in this way again.

Working to repair the fracture caused by my carceral dissonance helped me to realize that the story of my last summer in Cleveland proper, before we moved to the Cleveland Heights suburb, never had to be a story about a boy who blew up my childhood. That was just the story I'd learned to be comfortable with. It could instead be a story about how my childhood being blown up by the same misafropedia I wielded against him had helped me reduce Black children to terrors for years since.

By understanding the power dynamics in how we tell the stories of our experiences in any particular time, I can better recognize Black children outside of the flattening descriptors the world places on them. I can better learn to see my own childhood self outside of these patholo-gies, too. Giving space for Black children to be complex and multidimensional, and that leading to offering an apology to someone who deserves it and should have always been a friend, feels as freeing as I remember the piles of Nowalaters in a backyard clubhouse feeling as a kid. It feels like the imagination Mata worked so hard to safeguard in her children.

~

Though we certainly learned a lot during those years, I realize now that Mata insisted on her children being homeschooled primarily so that we didn't *unlearn* critical aspects of ourselves. It was the slow unlearning of a more tender care, one that allowed room for other stories, that kept me from regarding the Robertos and Sarahs in my life with the kindness they deserve today. It was replacing the openheartedness of a Black child with something else—something judgmental, self-policing, and punitive— marked by fear of how the outside world might respond to us.

Ironically, it was Mata's steadily intensifying policing of my gender expression that most exemplified this unlearning. As I grew older, her increasing vigilance around the femininity in how I dressed or walked or spoke suggested that the protection she sought for me by refusing "this material world" was limited, at least in critical aspects, to only the beginning of my life. This limitation is also a question of whose timeline we follow and why.

There are many different perspectives on when "the end of child-hood" arrives. The end date that we cling to, and the meaning we ascribe to that end, also matters. There is the version the state promotes, where immediately after a child hits an arbitrary age, it is suddenly legal to manipulate them into fighting unjust wars. In this version, this same age indicates a time when society will condone people much older and with much more power manipulating these teenagers into sexually exploit-ative relationships. And I believe these rigid ideas about when protect-ing childhood should be honored and when that protection should be withdrawn influenced Mata when it came to my gender.

In Mata's version, immediately after hitting another arbitrary age, queerness was suddenly no longer an option, even though my queerness was so linked to what she had been safeguarding in me before. And since I wasn't discerning enough to distinguish between homeschooling itself and the lens it had fostered in me, the lens through which I could view myself and other Black children with care, I rejected them both, especially when being at home longer seemed to buy me the safety I required.

~

Imagining how a younger me might have had more space to love and be loved is liberating, but it can also be discomforting. Reclaiming freedom often means exploring again how I lost it, and all the things I lost with it. Things like my hair.

It was more than just hair, when I had it. It was that getting my hair braided brought me near to the people I cared for most. It was the affection my sisters and mother could put into the top of my head that they sometimes could not put into words. When Mata would braid my hair, she'd sit me between her legs as she watched the latest *Oprah* or listened to her favorite bhajans, and everything was all right. I was proud of the way my hang time dropped past my small shoulders, curving at the ends like snakes at attention, as if I knew Medusa had never been the villain either, that she didn't ask to be cursed. But more than that, I was proud of my relationships with the women who gathered me to them weekly to leave my hair as fly as they could manage. For five years, my hair was a part of who I was. For five years, I was allowed to determine that, and I loved who I had determined myself to be.

Not long after the final time Mata did my hair, she told me, "You're becoming a young man now." It was only a few weeks before my fifth birthday, and what did I know about being a man? A melancholy bhajan about a woman longing for Kṛṣṇa might have played in the background on a tape player. Mata's own hair was certainly covered, as it always was, in a head wrap that matched her Punjabi.

"Young men don't have long hair," Mata continued.

"Why not?" I asked.

"Long hair is for young ladies," she said, as if she hadn't previously encouraged me to think critically enough to know that this was no real explanation. "Why don't we celebrate becoming a young man on your birthday by shaving it off?"

I didn't want to become a young man, but I didn't have a choice. The world demanded it, and in contrast to her resistance to the world in so many other examples of my life, now Mata demanded the same. A part of me refused cutting my hair for as long as I could. That part had to be the same one that I'm desperately trying to find now.

The day of my haircut, Mata bribed me with presents and my favorite food, a creamy Indian-inspired potato pie dish called Gauranga Potatoes, bartering with whatever she could to make me buy into my own rupturing.

"Can I at least save it?" I asked, holding back tears in our living room. My older brother Mohan's hand rested on my shoulder, his other hand buzzing in the air as it clutched the clippers, sounding like I imagined an electric chair might. At some point during their childhoods, all my brothers, in one form or another, had similarly been told it was time to be men. Mohan might not have known that he'd been enlisted to help take from me the same thing the state had been trying to take from him—his own tenderness. I'd go on to replace my sisters braiding their affection into my head with him cutting his into it, and like every boy who's thrust into manhood too soon, I would learn to call this love.

"Save it?" Mohan laughed, not noticing how emotional I was becoming as he removed his Kangol to wipe his forehead and reveal the same receding hairline that I would later inherit. Mata saw my face and let the weight of the world pull her high cheekbones down into a frown. She disappeared into the kitchen for a brief moment, and when she returned, it was with a Styrofoam cup full of water in her gentle hands.

"You can freeze some of it," she said with a smile that seemed to mask the hurt she felt from hurting me, a hurt that had taken her by surprise. I think it was her own carceral dissonance revealing itself as she told her barely five-year-old son that it was time to be a man.

We kept a cup full of ice with a tuft of my hair inside the freezer for months, until it mysteriously disappeared. For some reason, I never asked where it went.

There will forever be distinctions between different stages of life, and there should be. I needed a different type of protection and guidance as a child than I do now, and often children need adults to make decisions for them. But those distinctions never have to mean what the state says they mean. Those distinctions don't have to mean children have no say over their bodies, desires, wants, and needs. That only we, as adults, have the right answers. That they can't make decisions differently than we might make them, that they can't make mistakes and get into fights and have conflicts without something fundamentally wrong with them needing to be fixed. Or that they can't be queer. Protecting children shouldn't be conflated with controlling them and their perspectives along their journey into adulthood. Misafropedia ensures it always is.

All Black children are subjected to the harm that comes with erasing the complexity of their childhood experiences as they are forced into the categories of "young men" or "young women." This expression of misafropedia also comes for our girl children, in how we project designations like "fast" onto those like Tierra. And it comes for Black children who don't conform to either of the state's binary gender categories entirely, which is all of us before we are forced to conform. By joining in this process of denying Black children the space to exist freely, we have no recourse when the state does the same.

In 2014, twelve-year-old Tamir Rice was killed by police while playing with a toy gun not too far from my old house on East 128th. Afterward, newspapers referred to him as a "young man." They hardly mentioned his fourteen-year-old sister, who was handcuffed when she tried to reach her baby brother after she saw him murdered, nor how this trauma played a role in stealing her childhood, too. Rice's murderer insisted he thought the child was no less than twenty years old in order to justify his actions, building on the groundwork already laid for our acceptance of such childhood-thieving narratives.

Like many Black children, I was coaxed by the state, and by those who had adopted the state's messages, out of my childhood, in order to try and fit a definition of manhood that was never compatible with me. That haircut was the early part of a sustained project of gender policing that my parents adopted to prevent me from growing freely into my queerness. This project would include shame and isolation, neglect, and the memory of at least one beating.

It wasn't just my hair. It was that, in an attempt to make us ready for the world and to shape me into their inflexible and supposedly objective idea of what it meant to be a man, my parents would now compromise their strongest beliefs about how important it was for their children to safeguard against inflexible perspectives and a false sense of objectivity. I, in turn, would come to compromise those beliefs, too.

The summer we disinvited Roberto was the last summer we ever built a clubhouse. I soon began to make bigger fragile houses, and from them I only got better at throwing stones at the Black children whom I could most easily criminalize in my life (and the parts of me that, like them, I could not reconcile with white society).

My family moved to Cleveland Heights when I was ten years old. The move marked a shift into some semblance of middle-class life, even though we were still surviving on my father's poverty salary and food stamps. I didn't really know what "middle-class" meant at the time, but I knew that our new home had not only a sunroom but a side porch and a basketball hoop on the garage. I still didn't have my own room, and never would until I moved out from under my parents, but I knew that our new house was now considered "nice," even though Kiss still really loves our old one with the dandelion lawn. I knew that we had to separate ourselves, with the "nice," "respectable" neighbors, away from the "ghetto" ones—who were so much more like the dear friends who'd helped us build our clubhouse year after year.

The state allows adults to tell only specific stories about growing up in a poor Black city. Stories about danger and gunshots and how no one cares for one another. Stories of how we were stripped of our agency but never of how free we felt when we still had it. Stories where it would only make sense to want to leave, to hate all the dandelions, even if you really didn't.

The compulsion to tell these stories is an extension of how the state frames the Black past in general. The state relies on progress narratives that insist Black people are constantly moving forward from horrible events and that we must keep running in the same direction. This is why, for instance, popular media propagates the idea that New York City's Blackest neighborhoods were "bad" in the eighties, overrun with gangs and drugs, until the police state increased its presence, ensuring that those areas are now whiter and "better."

This story disregards the indisputable creativity and revolutionary spirit of that same time—and indeed of many of the gang members and drug dealers—a spirit that has survived in the people who lived through it and are still here. It is a story that disregards anything we might learn to make it through the difficulties of today by embracing their guidance. With the narratives of our pasts being so devastatingly flattened, it's only fitting that "doing time" has become a reference to our literal imprisonment in the carceral state. To understand history as the state does, as a singular narrative of the past that it projects onto everyone, as if proximity to power has no bearing on how a story is told, is central to criminalizing Black children and adults in the present. When the state tells history, our singular past is always that of enslaved people "freed" into an anti-Black, carceral system.

I told these flattened stories of my own past for so long that sometimes I still get an involuntary chill when walking through the same type of "dangerous" neighborhoods where my little yellow house resided, neighborhoods where sisters like Sarah and Tierra and Marissa and Titi sometimes fight on the streets, but only because they want nothing more than to protect and be there for their siblings. I feel that chill even though far more harm has come to me in "safely" white neighborhoods, where cops and citizens and even white children with guns and fists remind Black people over and over again that we don't belong.

~

Black people have always carried multiple sets of memories, multiple perspectives of the past, living with the dissonance this country requires of us in order to survive. That we can carry them all at once, without punitive inflexibility defining our histories along one singular timeline, is important. The perspectives we attempt to grow away from must be acknowledged alongside all others because it takes acknowledgment to heal, to be held accountable. But we can hold all these perspectives together and grow from the failures of each only when we stop considering any single outlook as the *only* one, as above critique.

There are the memories of Cleveland as a place of lack, of hating homeschooling, of my grandmother as a terrifying and tormenting presence, of difficult little Black boys and combative little Black girls . . . and then there are the memories of the freedom that I lost, of sitting between my mother's legs and having her tenderly braid my hair, of Black boys and girls who were complex enough not to pathologize each other even in the midst of conflict.

There are memories of me yearning for another life where I wouldn't be so different from everyone else, of difficult tensions with people who had different needs and desires from mine; and then there are memories of that summer building a clubhouse with all my differentness on full display being one of the best times I've ever had, and of the kids who loved us despite it all. There are memories I don't have full access to.

And reconciling all these memories, repairing the fracture caused by carceral dissonance, is a type of time disruption that is just as magical as a palm full of Nowalaters. Because as sure as there are many different ways to tell stories of the past and the present that aren't reducible to the only one the state tells us is possible, there can also be different stories of the future. There can be stories where we are free.

CHAPTER FOUR

A PRAYER FOR REST

Hari-Gaura,

Another night of no sleep, and I feel it coming like a storm creeping just beyond the horizon before I even lie down. Or it comes because I feel it, like when you think about yawning and then you do. I excel at keeping myself awake with fears of keeping myself awake.

I've found excellence in many such practices since I lost you.

Not all of them leave me feeling like the loneliest person on the planet—at least not immediately. Most of them, in fact, serve to foster a kind of community, the kind that cheers on a person for acing tests that measure only how good they are at taking tests, not their intelligence; for having more of the skills others will celebrate than anyone else in the room, even if they don't have more of the skills others will need; for mostly successfully assimilating into spaces filled with powerful people when they themselves are weak. And I think mastering these practices has historically been a way to replace the companionship you provided me, however inadequate.

It took a lot of discipline to achieve this excellence, to graduate with the second-highest grade point average in my high school class; to attain multiple student leadership positions and honors programs while I was there; to manage, in my guidance counselor's words, a "near-perfect college application." Discipline like, "You idiot, you should have been first in class," or, "Only losers follow," or, "What am I doing wrong that my application isn't perfect?"

What I mean is, the idea of excellence that I learned, that I adopted, after you left, is one that travels hand in hand with harm. Capitalism is a system in which individuals are given value only through competing, often violently, to own the means of producing goods, exploiting those goods for personal profit. Under this system, how I came to value myself since high school, and even more so when I began to have some semblance of financial success in my career, meant that I had to beat someone down, even if that must be myself, to climb over them. And if I wasn't climbing, life wasn't worth it.

I've been climbing for more and more top spots and accolades and money ever since. I thought that was what I would have to do to have a meaningful life. I didn't know it was an option to find meaning in getting you back, in nurturing a love for myself. I had to be the best at not settling;

otherwise, what I settled for would be all I would ever get, and I didn't understand that to be able to reclaim my sense of wholeness would be enough.

I just didn't want to only ever get picked last, to only ever get locked out of power, to only ever not matter, and I saw that's what happens when you do nothing more than be Black and live life. So I couldn't just be Black and live; I had to become an example of Black Excellence, which I know now is just another expression of respectability. And that meant whenever I was or felt powerless or worthless, whenever I got complacent in my Black life, I had to punish myself for it, even if I wasn't the one who had made myself feel that way.

I didn't call Mata this week, and I am now so excellent at being a good child, at being the young man she always wanted me to be, that I will not rest tonight. I am so excellent at being that person that I won't even consider why I cannot be it for her all the time, through no fault of my own. I won't even consider that I might get too tired and too sad and too overwhelmed and too resentful, even if I feel all these things for valid reasons; it feels like this capitalist economy is collapsing, but I am still somehow being overworked, and I do not remember how it feels to be rested.

You can become so good at punishing yourself this way that it almost feels like a superpower. No, really—I can hear everything outside for what must be miles, blaring louder every time that my body approaches relaxation, all because I can't stop thinking about missing a phone call.

Someone is dribbling a basketball a few streets over, but she might as well be dribbling on my head for how adept my body is at amplifying the sound to penalize me. A car alarm keeps going off blocks and blocks away, but the car may as well be floating right outside my fourth-story window. My fiancé is grinding his teeth so loudly that I fear that they will fall out any second and chew me to pieces.

My superpowered body can even metamorphize in mere seconds through extreme temperatures, ranging from raging hellfire to the center of an iceberg, prompting a never-ending cycle of sticking my limbs out from underneath the covers and then wrapping the covers around myself so tightly I can hardly move. My body can make time meaningless. In two seconds, the sun will rise, even though it was only just midnight, and with it will come a light so blinding no pillow held across my face can keep it at bay. Though that won't stop me from trying and nearly suffocating myself in the process.

If my anxiety is just my mind being colonized in the ways that my external world has always been, then this burning heart and cratering chest and famine of rest are the final frontier. In this search for excellence that I've undertaken ever since you were gone, my body is doing only what my colonized mind trained it to do, better than it ever did before. In a warped way, I feel proud of what it has accomplished. It has gotten so good at trying to be good that it won't allow me anything else, even when it has no choice. Even when everything around it is so conspicuously bad. I wish that my body knew good outside of punishment, like you did. I know there was a time you wanted to be good at being free.

But knowing that you could be in this unsettled mind with me means that filling it with the constant punishment of myself and others in search of excellence isn't the only solution. I don't have to wander through this emptiness without a guide to show me a way out. I can ask you to lead. I can ask you, what is *your* purpose? What do you need to fulfill it? How can I help? Trying for another type of purpose that doesn't turn on harming Black people who refuse to climb endlessly is possible, if you are. There must be some other way to live life outside of the constant attempts to build a feeble sense of self atop the bodies of the people whom I have harmed and discarded.

And strangely, as I talk to you about all this, I find it a little bit easier to relax. In the calm, I can feel my body cautiously begin to lose its superhuman abilities, but if that means waking up tomorrow without feeling like shit, I guess I have to start being okay with that.

CHAPTER FIVE

D*MB SMART

"It was all Kṛṣṇa's mercy," Mata responded when I asked how we afforded the move to Cleveland Heights, a question that for some reason I'd never thought to ask before. We were sitting in the bedroom she shared with my father, a converted attic that had gone unfinished for more than a decade, filled with neatly stacked piles of books and magazines that smelled faintly of sawdust. The room was mostly off limits to her children before I moved to New York for college. She said she was talking to me inside it now only because she had work to do there, but I could tell it was really because she was tired. She had on her head wrap but had otherwise put little effort into getting dressed—wearing only a robe—which was markedly unfamiliar. I didn't know it yet, but she wouldn't leave the room for the whole time I was in town.

"We needed to get you out of that house," my father followed up, taking the baton of storyteller. He does this sometimes, forcing her unwillingly into a conversational relay race. I used to think she was okay with it in that same mystically charitable way I'd always mythologized her to act because she never stopped him. This time I think I caught her rolling her eyes before giving the more customary warm smile and placing an encouraging hand on his shoulder.

"Once you passed out, we realized we couldn't live there any-more," my father continued.

He asked if I remembered. I told him of course, but he still recounted the tale of how, at the yellow house, I developed terrible breathing problems that nearly killed me.

"Just walking down that old carpet-lined staircase took all the breath out of you." He'd probably spit at the word "carpet" if he were outside and had less couth, his anti–floor covering crusade kicking into high gear.

"I try to warn everybody about them carpets. Death traps."

Like with his excessive hatred of microwaves and GMOs, I might otherwise have dismissed my father's incessant war on carpeting as irrational, but I could almost feel the air siphoning out of my lungs again as if it were helium in a just-punctured balloon, the foul coughing fit hitting me like a tornado the air escaped to create, and I found myself sympathetic to this cause. I can only imagine the horror Mata must have felt when she saw me start sprinting in desperate circles around the landing area at the bottom of the steps as I tried and tried to outrun death, before everything went black.

An acute case of chronic bronchitis, the doctor said when I woke up in the hospital. My lungs have never been the strongest, and my breathing issues had been greatly exacerbated by the dust collecting in our carpet. After the diagnosis, I had to wear a breathing machine every night for days on end.

"It didn't help when we had the carpets throughout the whole house cleaned," Mata began to explain before Daddy finished for her: "At that point, everything we did was like, are you working hard or hardly working? We weren't allowed to remove the carpets, so we knew we had to move." Even though, he continued as Mata laid her own ailing body down in their bed, they didn't really have the money for this.

"We were looking at homes in East Cleveland first," Mata said. East Cleveland was the first established suburb in the Cleveland area. It is just as neglected by the state as Cleveland proper, and—or because—it is even Blacker, the state has successfully redlined and drained it of resources through their anti-Black systems of urban planning.

"We wanted to be part of a Black community. But all of our applications for houses in East Cleveland fell through." Eventually, they applied for a house in Cleveland Heights, a more "diverse" suburb nearby that wasn't yet fully drained of resources by white flight. But as more Black people have trickled in during the past few decades, they've fallen prey to predatory banks and police looking for ripe targets. The house on which my parents ultimately put a down payment required a lot of fixing up, "which is part of how we could afford it," Daddy explained, revealing that they also received assistance from a government housing program. We stayed in the upstairs apartment of my godmother's duplex in East Cleveland for a year while the house in Cleveland Heights was fixed up.

"But really, it was the devotees who helped us make that move possible," Mata said. "A lot of that work on the house they did for free."

Because our religion reached its pinnacle of popular-culture awareness in the seventies, many people still associate Hare Kṛṣṇa devotees with chanting monks in saffron robes who handed out books at airports and who were so easy to parody in films of the time. But most devotees—and particularly those of us who didn't live in insulated temple communities—are people with typical jobs, dress, and problems. And though devotees are supposed to be beyond race because we're taught to believe that we are all just souls trapped in differently colored bodies, we have always had typical experiences with it, too. But many members of our religious community—which genuinely has shown up for our family's material needs more times than I can count—obscured the reality of our racial experiences under the guise that following a religion that considers people as spirits instead of bodies meant that they could never hold anti-Black beliefs.

Mata ran weekly Hare Kṛṣṇa programs out of different devotees' homes (most often ours) from the temple in Cleveland's closure just before I was born until she traveled to India for her cancer treatment. "Class," as we called these programs, began every Sunday at 3:00 p.m. Devotees would assemble to listen to a teacher, usually Mata, as they led a lecture on the Bhagavad Gītā. This was more or less my only exposure to non-Black people before moving to Cleveland Heights, and it helped lay the foundation for my belief in the respectable quest for Black exceptionalism, the idea that I could become somehow different and more deserving than the Black people around me if only I met certain criteria. It was the clearest message I received from the distinct treatment of my family by the devotee community, in contrast with their treatment of the Black non-devotees living around us.

"When Charanjit Swami came for a class at the old house," Mata added from her bed, referring to a renowned Hare Kṛṣṇa guru who is white, "he told me it was time to find a better neighborhood, so I knew we had to." It was the third explanation for how we afforded to move to Cleveland Heights, and all three of them rang true: God's mercy made it possible. We had to move to save my life. Because a white man didn't feel safe in a Black neighborhood (although Mata insists this wasn't what the swami meant). But none of them answer how we afforded what we paid: a deeper connection to ourselves and to each other that I had experienced before moving to Heights.

When Mata and Mother Bhūmi first learned about the man who would later become their guru, Srila Prabhupada, who was also responsible for bringing this branch of Hinduism from India to the States and much of the rest of the world, it wasn't as if they were under the illusion that anti-Blackness magically bypassed the Hare Kṛṣṇa community even while having obviously influenced the lives of everyone who converted into it. After crossing paths with Hare

Kṛṣṇa preachers and being enraptured with what they heard about this exuberant song-and-dance-centered path to self-realization, Mother Bhūmi and her children sought membership in the old Cleveland temple. When they arrived, they were stopped by the temple president, who told them in no uncertain terms that Black people were unworthy of being in Kṛṣṇa's presence. When Mother Bhūmi protested, the temple president called the police and had them arrested.

This familiar violence didn't deter my mother and grandmother. They interpreted the temple president's actions as a mere perversion of Prabhupada's teachings, and Mata later wrote her future guru a letter to make sure he knew the discrimination being done in his name.

"He wrote back and said, 'If someone discriminates against you based on your skin color, that's their problem. If you let it get to you, that's yours.' I'll never forget that," Mata recalled with adoration.

I wanted to ask how she could find liberation in a belief system that puts the onus of eradicating anti-Blackness on those who are destroyed by it, that asks that they achieve excellence by skillfully overlooking their own destruction. I wanted to ask what we are supposed to do with the Black people who don't or can't overlook this violence, like Korryn Gaines, like our neighbors in the "dangerous" Cleveland community we moved away from, or—in my wildest thoughts, which I was often too afraid to speak growing up—like me.

I wanted to ask how she could still perceive these words as so admirable when her own mother was proof the problem was around long before any of us "let it get to us," proof that being exceptional in the amount of suffering we can accept is never going to save us. I wanted to know what she would say it looked like to refuse to let someone who is denying your existence, or abusing you or threatening to harm your children, get to you in the first place.

But I already knew what it looked like; it was lying down in front of me, trying to appear strong when she was sick. Trying to reconcile her earthly Blackness and desire to be "part of a Black community" with the transcendent idea that "we are not these bodies." And I already knew how she could consider this liberating, too; it was the same reason I tried to find liberation in my separation from my childhood. We had been conditioned to recognize Black life only if it came alongside Black pain, and so we embraced these painful dissonances in an attempt to stay alive.

In 1990, Kīrtanānanda Swami, one of the first white devotees Prabhupada initiated into the Hare Kṛṣṇa religion and the former leader of one of the largest Hare Kṛṣṇa communes, New Vṛindaban in Marshall County, West Virginia, was arrested on charges of racketeering, mail fraud, and conspiracy to murder two devotees who were killed after criticizing him. Steven "Sulocana" Bryant and Charles "Chakradara" St. Denis had tried to expose Kīrtanānanda for his alleged persistent rapes of young boys in the community, the beginnings of a global child sex abuse scandal that would show this sickening violence to be as pervasive throughout the Hare Kṛṣṇa community as anything the Catholic Church has ever seen. Kīrtanānanda was initially convicted on nine of the eleven counts related to Bryant's and St. Denis's murder before hiring Alan Dershowitz, who would later defend Jeffrey Epstein against child sex abuse accusations, to lead an appeal that resulted in the ruling being overturned, and the swami later pleaded guilty to racketeering during the retrial.

We visited the New Vṛindaban community more than once a year growing up, and although Kīrtanānanda had been belatedly expelled from the movement by then (only after he was officially charged, despite the accusations and suspicious murders that had been occurring for years), many members of the community's leadership who have been accused of covering up his abuses remain in positions of power—including Charanjit Swami—and other child abuse cases have arisen in Kīrtanānanda's wake. Charanjit never suggested Mata and her young children leave *this* dangerous place for a "better neighborhood," because misafropedia means endangering Black children is always more acceptable than the danger thoughtlessly ascribed to them.

Although Mata would later go back to that same temple led by the white temple president who hated Black people with Prabhupada's blessing—and although she heeded Charanjit Swami's concerns and moved away from the Black community in which she said she wanted to build a home—her closest devotee relationships were always with other Black devotees.

The Cleveland community that Mata led still has a larger percentage of Black Hare Kṛṣṇas than almost any other Hare Kṛṣṇa community in the States, and I don't think her recruitment of souls trapped in Black bodies was ever a coincidence. Her relationship to race and religion is more complicated than any simple criticism. It would be easy to judge her for the mistakes along her own journey to make herself whole again, but I think it's time I learned from them.

~ ·

Just before ninth grade began, I finally won. I had been pleading with my parents for the previous four years to let me attend school with my friends, and after all that time and effort and tears, they had relented at last. Mata usually allowed her children to enroll at a school outside the home when they reached the ninth grade, but this still felt like a hard-fought victory. I had forged my weapons for this battle meticulously. As a last-ditch effort, I spent weeks writing out a precocious three-page letter listing all the reasons why I should be permitted to go, giving myself debate prep worthy of a presidential candidate before turning it in to my parents.

"You should trust me," I wrote in conclusion, "and everything you taught me. I know who I am, and I won't let any environment take that from me."

The reality was that I knew myself less than I ever had before, but the letter was enough to sway my parents. I can still understand the desire I had to spend more time around my peers back then, especially as my last two older siblings who were living in the home, Ganga and Ghanasyam, were gearing up to head for college. But if I had the choice now between being with my mother and being forced for the majority of the day to work on things in which I had sparingly little interest, I would make a very different one. What I would do to have it.

That isn't to say I didn't thrive in high school. My friend Betty constantly referred to me jokingly as a "homeschooled jungle freak," referencing Lindsay Lohan's character in the movie *Mean Girls*. But like Cady Heron, I didn't have too much trouble making friends, even if I also experienced an array of identity crises in my attempts to fit in. In another similarity, I would ultimately end up being crowned homecoming king, although I surely benefited from a nominal voting turnout propelled by the fact that ballots weren't collected in class as they had been in years past. I also had my horde of siblings and my friends across the Hare Kṛṣṇa community, and Mata had scraped up what I didn't know then was far too rare money for me to take tae kwon do classes and play rec-league basketball for years, which helped make developing relationships with kids my age fairly seamless. Many of the friends I'd collected in these activities ended up at Cleveland Heights High with me.

My class of 2009 was one of the first at Heights to be split into five "small schools." Administrators said this would make the institution, which held two thousand students, a more manageable size, because a student's classes would be primarily in the section of the building where their small school was housed. But most of the honors and advanced placement classes were conspicuously situated on the first and third floors, in the Mosaic and Renaissance schools. These were, coincidentally, the small schools that almost all the white students—who made up only about 20 percent of the school but more than 50 percent of the suburb—chose to attend.

Mimicking a group of my friends, I picked the Pride school. (In hindsight, this was a fitting choice, in light of my burgeoning queerness.) Pride shared the second floor with the equally Black Real school, so the small school split didn't much help the commutes of Black students in honors and AP classes, who still usually had to journey to other floors to reach them. The students who previously would have been sent to the recently closed alternative school Taylor Academy were automatically assigned to Transition, which was immediately stigmatized as the "d*mb school," and so it certainly didn't help those students either.

In fact, it seemed small schools functioned to give white students yet another way to separate themselves from the rest of us, the administration's solution to appeasing the increasing numbers of white parents who would send their kids to private schools to avoid exposure to Black people. It also perpetuated separations between "high-achieving" and other Black students, ensuring white wholeness and cohesion by paying with the currency of Black division. I didn't fully understand it at the time, but this experience was a predictable evolution of anti-Black school-zoning laws, the charter-school push, and redlining, all of which have had a similar effect of continuing the separate and unequal access to schooling between Black and white families that is worsening today.[23]

For the first semester of high school, I shared more than half of my classes with Betty, who was also Black and in Pride. Her jungle-freak quip didn't start off as a rib nudge between good friends—it was anything but. A grade ahead and only five feet tall, I was small even for my thirteen years, and given the unfortunate popular styles of the time and my assimilationist willingness to unquestionably adopt them, my clothes usually swallowed me whole. In my oversize Girbaud jeans, knockoff T.J. Maxx Iverson jerseys, and fitted caps that didn't really fit because I had stolen them from my brother Mohan, I looked flimsy and breakable next to Betty. She was tall and boisterous and willing to get hood if the moment called for it, and sometimes even when it didn't. She made me feel as insecure as Roberto had, and I was well on the way toward being unable to reckon with those feelings without wrapping them up in righteous superiority.

Though she excelled academically, Betty hadn't initially shown any interest in competing with me, but that didn't stop me from making sure I beat her. When teachers passed out graded homework, I'd try to burglarize a peek at Betty's results, smiling smugly when they fell beneath mine. I felt vindicated whenever I could correct her, and so I made it my mission to correct her regularly.

I didn't question why I did these things, but it felt right. Betty had unjustly become a representation of all my worst fears—that even if I was smart, I might not be smart enough, that even in white spaces, I might still be too Black—and so I did everything in my power to distance myself from her and the possibilities she offered. No one corrected me. If anything, teachers encouraged my efforts to be better than the Black people around me, of whom Betty was but one example. And she was an example who was also considered "gifted," so you can imagine the distance I sought to make between myself and those who weren't.

"You aren't like these other Negroes," a Black high school guidance counselor once told me with a laugh and a pat on the back. I was trying to prove him right. Being unlike everyday Black people—or even just Black people whom I could position as more everyday than me—was what it meant to succeed in the culture I was learning to be part of at this school. It's what respectability politics always means.

To be Black and exceptional in this world requires seeing yourself not in your people but in whiteness. I wiped that mirror over and over again to find a face less like those of the other Negroes looking back, pressing harder and harder with every unsuccessful motion across it, until the mirror cracked.

Freshman year, I had two classes with Paul, which we both shared with Betty, too. Paul was a white boy who was even smaller than me, wiry enough to twang if you flicked his arm. He wore round glasses that made him look like a skeletal Harry Potter. For the entire school day, he carried around a viola strapped to his back, the instrument twice as big as his body. It admittedly made for a laughable sight, but I pitied him when the chuckles came his way. I assumed he had some sort of social disorder, as he didn't seem to be able to engage with anyone, and I pitied him for that, too. I leaned into the same ableist ideas about disabilities being to blame for unwanted behaviors, the same ideas I'd wielded against my grandmother. It was as easy for me to shower Paul with pity as it was for me to be afraid of Mother Bhūmi or to resent Betty. Maybe even easier.

"Give me my viola!" I heard Paul's nasally voice pierce the laughter of a crowd in the hallway. I could just make out his instrument floating above the crowd like a thundercloud, and I groaned as I stepped closer and saw the person who had created this storm.

"Give me my viola!" Betty repeated, mocking him, as giggles rippled through the small crowd again. Paul bounced up and down like a bespectacled grasshopper, but he could not make up the distance created by Betty's towering figure.

"Give it back to him, Betty," I implored.

She looked at me and rolled her eyes. "Or what?"

"Or . . . or we'll all be late to class," I said, my brief burst of "bravery" deflating. "Just give it back to him and let's go."

Betty looked from me to Paul, who just kept jumping and clawing at her arm, face redder than a well-fed mosquito. The crowd had already begun dispersing.

"Here," Betty said, smacking her lips, thrusting the viola into Paul's arms, nearly knocking him over backward in the process. "Say 'excuse me' next time!"

But Paul said nothing, just scrunched up his face and powered directly toward me, no "excuse me" as he crashed into me either.

"Bitch," I heard him mumble in Betty's direction as he walked by, taking me aback.

"I swear to fucking god. He bumps into me every day. Every day!" Betty threw up her arms, exasperated. "Racist motherfucker."

"What do you mean?"

I wasn't sure I really wanted to engage, but we were heading to the same class anyway.

"The other day he called me a nigger, and I almost tore his head off. I'm sure you just heard him call me a bitch."

I nodded reluctantly.

"He's always been like that. And no one wants to do anything because he's, well, Paul. Hell, I don't want to seem like I'm picking on him either. But he's fucking terrible, and I don't care anymore."

I would later hear from other students more stories about Paul being hateful, which had apparently been a regular preoccupation of his since at least middle school. His outbursts seemed largely reserved for Black women. Usually they just let him slide. Some even defended him, like I did.

As the year progressed, it didn't take long for Paul to begin crashing into me more in hallways, too, and he never said "excuse me" those times either. For a while, I still felt compelled to let it slide. But when I also began noticing his smug smirk when he did better on a test than the rest of us, how much he loved correcting us, I started to consider that maybe there was such a thing as doing too well at living up to my guidance counselor's statement. That there was a damaging side to excelling in the way that I had, which seemed in such proximity to the way Paul did, too. The narcissism of regarding this violence as a problem only when it came down on me was real, but only part of my realization. The other part was that my reflection had become clearer than ever in his violence, and I did not like how I looked. Or maybe that's ultimately just narcissism, too.

"I'm sick of just letting that slide," Betty reiterated, and as our friendship developed, I let her weariness wash over me. I was embarrassed that I had let Paul's feelings—or what I'd perceived of them—wash over me instead for so long. I was embarrassed at how easily I could identify harms done to this white student who had no love for me, but not the harms he'd done—not the harms I'd done—to Black students who I'd never even considered might have some love for me themselves. I was embarrassed at how excellent I'd become at identifying with whiteness.

I learned to be excellent at school the most from teachers like Mr. Smith, a white man who taught my Advanced Placement English class that same year. Mr. Smith was the kind of serious whose resentment for not working on the college level bled out of his grading pen. His appreciation for the work of the other old white men he taught in our class—F. Scott Fitzgerald, William Faulkner, William Golding—was rivaled only by his reverence for rules, or maybe those are just two names for the same thing.

Mr. Smith was one of those teachers who would make students feel foolish whenever they asked a question he thought they should know. One of those teachers who would not open the door no matter what after the bell rang, regardless of whether, it seemed, you had a death in the family, had broken a leg, or had passed out right in front of him. This inflexible view of timeliness is entrenched in our education system through capitalism. During the industrialization of the eighteenth and nineteenth centuries, it became more important to business owners that workers turn up at their stations at the same time each day. Workers learned to think of their time as belonging to the people they worked for, and schools became a prime opportunity to reinforce this idea.[24]

When I made it through a stampede of students only to find Mr. Smith's classroom locked one morning, I started wringing the sweat from my palms. I was convinced I'd lost track of time and somehow missed the bell, and was terrified of the consequences for my mistake. Then other students arrived, and we all just sat there. We were still waiting when the bell rang. It was so out of the ordinary that Mr. Smith wasn't there that I was sure something terrible had happened, and my anxieties for being late morphed into worries about the white man who made me anxious in the first place—or maybe those are just two names for the same thing, too. But when Mr. Smith finally showed up minutes later, he didn't even acknowledge his own tardiness to his class. He started normally, affirming that punishments for failing to follow these rules applied to us and only us.

Mr. Smith's punitive view of tardiness is inextricable from the legacy of white administrators' and educators' adherence to school-disturbance laws and zero-tolerance policies, which all lead to the accelerated incarceration of Black youth. According to a 2015 study, Black youth are five times more likely to be detained or committed compared to white youth, in large part due to how the enforcement of these rules fuels the school-to-prison pipeline.[25] As schools impose more rules based on state-dictated standards, they create more ideals with which Black people in particular are incompatible and more punishments that apply only to us. It creates the reality education scholar Dr. Michael Dumas is referencing when he calls schooling "a site of Black suffering."[26]

A few weeks after Mr. Smith showed up well past his own bell with a shrug, Betty switched out of his class after being disciplined for being late one last time. I used to think she deserved Mr. Smith's wrath for her tardiness, taking my own ability to be more punctual as another example of what made me better than her. But if her being late to these classes was an inherent disruption of learning, perhaps it was because Mr. Smith's way of teaching inherently needed disruption.

My way of learning to empathize with Mr. Smith and Paul over Betty, and even more so over the students who didn't make it into these mostly white classes in the first place, required disruption. Only once it had been disrupted could I understand Betty's weariness. Only then could I understand her unwillingness to let shit slide just because letting it slide was how she might find more success in a society that protects the Pauls of the world at the expense of others. Only once my way of learning had been disrupted could I understand that I needed to be unwilling to let Mr. Smith's abuse of authority slide, too, even when it seemed to more often spare me.

By modeling teachers like Mr. Smith, I had come to think of the tardiness of my peers and Black folks in general not only as inconvenient but as an indictment of their character. As something indicating an inherent failure. As justification for their disposability. My parents were always late, and adopting this politic of excellence by white standards meant that even though my father was available and willing to drive me to school (and generously offered to drive friends who lived on my street as well), I often refused his kindness just to avoid the possibility of tardiness he carried like the plague. I would ultimately be *losing* time by trading a five-minute car ride for a twenty-minute walk, but at least it wasn't *Mr. Smith's* time. In order to embrace the rules of the state and the school system, I had to refuse so much kindness that Black folks like my father had to offer; otherwise I believed everything would devolve into chaos. But there are other ways to live, and there always have been.

~

Under capitalism, time is just another resource to be exploited, and it's no coincidence that poor people—who are more likely to have multiple jobs and responsibilities and obligations they need to fulfill in order to survive—have less of it, any more than it's a coincidence that poor people are also more likely to be Black. Being punished for lacking time is more likely to affect the poor and the Black, too. Even though my mother didn't work a typical job outside the home, because my father's salary was never enough to keep us above the poverty line, both of them still spent any "free time" they could manage working—teaching us, cooking, writing grants and giving classes and trying to find rest. Maybe Colored-People Time was only ever a form of resistance. A demand to retrain our responses to the "problems" caused when Black people don't show up exactly when we are told to. A demand to focus on how we have been forced into insecure home lives, or into lacking food, or into having inconsistent transportation, by the anti-Black and unequal distribution of resources.

Maybe Colored-People Time is a call to actually deal with the physical and mental health issues our communities don't always have the means to manage because the world hoards those resources to protect the Pauls instead. Because it does so in the same way that the state hoarded resources to turn the white faces of the opioid crisis into sympathetic victims while it made out the Black faces of the crack epidemic to be monsters deserving of their lot. There is no situation in which we can't afford to give Black people who fail at state-sanctioned behaviors more care and grace.

Of course anyone being late can lead to problems, and I'm not saying Black folks' lateness never does. I'm saying that the moments when we are late or miss engagements or get high or otherwise disrupt institutions that uphold the master's rules, that uphold respectability in an anti-Black, capitalistic society, are opportunities to think more deeply about where the problem truly stems.

Instead of a smug smirk and a patronizing correction, Black folks who are late or who fail tests can and should be met with caring inquisition. Why are so many engagements in this society structured so that if we are late or don't pass a test, we might lose everything? Would the stakes be so high if the old white men Mr. Smith revered so much weren't making money off everyone else doing everything on *their* schedule, if the tests weren't based on what *they* call skill or a schedule to which they themselves don't have to adhere to still find protection?

~

"You remember when you called me a homeschooled jungle freak?" I asked Betty as we caught up over drinks. I count her among my closest friends now, and she had just moved to the New York City area.

"I'm sorry, but you were so annoying," she laughed. "You knew you were d*mb smart, and always thought that meant you were better than the rest of us. I was just over it that day. But thank god we moved past that."

It would have been so easy to settle into a capitalistic idea of Black Excellence that helps perpetuate the punishing of Black children for not meeting white-supremacist standards for success, and in many ways I did. But it was having friends like Betty, who were generous enough to hold me accountable and challenge me on my anti-Blackness, even when I didn't understand it as generosity, that kept me just aware enough that I didn't lose myself completely on the condition that I was at least willing to grow. They, along with the far-from-inconsequential Black teachers and coaches who refused Mr. Smith's way of teaching, ensured there was always a way back.

It was easy for me to use my weird name and odd religion and homeschooled-jungle-freak past to shield against any critiques of my behavior—to claim my tensions with Betty rested only on her inability to accept my differences rather than on *my* ability to use any difference from her as a bargaining chip for proximity to whiteness. But she, and the many other Black students who might have had less regard for the rules of this school but often still possessed more intelligence than I did, didn't let me. I am eternally grateful for that, and I have a responsibility to them for it.

It's magical the things Black people create out of the scraps thrown at us. How we have taken the discarded parts of what's left after the masters finished eating and turned it into soul food. Hateful language meant to demean people with disabilities turned into signifiers of feats antithetical to demeaning—"d*mb smart," meaning "smart as fuck." Relationships molded by loathing and scorn turned into lasting friendships of accountability and understanding. We stay breaking the line between binary distinctions created to punish some for the sake of others. It's magical, but that doesn't mean how we create these new worlds doesn't take work.

As a person who's managed some proximity to whiteness by meeting the respectability standards of academia, acquiescing to the lived experiences of those who don't meet the same standards has required work, too. It's easy to say that those with less proximity to whiteness have agency and that their lives matter, but what does it mean to honor their capabilities, knowledge, and agency in my everyday life?

How do I rightly regard the Black children society calls "demons" or "no angels" just because they don't follow its rules, knowing that the state uses disregard for these children to avoid pushback for mowing them down in the street? Do I follow the lead of the Black man who is arguably most proximate to whiteness, President Barack Obama—the man who lectured Black people who fall short of white standards for not "taking full responsibility for our own lives" and succumbing to "despair or cynicism" in even his most famous speech to purportedly take on anti-Blackness?[27] Or do I consider that these children might be responding from a perspective I do not know and can learn from?

Finding excellence in the respectable ways I learned from teachers like Mr. Smith would always mean losing community with those who resisted this anti-Black system, but for a while I tried anyway. I tried even though I knew I needed this community just as much as

Mata needed it before me. I tried because I believed, just like Mata believed, that with some postracial god's mercy, I could afford to lose my wholeness. That's why I never asked Mata what price we paid for this more respectable life. I did not believe there could even exist a god who wouldn't ask such a steep price for deliverance. But here Betty was, thanking a god who didn't.

CANTO II

Queer

CHAPTER SIX
A PRAYER FOR LIMITLESSNESS

Hari-Gaura,

Have you met god yet, or is that just something that happens when you're taken from this world in myths and movies? Do you know for sure whether god even exists? If you do, don't tell me. I think I'd rather not know. What's the point of believing in anything if you don't have doubts sometimes? What would you have confronted and overcome to make having faith worth it?

I don't know what I believe anymore. When people ask, "Are you religious?" and I respond, "Not really, but I'm spiritual," it feels trite and indecisive, like I am desperate to hedge my bets. I set up an altar to my ancestors, but I don't study any scripture. I am exploring African traditional religions, but I haven't been initiated by any teachers. I know that I'm trying to have it both ways, and for some odd reason you're not supposed to eat the cake once you have it lest you be seen as gluttonous. But this is still the best answer I can muster, so it's the answer I must give.

I guess it's like how Daddy believes Allah and Kṛṣṇa are just two different names for the same being, despite Islam's injunction against sacred images and Hinduism's reliance upon them. "People get too caught up in what they call god, and what he does or doesn't look like, with too little concern for all that he does," he rationalizes.

But Daddy still believes god is a "he." I ask him why, ask him how this isn't just an example of getting too caught up in god's gender—in the binaries we force ourselves into at the expense of what god can do to expand existence limitlessly—and he says something about it being a problem of language rather than one of his beliefs, then changes the subject. I hate when he changes the subject after being presented with his contradictions instead of acknowledging the doubts that have been raised. Like last year when he claimed he was only trying to be health conscious in making an offhand comment about a woman's weight as we drove by where she stood on the sidewalk, minding her own business.

"You couldn't possibly know how healthy the woman was just from a drive-by observance of her body, and body-shaming has a proven detrimental effect on folks' health anyway," our baby sister Kiss admonished in the driver's seat, shaking her head.[28] I can't believe she's now old enough to drive. We were headed from Vegas to the Grand Canyon for Daddy's seventy-ninth birthday. He had been talking about how badly he wanted to see it for years. Kiss figured then was as good a time as any to start scratching items off our parents' bucket lists, and I didn't blame her.

"Look at that beautiful sunset over the mountains!" Daddy replied, staring out the window at the landscape the disappearing rays were merging into a gradient of purples, yellows, and reds, as if it were a melting box of crayons. I almost fell for the deceit. To not have to reckon with harms perpetuated in your presence is an enticingly comforting thing. Until you realize this only means you're now forced to deal with harms that are hidden from you or that might not even exist.

Daddy is still a conspiracy theorist.

"Don't fall for anything they tell you," he advises me often, pointing to instances of the government covering up dastardly deeds against Black communities that are only exposed later. The assassination of Black Panther Party deputy chairman Fred Hampton by the Chicago police and the FBI. The government's involvement in the destruction of Black Wall Street during the Tulsa Race Riot.

"These people have been liars since the inception of this country," he says.

He still doesn't believe in saying "hello," replacing it with "heaven-high" whenever he greets anyone.

"It's their way to keep your mind centered on hellish thoughts," he says. You trusted him on this, but I once tried parroting it to a less conspiratorial person, and they politely laughed at my hereditary obliviousness and explained that the word actually comes from the Old High German "Halôn," which means "to fetch" or "hail," as in what you do to signal a cab.

Daddy believes 9/11 was an inside job. He believes Black people in America are secretly indigenous to this country, and that we are only told we are from Africa so that we won't have any claim to this land. I point out that actual Indigenous Americans don't have their claim to this land recognized anyway, that there are Black diasporans all over the globe, not just here, and that colonizers are still stealing the lands of Indigenous Africans to this day, too, but he just changes the subject to you, Hari-Gaura.

"I always let your mother do her thing with you children, but I wish you all had come to the mosque more when you were little," he says when we reach our hotel in Arizona. He's been recounting the story of when he became a Muslim more recently, as if I need to really get it to understand why he does the things he does. After moving from Tennessee to Cleveland, he joined the Nation of Islam, a Black American Muslim movement founded in 1930, in his twenties. That was where he met Mother Bhūmi, who was exploring the religion, too. Mata was only a child then, and he wouldn't connect with her on any deeper level until many years later, after they had both been through three marriages each. By then, he and Mata were active in various multifaith initiatives together, and after observing how he moved within them, she asked him to be a mentor to her boys.

"I knew it was a trap," he half jokes, perhaps regretting some of the things he taught us, and some of the things he didn't, after the mentorship turned into something more—turned into you. Later, he left the Nation to become a member at the Mosque Cares ministry, which was established by Elijah Muhammad's son W. Deen Muhammad after the former's death. W. Deen disbanded his father's Nation of Islam (Minister Louis Farrakhan would later revive it) and pushed its members toward a more liberal direction than it had operated along in the days of Malcolm X's excommunication—although idolatry, or worshipping any sacred images, is still strictly forbidden.

"It's all about interpretation," Daddy responds whenever someone asks him how he reconciles this prohibition with his marriage to Mata and the paintings of different Hare Kṛṣṇa pastimes that hang all over their house. Aligning his practices with the woman he loves is one of the few contradictions for which he will never change the subject, that he is always willing to confront, even if the words he finds to confront it feel trite and indecisive. There is a lack of language for how to resolve his beliefs and his marriage, but he struggles to muster his own anyway.

"God is whatever helps us get to self-realization, regardless of the road you take. Bismillah ir-Rahman ir-Rahim," Daddy says.

In the name of Allah, the most compassionate, the most merciful. God's merciful acceptance of the sacrilegious way Mata raised us is why Daddy says he never really pushed us to go to the mosque and didn't protest when Mata brought all her children up almost entirely within her religion.

I hate when Daddy changes the subject after being presented with his contradictions, because it was he who showed me how powerful it could be to acknowledge the doubts that our contradictions raise. It was he who taught me that no matter how right I might think I am, I should always be willing to be wrong for something greater. It was Daddy who illuminated the necessity of struggling to name the unnameable, which ultimately brought me back to you, Hari-Gaura.

There are always exceptions and contexts and gray areas in the space between and outside of the binaries constructed to make sense of ourselves in this carceral world. To refuse to place all your bets on either side of these binaries doesn't mean one's beliefs about oneself are weak; it just means they are as expansive as any god should be. As the gods of our ancestors were, which is why those are so appealing to me. And Daddy taught me all this without always recognizing when he could apply it to himself.

"I don't have a problem with you being Hare Kṛṣṇas," he said, sitting on his hotel bed across from mine in Arizona, still mispronouncing it as "Kris-na" instead of "Krish-na" after all these years.

"But I regret that Islam didn't have more of a role in your lives," he continued.

"Sometimes, I feel very Muslim," I said, "even though I am not religious."

I tell him how my last name gave me away to the Muslim cashier at my local deli in Brooklyn, how the cashier asked me to pray with him, and how I remembered the Arabic again. I tell Daddy that I don't always trust the government's narrative of the events of 9/11 either, and I know he's not delusional for believing in things people who stay trying to kill us say he shouldn't believe.

I tell him how I thought of him when the controversy erupted over Barack Obama's former pastor Jeremiah Wright, when Wright argued after the twin towers fell that God will continue to damn America until it stops avoiding its own violent contradictions. I tell him how I knew Wright's was a correct assessment of the evils this government had enacted because Daddy is my Muslim father. Because of the rage I feel witnessing the violence that Muslim communities have experienced in the wake of that fateful day—communities that, through him, I have some kinship with. Because of the state-sanctioned Islamophobia that has only deepened since, and strengthened its grip across the globe—from Kashmir to Palestine.

I tell Daddy that Wright's "God damn America" sermon sounded a lot like, "These people have been liars since the inception of this country" to me, and that I never forgave Obama for abandoning someone he supposedly loved just because it contradicted his political ambitions. How I hope to never abandon what and who I love again just because it contradicts some ambition of mine, and how I learned this from how Daddy always reconciled loving Mata with his practice of Islam. And if I can make up for the abandonment I've done myself, if I can get you back, it's because Daddy showed me how, even amid the moments when he abandoned what he shouldn't have, too.

CHAPTER SEVEN

GUILT AND GODS

My baby brother Visnu swears I began my rebellion against my parents not long after I entered high school.

"Boy, I was finding cases of Mike's Hard in the closet every day when you were fifteen!" he chortled, as obnoxious as he is endearing, as he took a sip of a vodka soda himself. We were at our sister Kiss's friend's house, and Visnu had begun the conversation without prompting. Visnu isn't a heavy drinker, and he weighs less than me despite a benefit of at least three inches and my not being very heavy to begin with, so when he starts, the effects come on fast. I think his self-consciousness around the speed of the whole process might make him feel the need to deflect.

"Nah, you got the timeline all messed up," I insisted, but he would not be convinced.

"You were a teenage alcoholic!" he persisted, cutting an argumentative tone with a hint of laughter, as he does.

"Okay, I was probably drinking too much, but not until later."

He just shook his head, stroking his patchy beard, which still covers much more of his soft chin than my own beard, only now beginning to grow in, covers of mine. He thought I was in denial. Visnu may very well have learned the urge to steer the focus away from his tipsiness to me—I *am* overly defensive about my drinking—but in reality I didn't have my first drink until after the second semester of senior year, when Visnu was ten. I rarely even cursed before then, but by that summer I had become masterful at breaking my parents' rules, and I can see how the rapid escalation of this behavior might have warped my little brother's perception.

After high school had let out for the final time, at least once a week I would wait until I thought Mata and my father were asleep in their room on the third floor, tiptoe downstairs from the one I begrudgingly shared with Visnu on the second, and swipe the minivan key from the hook in the kitchen. Our driveway at the Heights house was narrow, with concrete, waist-high stumps painted yellow to guard the side porch on the right, and a steep ditch that, on more than one occasion, had caused the van to get stuck between the pavement and the neighbor's house on the left. Every year we tried to fill the ditch with dirt and gravel, but by the next it would inevitably sink significantly below the pavement again, as though being fed to some buried, insatiable beast.

The setup meant I couldn't reverse out quickly, making my escape a risky one. But I'd already been accepted into my dream school, and the worst I imagined could happen was that I might disappoint my parents—which wasn't much of a deterrent, as I already felt I had disappointed them as much as I ever could. I wouldn't have sneaked out of the house and had a drink for the first time that spring if I hadn't been convinced by unspoken promises that this could mitigate the excruciating identity crisis that their disappointment had brewed inside me.

Michael had become my best friend over the two years prior. We'd hit it off in our school's gospel choir, where he initially drew my attention because he had a voice of molten gold, and where I drew his because he couldn't understand why a Hindu was so excited to sing about Jesus. I explained to him that the way I was raised held space for other religious practices and that my enthusiasm for choir likely had something to do with how central music is in the Hare Kṛṣṇa tradition, and he found this fascinating. I told him how I'd grown up having to sing before sermons and before eating and how nearly every Vaiṣṇava event calls for music and dancing, a symphony of cymbals and drums, and he swore I was the most interesting person he'd ever met. I believed him, and it quickly became apparent that he was the same for me, too.

I was most taken by how he didn't seem to give a fuck about all the things I gave too much of a fuck about, but he didn't judge me all the same. Michael wasn't especially academic or religious or popular or active in anything outside of his music, and I think a part of me hoped that his carefree nature would rub off over my constant need to excel regardless of the sacrifices excelling required.

I have never been the best singer, and gospel choir didn't require me to be, but soon I also joined our school's show choir, with Michael's encouragement, and then the more demanding a cappella choir, too. I even quit the track team, which I'd been a part of for the first three years of high school, to make time for this new activity. Michael could do effortless Maxwell runs to every song that came on the radio, picking up the melody on just his first listen, and when I tried to do the same to impress him and failed, he never laughed too hard.

"No, that was all right," he would say after chuckling, still smiling a tickled, dazzling smile at my floundering attempts to harmonize in the passenger seat of his mother's Jeep.

"You're getting better," he would continue, even though I still felt that compulsion to beat myself up because I was sure that I *wasn't* getting better—or at least I had been sure before I heard the words leave his lips.

Michael welcomed me with open arms into his friend group, which included two other dedicated choir boys, Jon and Calvin. The three were inseparable. Jon and Calvin wanted to be musicians just like Michael and weren't as forgiving about my lack of skill, but Michael always defended me to them.

"Hari's not even a singer and still has just as good an ear as you, Jon," he'd chastise when Jon would playfully latch on to a mistake of mine, forcing Jon into silence. Michael was far more skilled with music than Jon, and he knew Jon wouldn't question his characterization of anyone's musicianship. Michael defended me so convincingly that sometimes he even made *me* believe that I had the ear of a real singer.

Michael, Jon, Calvin, and I hung out together and talked on the phone nightly, but as our friendship progressed, sometimes I would call Michael—just Michael—after we got off our four-way calls to talk about everything and nothing. He didn't seem to find this weird. Sometimes he would call me—just me—too.

"Can you come to the party?" Michael asked during one of our private calls the spring of our last year in high school together, after we'd rid ourselves of Jon and Calvin.

"You know my mother . . . ," I said, repeating an excuse I'd given him countless times.

"Yeah, but I thought it was worth a try."

He sounded defeated. Hurt, even. And somehow that hurt me, too, though I didn't have the words for why.

"I mean, I could try to sneak out?"

"Hari, sneaking out?!" He laughed that oddly understanding laugh of his, full of shock but lacking any real judgment.

At first I didn't know what made me want to break the rules for Michael. I'd had other very close friends before, and I'd have done anything to protect them from being hurt, but they'd never expressed pain for my absence the way Michael seemed to. I knew his feelings were different because his absence was excruciating for me, too, and I saw my pain reflected in his eyes. I saw myself when I looked into them.

"We're almost like brothers," I said to him one day in an attempt to explain my feelings.

"Yeah, like brothers." He smiled, but that light wasn't there when he said it, and nothing could ever be adequate without that.

When I showed up to the first party I sneaked out to attend, the joy I saw emanating from Michael's face no less than demanded I show up again to the next. It still wasn't a regular occurrence then, but whenever I stole my parents' van, it was almost always to be with Michael, to see that smile beaming back at me through a night I'd otherwise have spent shrouded in an indescribable loneliness away from him. I felt guilty, of course, but the alcohol came to help with that.

When Michael gave me my first drink, he didn't push it on me. I had noticed it seemed to help with his feeling carefree, and like I said, I wanted that, so I asked for his red Solo Cup, still fresh with the wet from his lips.

"Are you sure?" He smiled. I imagined tasting a hint of his breath on the rim, and I'd never been more sure of anything.

The drinking helped with the guilt only while I was drunk. It exacerbated it afterward, which only encouraged me to be drunk as often as possible. Drinking also gave me an excuse to be with Michael. High school kids seemed to understand why we spent so much time together when getting drunk was the reason, when they might not have been so understanding of any of the other reasons I could not yet name.

Sometimes when I sneaked out—the best times—there was no party to attend. It was just me and Michael, drinking in his basement, talking shit about choir and school and Cleveland Heights, anything or nothing. His parents never discovered I was in their house or that we had stolen their alcohol, even when we crept up to Michael's room, right across from theirs.

"Why don't you just sleep over?" Michael asked on one of these nights. My chest, in a prelude to its later persistent torment in my life, responded like a popular teen's phone buzzing with a hundred notifications at once when it's started up after a week being powered off.

"You know my mother . . . ," I said, trying to calm the fluttering.

"I do . . ."

I could almost see his chest rise and fall like waves in a high tide, matching mine.

I was drunk. I shouldn't have been driving anyway. I wanted to see him beam at me. I needed to.

"I can just leave early in the morning," I said, relenting, and there it was, that smile.

Michael had only one sibling still living in the house, an older sister, and she had her own room, but for some reason he had a second bed in his. When I asked him why, he just shrugged and laughed. I was happy to fill in the blank with the fantasy that he had insisted it be there as he lay in wait for the perfect person to share a room with—for me.

He'd brought drinks up from the basement, and he poured me another before plopping down on his bed. I kicked off my shoes and sat on what you could no longer tell me wasn't my bed, too, as Michael turned on some singing-competition show. He sang along with the auditions and sounded better than any of the contestants. I never looked at the screen. I took constant sips of my drink, watching him and waiting for the night to brighten when he returned my glance.

"Do you want to lie on the floor?" he finally asked, taking a large gulp from his glass.

It shouldn't have made any sense that we would move to the floor when we had two comfortable beds between us, but it was the only thing that felt logical at the time.

"Sure!"

Michael laughed with a noticeable discomfort I'd never seen on him as he unrolled a blanket on the ground, threw the pillows from his bed on top of it, and lay down on the pallet. I grabbed my pillow and lay down beside him.

"Come closer," he said. And I did.

When I visibly tried my best not to touch him, he laughed again, as if I had sung the wrong note in the passenger seat of his mother's car, then wrapped me in his arms, and I realized that was what he'd meant for me to do. I realized I was always supposed to have done this. And I held him back, as much as you can hold the sun.

When I awoke at 4:00 a.m., I had sobered up. We hadn't gone any further than holding each other that night, but still the guilt was suffocating. The most depressing thing about being queer in this world is the fact that it isn't just the possibility of your sexuality that you are taught to be afraid of: a world where you can hold the person you love without guilt terrifies you, too. I had never held another boy in my arms. I had never been held that way with my consent either, and I had been taught that I was never supposed to feel that much joy, so I could only beat myself up when I did.

"I have to go," I said, gasping for air and pushing him away.

"Are you sure?" he asked.

"You know my mother."

I held my breath for what couldn't biologically have been the entire ten-minute drive home but felt like it. When I pulled into the driveway, I found Mata waiting up for me.

"Shit," I mumbled to myself. "Shit, shit, shit."

Though I'd made sure to shut off the van's headlights before I inched back past the yellow stumps, it was futile. The shadow of Mata's small frame behind the curtains of the living room, gusting around like the winds preceding a thunderstorm, seemed to jump through the window, piercing my stomach and morphing into a black hole inside me.

In silhouette, the shape of the head wrap Mata wore every day for the sake of modesty became the plume after a bomb. Even before I cracked open the back door, I heard the chanting—"Kṛṣṇa, Kṛṣṇa!"— and my heart began to sprint. I sat in the vestibule between the door and the kitchen for what seemed like hours waiting for her to go to bed so that I wouldn't have to face her. But she just chanted and chanted and chanted, her voice full of sorrow for all my sins. And in that vestibule, amid the sound of her prayers and the tangy smell of all the shoes lining its walls and the Bacardi on my breath, I had the second anxiety attack of my life.

Mata believes that the Hare Kṛṣṇa principle of "no illicit sex" refers to queer sexuality. I think this belief was shaped by losing her own childhood in a fundamentalist Christian upbringing, marred by colonized and anti-Black interpretations of sex, but she would be able to find some way to use Kṛṣṇa to justify it—just as white devotees had for their anti-Blackness.

When I was twelve, my brother Mohan discovered a new book series by Mercedes Lackey. The first book, *Magic's Pawn*, featured an anguished young man and a beautiful white stallion on the cover, which, along with the word "magic" in the title, was more than enough to pique my interest. It looked like many of the other fantasy novels Mohan devoured, and the books he'd finished composed the bulk of my reading list at the time.

But *Magic's Pawn* was different from any of Mohan's other hand-me-downs. In the first few chapters, the main character, the sad boy on the cover, was clearly beginning to develop feelings for another magical boy, and my heart pulsed faster with every new page that the story unfolded. I knew those feelings. They were mine, even though there was no other magical boy yet. I knew them, but I did not want to. Reading the book did nothing to lessen my fears of being queer, but it did everything to make me feel like maybe I wasn't alone with them. Those fears grew so large that I began to sneak into the bathroom and read the book at night when I was supposed to be asleep, so that no one would catch me with it. One time, I got so tired reading late into the night that I accidentally left the novel in the bathroom. Mata found it, read from the bookmarked page with disgust, and gave a stern talk to my brother about influencing me with these sinful thoughts. He never brought any more Mercedes Lackey books into the house, and I never got any closure on my fears or feelings, or on what happens when two magical boys choose to love each other. Until Michael.

I grew up hearing the Vaiṣṇava dictum that "we are not the body, but spirit souls" repeated over and over again, and many interpretations of Hinduism embrace queer and transgender people (which is not to say Hindu scripture regarding gender and sexuality is without its own gendered violence). But to my mother, my body—which my existence supposedly wasn't limited to—still determined that I could never love other people who inhabited bodies like it. For my body to share specific attributes with my lover's was such a horrible thought to her that when I finally confirmed I was queer two years after sneaking back into my house that night, she refused to sign off on the loans I needed to attend college, nearly forcing me to drop out as punishment, until an administrator in LGBTQ student services pulled some strings for me.

"If this is what that school will teach you," she said, "I won't support it." She spoke to me only in scripture verses condemning sexual sin for almost the entire next year. Our relationship has never quite been the same.

Whenever I had asked for permission first to use the van to go out with Michael, Mata had always said no. She swears today that she didn't know I felt this kind of love for him, but she didn't need to consciously know it was true in order to fear the possibility, to punish me for it, and for me to internalize her fear and punishment. She didn't need to consciously know it to always assume that when I sneaked out, it was to be with him, and to always be right. She didn't need to know for her to constantly warn me of how he gave her "a bad vibe," for her to tell me often that I should be wary of him "getting too close," and for her to also make it known, in no uncertain terms, that I would never be accepted if I was anything like she rightly assumed he was.

My mother didn't need to know how I felt about Michael to look at me with the most distress I had ever seen in her eyes when I finally walked into the kitchen after my panic attack. She didn't put me on punishment or take away my phone or yell; she just never looked at me the same way she used to after that. And when I couldn't get her to see me as she used to see me, to show the love I know she still had for me, like she used to show love for me, I gave up.

Michael had illuminated how painful it was to be trapped between the conflicting ideas of my mother's faith, within the contradiction of praying for liberation to a god who wouldn't allow me to be free enough to be queer, and I did not know how to reconcile that. I did not know that I could. So I ran away.

I rebelled against my parents' rules and the gods who had dictated them because I had gotten tired of tearing myself apart between mutually exclusive ideas of who I needed to be and who they said god wanted me to be. But running away made me into just another person who had hurt my mother, like so many had before me. And it wasn't completely her fault, but when I walked up the stairs, clouded with shame, Mata was still apologizing to her god: "Rāma, Rāma!" And I knew it wasn't my fault for wanting to be free to feel Michael's love either, so I couldn't work up the words to say I was sorry. And my inability to find faith in a world where both Michael and my mother could coexist helped spur a perfect storm of avoidance and substance abuse and self-destructive tendencies that were easily recognizable even to my ten-year-old brother, and that have plagued me ever since.

"Naw, I get it," Visnu said solemnly after getting bored of teasing at my sister's friend's house a decade later. "You were going through a lot . . ."

"Yeah . . ."

The silence that fell was abnormally long for a conversation with my little brother.

"You okay?" I finally asked.

"Yeah," he said, taking another drink. He couldn't be more my brother.

My propensity to run away, to sneak out from under tense situations, and to avoid what needs confronting would later lead to my breakup with Michael only a year after that night we spent in his room together, after he became my first boyfriend. We'd both gotten comfortable avoiding too much, especially for a long-distance relationship, and I used too many lies and substances to fill the gaps between us.

Embracing avoidance was the central mistake of our relationship, but it has nonetheless remained a consistent crutch for my anxiety. It is the easiest way to cop out of managing this ever-present guilt of internalizing a critical part of myself as a sin. And embracing avoidance has created problems in all my relationships that followed.

~

Despite the lack of space, in each home she has had, Mata has dedicated one room to her deities and the worship of them. Her deity room is filled with elaborate altars and garlands and the incurable smell of incense. When her children were young and we would get in trouble with Mata, we would run into the room and bow down in front of the bronze statuettes of Kṛṣṇa and his consort, Radha. We knew that Mata would never punish us in this spiritual sanctuary, and she didn't try to hide the fact that she wouldn't even discipline us after we exited.

"You took shelter of god," she would say, "so I will let him take care of it." She hoped that this would teach us to always take shelter of god when we were in trouble.

If my father is right, and we should pay the most attention to what god *does* rather than the traits we project onto them, then god is defined by what liberates a person. If that's the case, then god for me is in fully embracing myself, my joys, and my freedom, without excuses or avoidance or shame. This god may look different from my mother's, but I was raised to hold space for other spiritual practices. God for me is in fostering a true connection with myself, which means reclaiming my childhood—reclaiming who I was before I was taught to fear the parts of me that don't fit neatly into the world—and repairing the fracture caused by my carceral dissonance.

God is in challenging misafropedia wherever it rears its ugly head. The prayers I discover can be offered to only a god who doesn't force me into choosing between one necessary love and another. A god who doesn't push Black children into irreconcilable binaries at the expense of their wholeness. My ancestors modeled these prayers for me. I hope that I can model these prayers for Visnu, too. It only makes sense that in order to refrain from punishing myself the way I was taught by our mother and she was taught by the state, I would have to learn to see myself the way I want her to see me again. That might be the only god who can provide me shelter once more.

CHAPTER EIGHT

A PRAYER FOR ANOTHER WORLD

Hari-Gaura,

I wonder why so often the mind tries to manifest what it cannot have. Right now, I'm stuck within the recollection of a birthday party held last year for the mother of one of my best friends, Ahmad. And all the old heads stand one right after another like a swelling current, but the wave stops at my shore.

It's the kind of tide that makes onlookers sit straighter, on high alert—*what happened?* Then I hear, "You can't seeeee it, it's electric!" and I have to believe these lyrics. Nothing less than lightning animates the elders' bodies as they Electric Slide. Each of them is moving like that pain in her hip was just a bit of joy caught in the joint, a bit of joy that can be let out only when she sways in sync with everyone else. Every line dancer outdoes the next—flipping a wig, kicking up a leg as they spin—and yet they are all in perfect harmony.

Every person puts the next to shame, and yet no one is ashamed, because Blackness is a meritocracy that doesn't require suppression.

The birthday party was in Newark, New Jersey, but for a brief moment I was home. For a brief moment, I was sharing this body with you again, and Auntie Grace was stepping away from the grill to join the dance floor her driveway had turned into.

Our cousin Eric was out of prison and dancing like he ain't never been accused of killing nobody, because in this universe he hadn't. Even Mata, who has long forsaken secular dance, gingerly boogie-woogie-woogied into the crowd, tepidly relearning the steps she looked embarrassed to have forgotten, but that brought her more joy than anything. For a brief moment. Then this world appeared before me again.

Eric has been in prison for as long as I can remember. Our cousin D has been locked up for a stretch, too, for allegedly stealing shit. He's only twenty-three. I used to babysit for that kid, man. I used to wash his face when it was dirty, put his toys away after he fell asleep, back when he would stay with us for spells while his parents were going through some things. I remember thinking he should have had more of them, that he never had enough things to play with for a child.

D's younger sister, Justus, says some boys in Lorain are looking for our cousin Ali. He's in his early twenties now, too, and he's still a smart-ass. When he was younger, he would stay laughing

about things that I could never understand and rib
me for not being able to grasp them. The boys told
Justus that if they ever saw him on the street, they
would kill him for some shady shit they say he did
to them. I don't know if Ali is scared or not, or if
fear just doesn't really matter to him, because he
keeps doing the same shit anyway.

I've been reaching out to him more recently.
Each time I don't know if it will be the last that he
responds, at least with his freedom. I miss him.
Even talking to him more regularly doesn't really
fix that. I understand too much now, and there is
too little of his laughter left for me.

Justus and D's brother Tay, the middle child
between them, has been in and out, too. He lost
his baby while he was behind bars, and then someone stole her ashes, which he'd kept in a locket.
Justus told me that she thinks his baby was the
only thing he was really still living for. Now he
keeps getting into fights and being thrown into
the hole only to be tortured with more loneliness.
I never got a chance to meet his daughter.

I miss all our fucking family, and I don't feel
like I have anyone to talk to about it without elic-
iting fake empathy or judgment, because people don't understand how, as a group, we could
be so affected by criminalization. So I don't. Or
I didn't. I don't think my therapist really gets it
either, but he tells me that maybe you might. That
you would know the indescribable hatred I have
stewing because of how many people have been
taken away from me, one after another. That I

might share with you the rage I have on behalf of the many people I've loved whom I'll never see again, and the many others I'll never see the way we used to see each other, and together we can make space for each other to feel it.

I'm tired of looking at faces behind bars and in coffins. I feel like the next thing I lose will be the last thing I'm really living for, too, if I don't figure out another way to live. That I'll also be constantly tortured with loneliness, if in a different kind of way than Tay, if I don't figure out how to hold on to the flashes of other possible universes that moments like dancing to the Electric Slide at a Black family party can create. Maybe that's why my mind keeps bringing me back there now in this time when I feel so isolated.

I would have joined the elders on the dance floor, but my friend Sevonna had brought her three-month-old baby, Tiger, and he's just the cutest thing, soaking up all our attention. Our mutual friend Henry was playing peekaboo with him. When Henry's face reappeared from behind his hands, Tiger brightened, lightning animating his body like it did the elders'.

"He doesn't have object permanence yet," Henry, a sage who rarely meets knowledge he is selfish enough to keep to himself, explained. "When I put my hands in front of my face, he thinks my face just disappears. He won't learn that things continue to exist outside of his field of vision until he's a little older."

I'd heard of this concept before, almost always with a soot-thickened air of "awww, silly little babies" suffocating the discussion. But Tiger's face looked to have caught all the joy spilling from the old folks' hips, and it was not silly at all. His face looked like maybe he knew something Sevonna, Henry, Ahmad, and I didn't, not the other way around. Like he understood that the things adults now believe are too established to disappear still can, and that those things can still make their way back even if we don't yet understand how. Like he believed in other worlds we can escape to and return from and that nothing is limited to this carceral one. Like he still believed in a god who can save us from carceral dissonance, from losing ourselves and each other to this world's systematic ways of breaking us and our families apart with its prisons. Like he still saw your reflection in my eyes.

Growing up with eighteen siblings, it must have been impossible for you not to feel invisible sometimes. It was impossible not to "disappear," your whereabouts or emotional states going unseen by a mother and father who had their hands full with their gods and their homeschooling and all the kids they'd built this life for. But you found a magic in this where I would later discover only bitterness, imagining yourself as one of the X-Men with invisibility as a superpower.

I don't know where the heroism of stealthily making your way into spaces you would otherwise be forbidden from entering went—the feeling of accomplishment that came with sneaking a spoonful of strawberry jam from the refrigerator when you were supposed to be done with sweets for the day, with no one ever being any the wiser—I know only that it did go. I know only that I resented our parents for having so many children that I couldn't soak up all their attention no matter how hard I tried to be just the cutest thing, and the magic of disappearing was lost with time. I embraced becoming an object that could be commodified by others, because I wanted to be permanent, too.

I almost forgot the names of your imaginary friends, but I still remember how they were there to keep you company during those moments of feeling invisible. I still remember how our older sister Ganga would ask you the same questions about them, and you always had the same answers because they truly weren't made up. You told her how Kula really grew up, and real stories about her family. How Saia really did her hair, and what type of food she liked. How India really came to be named after a country, and what she felt about it.

"But you know they're imaginary?" Ganga probed, just to confirm your level of awareness. You were four years old.

"Yes," you replied. But that didn't mean they weren't real. You loved them, sight unseen.

We were all invisible together, so it wasn't like I stopped seeing them and then that made me stop engaging with them as you had engaged with them. At some point, I was just too old for imaginary friends. I was just too old for "real" to mean that Kula and Saia and India were really there for us whenever we needed them, even though they were. I was too old for "real" to mean that imagining them drying our tears when we cried was really a comfort. I was too old for "real" to mean that they really supported us through all our most difficult decisions, and that they never made us feel ashamed for being wrong. So I told them goodbye. They respected my decision, like lovers are supposed to but hardly any have since, and I never saw them again. But, oh, how I miss them, too.

Hari-Gaura, writing to you has me drowning in nostalgia, rediscovering so many of the other things I've pined to reclaim since losing you. The other day I came across the earliest home video that you created and I still possess. It's a recording of you dressed in faded denim overalls just before you turned five, head still full of hair. You stand in front of the camera for a few seconds before—poof—you are gone. There are countless clips of you disappearing and reappearing somewhere else, beaming a smile. One is modeled after a Toys"R"Us commercial, with you singing the jingle: *I don't want to grow up, 'cause, baby, if I did, I couldn't be a Toys"R"Us kid!*

It looks like the trick was the most fun you'd ever had.

By four years old, a child should have well-developed object permanence, but this video was evidence that finding joy in disappearing doesn't have to end as soon as a person learns that things continue to exist outside of their vision. Daddy had recently bought a new camcorder that allowed you to splice video of yourself standing in front of a static background with an image of just the background to create this trick.

I imagine Mata was frustrated with him for the purchase, thinking it just another gadget for his dusty collection of endless tools and books and electronics we couldn't afford and didn't use much. But you managed what I have too hard a time doing nowadays. You found something loving beneath the infuriating surface of our father's hoarding habits: a search to fill a void he did not create but I think he feels responsible for. And sometimes, the love that is buried underneath behaviors informed by the trauma of being Black in this world can be recovered, when you haven't given up hope in what you can't see under the rubble.

I might never see many of the family members I love again in this world. The carceral state intentionally draws a hard line between the world out here and the one inside its prisons, and that will never be acceptable. But there are things that can allow me to still have something to live for even while knowing this. There is something that can allow me to still find joy despite the likelihood of never seeing so many of the people I love again, and that is understanding the possibility of other worlds where those inside prisons are free.

The love given to me by the people I have lost and am losing to carceral logics doesn't have to stay gone just because they are, and I should never give up on it. I should never stop believing in the ability to see my family in other lights, knowing that we are worthy of care regardless of how deep into the hole of criminality we are forced. The state can never take something far enough away from me that it doesn't matter anymore—that it cannot exist anymore. There are always other universes where reuniting is possible, if I fight for them.

And this fight feels like my mother must have felt at the family reunions I haven't attended in too long, following the examples of you and Tiger and Black children everywhere to remaster the simple steps I am embarrassed to have forgotten.

Teach you, teach you, teach you, I'll teach you the Electric Sliiiiide.

CHAPTER NINE

REPRESENTATION MATTERS?

"Now we're cooking with gas!" my dad announced in the parlance only he knows as we took off from the Beechwood house toward New York City, where I would soon be attending New York University's film school. I huffed as his curls, already fully slate gray then, billowed in the wind that vacuumed through the windows of our van while we inched along the highway well under the speed limit. I'd be lucky if the typically eight-hour trip stayed under ten.

I was going to live away from my parents for the first time, but I had little hesitation to go off for college. In a way, I had already lived away from them, if you considered how much of myself I kept secret in the midst of my rebellions or in the invisible worlds I'd imagined for myself as a child. I thought of New York as the place I could finally explore my queerness unencumbered. I could finally leave Cleveland behind. Leave my father's plodding and corny sayings and hoarding behind. Our poorness behind. The unimaginable smell of Lake Erie polluted by the environmental destruction wreaked by capitalism. The snow the lake caused. Or at least I could tuck it all away, like old, stained clothes you won't throw out because deep down they mean too much . . . even if you never plan to wear them again.

"Don't lose yourself out there, now," my dad warned. "New York is too much. It's just too much."

"Not for us," I assured him. "Not for a Ziyad."

But I hadn't before been surrounded by so few Black faces as I was at NYU, which assisted in my forgetting who I was, despite my assurances to my father. It had been a long time since I'd known the joy of disappearing. I had seen the ways being Black and visible in a misafropedic world intent on harming Black children could be dangerous, and had begun to see that my own recognition in high school always seemed to come alongside harm for my peers whom the institution considered undeserving. But I didn't fully understand the implications: that recognizing the harm that can accompany visibility also means questioning the idea of representation, on its own, as liberation. Instead, now *I* was the student who was considered undeserving of recognition, and gaining that recognition was supposed to be a solution to all my problems, harms be damned.

Before starting college, I committed to the idea that if I could only tell my story, only make the Black, queer boy I used to be appear on as many screens as possible, all audiences would be forced to believe that he mattered without doing any difficult work. I myself wanted to be able to believe that the child I used to be mattered without putting in the effort to show myself that he did, without repairing the fracture caused by my carceral dissonance and caring for him the way he deserves to be cared for. I thought that if I could just make my presence known in the midst of all the violence directed at me, those who enacted it would find it in their hearts to direct their violence elsewhere. Instead, they only gained clarity on where their target was.

I tried to create what I told myself would be the Blackest, queerest films and scripts in my film classes. In my freshman production class, I wrote and directed a comedy about Arielle, a Black, genderqueer woman who turns her white partner's guilt-inspired fears of being seen as anti-Black on their head by accusing him of calling her a nigger in public after catching him cheating. In my sound class, I recorded an audio-movie re-creation of the life of a Black Chicago boy before he was killed in an act of "senseless" violence. I was sure that my *Game of Thrones*–inspired take on the Greek gods' competition to rule Mount Olympus, where the gods were all people of color and many were queer, was revolutionary.

As my peers did with all final film projects for that course, I screened the short about Arielle in a large studio in front of my entire class. Just before my film, another student screened hers, which featured a story line I don't recall except for one scene showing a character bathing in a tub of milk.

"It took a hundred gallons of dairy," the student director explained as she came up and stood behind the lectern in front of the massive screen to respond to feedback, laughing behind huge circle-framed Ray-Ban sunglasses that rested underneath her meticulously unkempt blonde hair. Even with the studio lights up, it was no brighter than the inside of a car with tinted windows parked under a streetlight after dark.

My fellow Black classmate and friend Kristen nudged me and rolled her eyes, and I laughed knowingly. As if on cue, the director took a sip from her Starbucks cup while one of the other students began telling her how "brilliant" the film's cinematography was.

"I shot it on an Alexa," the director replied, referring to a state-of-the-art camera that wasn't provided by the school but that many of the well-off students in the program would sometimes rent out with their own money. Those students could afford a hundred gallons of milk and more for their student films. Kristen and I could afford only to roll our eyes if we wanted to go on being tolerated by them.

The lights went down for the start of my short. The blonde director went back to her seat, sunglasses firmly in place. The film began with a close-up of the freshly painted nails of the actor playing Arielle, which I boorishly—but rightly—assumed would provoke humor when she was revealed as being played by one of the male students in our class.

Before the camera panned up, the character started talking to someone off-screen. It immediately became clear that it was her boyfriend, and he was breaking up with her after falling for someone else.

The audience's laughter crescendoed as Arielle morphed into an unhinged woman scorned, with more than a few hints of an angry-Black-woman caricature thrown in for good measure. I soaked in the roaring as it reached a fever pitch with the reveal of the actor and exceeded even that when Arielle started to scream, "You called me a nigger!" at her white boyfriend in the middle of a crowded park.

So many flaws with the work I was creating in college could have used careful critique. In this film, for instance, not only did I have a cisgender man play Arielle, but he played her in crude stereotypes of transgender and Black women for white, cisgender people to laugh at. The audio movie I created in sound class was based on a true story, but I had made no effort to reach out to the people involved and had almost entirely fictionalized what was a very real trauma for a whole community just to reify the myth that "Black on Black" violence is its own especially heinous and irrational form of intracommunal strife. The main conflict in my Greek-god story was too similar to *Thrones*, and I'd mostly just copied the characters and added more diverse identities. But when I got feedback from my classmates and students, these were not the primary critiques.

"I think something like this would need more diversity to sell," a white student who had laughed the loudest at Arielle's "nigger" moment said when it was time for him to comment, pointing out the very different audience demographics of similar shows the professor had asked us to research the week prior. "You want it to reach the widest audience possible. People want to see themselves in it." I could have easily deduced then that I wasn't "people" to him and stopped trying to get him to see himself in me, but I didn't want to.

My reality—my motivations, wants, hopes, dreams, and life—was too foreign a concept for many of my largely white colleagues and professors to comprehend. But I kept trying anyway, rather than working to more carefully and intentionally comprehend my own life. Even when they did enjoy the Blackest, queerest work I produced, these colleagues and professors often missed what I was trying to say. And because I thought all I wanted was for them to understand what I was saying, I edited my ideas to suit them. "Diversified" the Greek gods by adding back in more white characters. Made my stories more "universal." Less about me. Stripped them of their Blackness. Stripped my stories of myself. Stripped myself of my stories. The same thing I had already done to my Inner Child.

By the time I discovered communities of Black and queer people off campus, discovered where all the mirrors were hiding—or rather, where I had been hiding them by not seeking them out—there was hardly anything reflected back in my face. To make your body seen in a world that finds your light too bright, you must first put it out.

～〰

"I don't know why I expected to just graduate and immediately start working on real films," Kristen laughed as we caught up over lunch at Dallas BBQ in Chelsea. She is queer, too. She laughs a lot at the fucked-up things in her life, but it's in a completely different pitch from the sound that escaped from the white kids at the word "nigger" in our class. Like she isn't turning our shared pain into comedy because the transformation brings her joy but is expressing it however it comes out because otherwise the pain would simply fester.

"Because they taught us film as if we all had money and could finance our own shit," I replied. "They taught film for white people."

"You went straight into the field, though!" she pointed out.

After graduating, I was accepted into the page program at a major television network, a yearlong fellowship that was sold on the fact that it was more selective than Harvard, accepting less than 2 percent of its applicants. In reality, this meant not so much that those who were hired were highly skilled but that we were likely to have significant industry connections, or had been lucky enough to take advantage of rare opportunities to make lasting face-to-face impressions on the recruiters. (I'd attended a fair at NYU, where I was able to do the latter.) Of course, Harvard, which admits legacy students at five times the rate of students without university connections, could be accused of the same, as could any "exclusive" institution in a capitalistic world where even our favorite celebrities regularly bribe their children's way to success.[29]

"But the industry I went straight into was for white people, too," I told Kristen, explaining how Black employees were routinely disciplined for speaking out about anti-Black experiences, and that the page program paid only twelve dollars an hour (less than the current minimum wage) in a city with one of the highest costs of living in the country. This was almost as unworkable for me as any other fantastical dreams we had for our careers, as it would be for most people without a significant amount of money to fall back on. I scraped by that year only because my partner at the time supplemented my income and offered me a place to stay at an otherwise impossible price, and because I hardly ever ate.

Supposedly, pages have access to many exciting "assignments" that last for a couple of months in different areas of television. This is alleged to help them build skills and set them up for jobs with the company. The reality was that these assignments were often dependent on one's relationships with hiring managers or older pages who had worked the assignments before, and of course these relationships were usually made much easier if you shared a cultural background (i.e., if you were white).

While more than a few pages made it through the full year without getting an assignment, I managed to acquire two of the less coveted ones working in news production. This helped me land my next job as an assistant to a talent agent whose clients were mostly news and sports personalities, which was admittedly a little closer to the idea both Kristen and I had once had of "working on real films" just after college.

There were only two other assistants at the small talent agency. They sat in cubicles at different parts of the office, so I interacted with my boss and the office manager, Morgan, most regularly. By industry standards, we were as low-key an office as they come. I had expected work at a TV agency to be as cutthroat and cruel as the television show *Entourage* portrayed it to be, but we managed to do our jobs without many of the abuses that I soon found were in fact regular in quite a few other agencies and management companies we did business with.

One day in 2015, I came into work to find Morgan with the volume on the TV that sat on her desk turned up to the point that it couldn't be ignored. The bystander video she was watching intently on the news was damning and clear, the newscaster implied, as I turned on my own TV to listen in curiosity.

The footage replayed over and over, like another police body camera recording of an unarmed Black person being murdered that never leads to a conviction. But this time a jury would convict, even though this time no one died. No one even went to the hospital. By far, it wasn't the most brutal fight I had witnessed, even just counting the ones in high school. But, the reporter insisted, Bayna-Lehkeim El-Amin hitting Jonathan Snipes over the back with a chair—at the same Dallas BBQ where Kristen and I would meet for lunch, four years later—was one of the most disgustingly hateful acts he'd reported on.

"What a monster," Morgan agreed, still watching the footage on her screen behind me. "I don't know how a person could be so homophobic."

El-Amin was a six-feet-six Black man who would later be called a "hulking brute" in a *New York Daily News* story about his conviction. Like the language I'd used to describe Roberto from East 128th Street. Like the language that Officer Darren Wilson used to justify killing Mike Brown. This is the standard description for Black people who experience conflict in a carceral state, and sometimes Black people absorb the media's messages about ourselves, even without knowing.

Jonathan Snipes, a white, gay man, said the Dallas BBQ fight escalated when El-Amin called Snipes and his boyfriend, Ethan Adams, "white faggots," and derided them for "spilling [their] drinks." Snipes admitted to being drunk and hitting El-Amin first, and video from the scene corroborated this. But prosecutor Leah Saxtein, a white woman, still argued El-Amin was motivated by animus against "these girly men (Snipes and Adams)," an argument supported by a torrent of reporting that framed the incident as a "gay bashing."

When I first saw the breaking news story, I knew immediately that something was off. This particular Dallas BBQ is heavily frequented by Black, queer people, which was what made Kristen and me choose it that day for catching up. Morgan, who was straight, may not have known this, but regardless of whether El-Amin was queer himself, he likely was comfortable in the midst of queerness if he had any awareness of the establishment before going. I started asking around about the case, which eventually connected me to Mitchyll Mora, a founding member of Freedom 2 Live (F2L), a volunteer network aiming to support queer and trans people of color facing felony-level offenses in New York City.

Mora, whose organizing around the case helped establish El-Amin's defense, confirmed what I had suspected: not only was El-Amin queer himself, but he was actively involved in the LGBTQ community in the city. Many organizers focused on the issues of Black, queer people worked tirelessly to bring this information to mainstream LGBTQ organizations in an attempt to rally the community to defend El-Amin. Instead, a group of these mainstream LGBTQ organizations partnered with city council member Corey Johnson to hold a rally against "anti-gay" hate violence just after the incident. Instead, the *New York Daily News* put a photo of the "brute" El-Amin on the front page above the story of this imagined "gay bashing." And instead, the NYPD, under the guidance of LGBTQ liaison Tim Duffy, publicly announced they were investigating the incident as a possible hate crime.

As a budding writer who had just launched my own publication, RaceBaitr, I joined a collective of activists and other Black journalists coordinating responses to illuminate El-Amin's queerness and the fact that he was attacked first. I had some of my first major bylines at Mic and Slate writing about the case, but the narrative would not be changed. It was not ours to change. Councilman Johnson never returned my repeated emails and phone calls. To him and many others in the city, El-Amin could only be a brute. That is the story that reaches the widest audience possible, and so that is the story that sells. These most popular stories are also the ones that build prisons and that built this country.

El-Amin's sexuality, as well as the reality that he acted in self-defense, was visible from the beginning, and we made sure it remained so. But in September 2016, the judge agreed that El-Amin's attack on Snipes was egregious and hateful. Even though hate-crime charges were never filed, El-Amin was sentenced to nine years in prison.

"It is uncomfortable for me to discuss," El-Amin told me in a letter recently, the weight of the whole ordeal raining down on him in his fourth year behind bars. He pointed out that Islamophobia likely also played a role in how the case proceeded, but "it has and could happen to any other Black man."

El-Amin's presence as a queer person, and a victim of an attack, was made known in the midst of all the violence directed at him. But our stories don't evoke sympathy from the carceral state, and so making them visible does not cause the state to direct its violence elsewhere. In El-Amin, in his "hulking" body, in his "brutish" Blackness, the visibility and representation of his full story could not save him.

El-Amin's case illuminates the specific failure of visibility and representation at the intersection of Blackness. For years I stewed on the injustice of his case without any logical way to explain it, until a doctoral student friend referred me to Frank Wilderson III's book of film criticism, *Red, White & Black: Cinema and the Structure of U.S. Antagonisms.* In the book, Wilderson revisits James Baldwin's essay "The Black Boy Looks at the White Boy," in which Baldwin explains the dynamic with his friend and white writer Norman Mailer as being one where Mailer "still imagines that he has something to save, whereas I have never had anything to lose." Wilderson argues that the "something to save" that Black people lack is the relationship an owner has with interchangeable objects: the relationship white people have with Black people within a slave system.[30] Reading *Red, White & Black*, along with Saidiya Hartman's *Scenes of Subjection*, most powerfully illuminated for me the reality that for visibility to effectively improve the plight of marginalized people, empathy must be evoked, and this world is specifically designed not to empathize with Black people.

For empathy to be activated, a witness has to interpret someone else's pain and see it as similar to their own. When Black pain not only is seen as dissimilar to the viewer but also gives them pleasure—when our bodies have been defined as inherently criminal—it's no wonder that police body camera footage of an unarmed Black person being murdered so rarely leads to a conviction. It's no wonder that news stations replay it over and over again anyway. It's no wonder that our retaliation for being attacked and killed is so consistently made out to be unconscionable.

Even for the mainstream organizations and politicians that claimed to protect and defend LGBTQ people, only Smith's queerness registered as in need of defending, while El-Amin's, if it even registered at all, did not. Hardly any of the politicians who called for El-Amin's head set the record straight or came to his defense when he was named queer or when video showed he was attacked first. The media organizations didn't issue corrections. None of these truths changed how the prosecutor classified El-Amin's act of self-defense as hateful or how the judge agreed. Pushing back against what seeks to destroy us almost always gets Black people labeled as bullyish brutes by the actors in this carceral system, no matter whether our being destroyed is represented and seen or not.

This truth informed my mission for RaceBaitr and all the work I have done as a journalist and editor at publications like Black Youth Project since El-Amin's case. If Black people are to have honest responses to our experiences, we will necessarily be attacked as "race baiters" by those who wield a carceral gaze and witness our bodies as inherently criminal.

My work and the work that the RaceBaitr editors feature on the site are not an appeal for those who wield the carceral gaze to change their minds. They are to provide a place for us to work through the dissonance the carceral gaze creates, without conforming, appealing, or pleading to it. I believe that providing this space is all that our writing can do. I encourage Black writers to write like writing won't save us. Like only what comes after will. Like something must come after. And if others want to call that race-baiting, if they want to call us brutes, if they want to call us undeserving of recognition, fine. The work is not in trying to transform the carceral gaze; it's in trying to destroy it.

"Remember El-Amin?" I asked Kristen, looking around at the crowded restaurant and the multicolored Texas-size margaritas lining every other table. It was still filled with Black and queer people, as if the restaurant hadn't shown us they didn't want us here. My friend and I were still sitting there as if we hadn't seen the antipathy for us that they'd made visible, too. Kristen just laughed that sorrowful laugh of hers.

"I just couldn't believe what I was seeing," she howled.

"I fucking hate Jonathan Snipes and Ethan Adams," I told her. "I fucking hate how many Black people have been taken away, one after another, because we aren't 'people' to them. I hate how long I tried to suppress that feeling. How easy it is to try and suppress it now, in an effort to be seen by them."

"We should try to find Snipes." She laughed, but she knew this wasn't funny.

"I don't know what I would do if I saw him."

"You don't have to," she said, more serious now. "You shouldn't have to always contain your anger before you can feel it."

~

I think I get it now. When I was a child, disappearing to steal jam from the fridge, I didn't worry that I might end up separated from my parents forever. To be unseen doesn't always have to mean that I am erased. We don't need to see ourselves on their screens to know that we are not monsters. We know this before we learn otherwise. We have other platforms, in our homes, in our neighborhoods, and in our communities, that show us this naturally. We don't need to be seen in their media to be valued. We just need whatever *is* seen not to be used to erase our value. We need whatever *is* represented in their media not to be shoved down our throats and internalized. Yes, representation matters, but we don't need our own versions of their propaganda. We represent ourselves in how we show up in our relationships with one another every day.

I had forgotten that a story that doesn't involve a person is different from a story that precludes their existence. The carceral state wants me to believe that I can matter only if I am the hero of its stories, because if I believe that, it still gets to tell those stories. Because then we have to keep begging to be let in, to not be the villain, to not be the criminal of their tales. We have to put our faith in "diversity" and changing the colors and genders of people on-screen without changing what is being said about those colors and genders. The carceral state wants us to believe we can't tell stories differently about how Blackness is criminalized, or tell those stories to other audiences, for purposes other than to communicate with the state, on its terms.

While reading Black studies scholar Christina Sharpe's groundbreaking book *In the Wake: On Blackness and Being*, I found further clarity on what makes this essential: "I am not interested in rescuing the Black being(s) for the category of 'Human,' misunderstood as 'Man,' . . . both of those languages and the material conditions they re/produce continue to produce our fast and slow deaths. I am interested in ways of seeing and imagining responses to the terror visited on Black life and the ways we inhabit it, are inhabited by it, and refuse it."

Sharpe argues that the work is not to increase our representation in media to try and humanize ourselves for the carceral gaze but to participate in what she calls processes of "Black annotation" and "Black redaction" in this media landscape built on carceral logics. She describes Black annotation and Black redaction as work "toward reading and seeing something in excess of what is caught in the frame."[31]

Like Sharpe (and, indeed, in part because of what I learned from her), I am no longer interested in telling my story to those wielding a carceral gaze. This story is not exceptional, and those who have told something like it to the world before me have not been spared. Those who have told something like it to the world are often stepping into the line of fire, being made to strip their Blackness from those stories, to put out their own light.

I no longer need to see myself in their tales to know that I can exist outside the world the tale describes. To know that it is not the only tale there is, just because it is the only tale they advertise. I no longer need to tell them our stories because their advertisements make it feel like "no one is talking about" those stories. To believe that is to erase the very people those stories pertain to, who obviously talk about their own lives, loves, struggles, and triumphs, sharing these stories among their own communities.

Transgender women whose sisters' deaths don't get media attention aren't "no one," and they are talking, even without being represented in films like the one I made about Arielle. Black, queer folks like El-Amin aren't "no one," and they tell their stories even when the media doesn't listen. Black, queer Cleveland boys like I was aren't "no one." They are real people whom we should love and care for and learn from regardless of whether they are given a platform to be represented to this world. And we can learn from them only if *their* platforms are made sacred— platforms that are not meant to advertise for this world. Platforms that don't always look as fancy as what we see on TV, platforms like the community center around the corner or your auntie's house down the street.

I no longer need to see myself in the tales told by and through the carceral state, but I have to be able to imagine myself outside of them.

The question isn't how to tell the stories that the carceral state's media isn't. The question is much bigger: How do I put Black annotation and redaction into practice to go beyond this limited way of telling stories? How do I understand the stories beneath the lies this world tells? How do I embrace and embolden those who stay away or are forced out from under the scorching limelight of the carceral gaze? How do I use any distance from carceral gazes to my advantage? What can that distance teach me about myself that I would never know otherwise?

CHAPTER TEN
A PRAYER FOR CHOICE

Hari-Gaura,

I still hate wearing button-down shirts. It's not just that they make my body look as boxy as if it were being rendered on an old Nintendo 64. I hate how they feel like stiff cotton hands itching to tighten fatally around my throat when fastened all the way up, threatening every next breath. How the top button sometimes pinches my Adam's apple when I manage it through its hole, calling to mind the excruciatingly long wait I suffered for the lump to develop, thinking I needed it to define my manhood. How that pinch almost feels like it did when Mata would squeeze your skin between her bone-thick nails if you were acting up in public, but hers left scars much easier to heal.

There are other scars all over this body reminding me of how you were lost. The gash above my left eyebrow from losing a fight at the basketball court, trying to prove myself tough and unafraid of other boys. The one on my elbow from scraping the ground while winning a fight trying to prove the same. Each carries within its lesser regenerated tissues a memory of how Black children who claim freedom to be themselves are discarded when they are allowed only to be what they are told. I don't own much formal wear because their typical gendered limitations only draw attention to the marks left behind from all these cotton-picked pinches I've endured to become who I am today, marks that together compose a map showing just how far I am from you now. Marks that remind me how, as a queer person in this world, I have been struggling to breathe.

But last summer, I had to buy a button-down shirt for our brother Syama's wedding because the formal long-sleeve I brought with me instead would have been too hot in the ninety-five-degree Houston heat. It was so hot in the city that if you stepped outside, you'd instantly crave to fight, either to prove yourself or not. I said I would wear it only that one time. But a month after Syama's wedding, there I was, choosing to put on that damn white button-down again. Forcing this body into discomfort for the sake of looking presentable again. Failing at bringing you back again.

I've been mostly successful at staying away from churches and temples and mosques since graduating high school and leaving choir, but a few months ago Aunt Cheryl passed away unexpectedly, and I flew back to Cleveland for her church funeral. You didn't know her well, and I never really got to know her much better after you left. She struggled with addiction most of the time you were here, but when she was around, she was always kind and generous to her nieces and nephews.

Aunt Cheryl was the type who would give us a few crumpled dollars from the bottom of her purse when she saw us and had it, and a prayer when she didn't. She didn't often have money, and so she was usually praying. A true God-fearing woman, like all Mother Bhūmi's children. All pillars of the same churches I now take great measures to avoid but somehow always seem to find my way back inside anyway.

I wasn't sure I would go to Aunt Cheryl's funeral. The insides of churches aren't always as hot as Houston had been just days prior, but when you're queer, they tend to make you feel the urge to fight, too. Funerals tend to tighten up in your throat like that button-down to remind you of what you're lacking, too. But I felt like I had to show up on Mata's behalf.

"It happened so fast," she told me over the phone as she drove back to Cleveland from Gita Nagari, the Hare Kṛṣṇa commune in Pennsylvania. I wondered whether she had been crying, and I wasn't sure whether it would be more comforting if she had been.

Mata couldn't make the funeral because the church where it was held wouldn't change the date, and she couldn't reschedule a previously set engagement with the Vaiṣṇava community in Toronto.

"Isn't that a shame?" she told me. She explained that Aunt Cheryl had given all her money to this church. "Basically funded it!" Mata exaggerated, shaking her head at their inflexibility. At how little a God-fearing woman gets in return for all her dollars and prayers, without mentioning the possibility of inflexibility on the part of a god who would have her miss her sister's funeral.

You wouldn't believe it, but Aunt Cheryl's daughter Taylor is a full-fledged evangelist now. To the point where it wouldn't be her mother's funeral if she didn't get up and preach. My fiancé, Timothy, is a slam poet, and he says half-jokingly that Black church preaching isn't that much different from spoken word: the performance gets a person more points than the substance. I half-jokingly agree. At the funeral, Taylor started her poem with a verse about how we give more energy to our favorite celebrities than to God and discussed how her mother's death was a reminder that we need to rectify this problem before it's too late.

"We stay up all night—amen—waiting for the new Jay-Z album to drop—praise God. But how long—amen—do we stay up for him?! Praise God!" she shouted, spinning on a single red heel, the other foot kicked up in front of her to cap off the show.

The judges held their hands up, snapped their fingers, and shouted—a perfect score of 10. But all I could think about were the things our aunt didn't rectify in life. All I could think about was how spoken-word scores are inherently biased against marginalized people because they rely on the reactions of random audience members—who, even though the spoken-word community is diverse, are still unlikely to share the most marginalized experiences with the most marginalized performer—and how I never did like the scoring part of the process all that much.

During the repast, Taylor came to hug me and remarked on how handsome I was in that ugly white button-down.

"You make sure to tell them girls no unless they are saved!" she said with a wink. I forced a smile and told her sincerely how sorry I was for her loss—our loss—and she earnestly thanked me. But I am almost positive she knew I was queer. She follows me on Facebook. She once warned my mother after I posted a picture of the tattoo on my back depicting a scene from a Hindu myth in which Kṛṣṇa takes a half-man, half-lion form that I was worshipping demons. It's the natural next step on the gay agenda, I guess. Mata told me afterward that she was actually worried by Taylor's message until she saw the picture; then she laughed. I was surprised at how quickly Mata would have believed it.

After Taylor's sermon, Auntie Grace went up to the lectern behind large black sunglasses that swallowed half of her face. She has always had a thing for flair, and I have always loved her for it. I am still closest to her of all Mata's siblings, and like all of them, she is still anti-queer in a "hate the sin, not the sinner" kind of way. I'm used to it.

It's one of the reasons I wore this button-down, to look less like the sinner I was. Distance from myself allows a type of proximity to the people I love that sometimes doesn't feel like closeness at all.

"I can't see," Auntie Grace said in her Kansan accent, which had been watered down only slightly by a decade of living back in Cleveland. After fussing with the glasses, she huffed and finally tossed them aside. All the congregants laughed, making a sound like bubbles pushing through boiling water, hissing sniffles left over from crying just the moment before.

Auntie Grace shared with the congregation how the family was so focused on Mata after her cancer diagnosis that the death of her other sister felt like being blindsided by a truck, and everybody laughed again at how funny God is. But if God stays reminding us to look both ways before crossing the street and we stay limiting his messages so that we can focus on just one side or the other, I think that makes us the funny ones.

Daddy says you were ambidextrous. He says it with such pride.

"Your mother and her mother didn't like that, though." He shakes his head at their inflexibility. I vaguely recall Mother Bhūmi slapping your fork away once when she saw you eating with your left hand, disgust bleeding from her shiny eyes.

"The left hand is unclean!" our grandmother said, pointing to scripture and using a term I would later hear Mata repeat to describe my sexuality. The two of them joined forces to pressure you to stop using your left hand all the way up until you were gone. Sometimes, I try to write with mine to bring you back, but the words just come out shaky and unfocused. The words just come out as this bizarre attempt at explaining away why I am still wearing a shirt that you never would have worn, while claiming to want you to return.

~

Most of the family showed up to the homegoing. I had seen our cousins only a few times since moving to New York nine years earlier, and at Aunt Cheryl's funeral, I told them the same thing I said at Mother Bhūmi's, the last time I saw them: "We have got to do a better job of keeping in touch!" But ever since losing you, the deaths of other family members have been the only things that have managed to bring everybody back together.

After the ceremony, most of the family headed to our cousin Kadeem's house around the corner from the church.

"I know you don't want any," Kadeem said after he brought out a case of beer and began to roll a blunt. "You're Kṛṣṇanandini's kids." *Your God doesn't let you grieve like us.*

Kadeem doesn't really know me well, and I guess he also didn't know you were gone yet. So I told him. I asked for a drink.

"Damn, what happened?!" he replied with a nervous laugh as he poured me a whiskey cranberry. I wanted to tell him how you were suffocated by limiting ideas about what boys like you should do, and sometimes that drives me to drink too much. Instead, I just laughed along with him. Then he asked me how I liked the girls in New York.

"They're cool," I said, before making up an excuse to escape the conversation, grateful for the Jameson.

Later that night, our cousin Richard grabbed my shoulder. I am closer to him, and he knows about my queerness.

"Step outside with me, Hari, man," Richard said, running his hands awkwardly through his locs. I gulped down the last of my drink and headed to the patio, unsure what to expect. I carried my empty cup as if it weren't empty at all, indistinctly aware of a strange hope that I might look down and see it had magically refilled itself.

"I been meaning to ask you," Richard said through a graceless chuckle. "What made you like boys?"

I wanted to tell him, "I didn't have a choice." That you had been attracted to boys for as long as I could remember. It's the same thing I told my parents in the letter I sent them in college explaining that I was queer. I assured them that nothing they could have done would have changed that fact. Lady Gaga proclaimed "Born This Way" was the answer to all my concerns around my sexuality, and I wanted so hard to believe this message, like so many of my gay NYU peers had in their deification of her, because that would make navigating this so much easier.

If you were born with your gayness, then the fact that everyone seemed to pick up on it just to pick it apart made sense. That it felt like your performance of gender was targeted every single day—that the only whupping I remember you receiving from Daddy was after you jokingly danced on a male friend, that it seemed like our parents made sure to criticize everything that could possibly be interpreted as queer in front of you—felt logical.

"You had to know," I wrote in the letter, but Mata insists that she didn't. None of our family admits that they knew, or that they could have ever even guessed.

I used to think they were all lying, that this just gave them plausible deniability for me turning out this way. Your queerness felt so loud to me. It was in everything you did. I wanted to tell Richard this, that he knew why I liked boys. That I didn't have a choice. That I was born this way. But the collar of the button-down was suddenly so tight I couldn't get the words out. At that moment, all my scars were visible again, and I was reminded that you are gone and I cannot speak for you—not without repairing the fracture caused by this carceral dissonance.

What is the story beneath this lie that the world tells about the certainty of sexuality? What made you like boys? Even in my earliest memories of experiencing what I interpret as attraction today, I'm not sure it was always entirely sexual. Did you want to have sex with everyone you were attracted to? Were you even completely sure what sex consisted of? Were you really born gay?

"Born This Way" made sense of the violence that had always targeted me, but claiming it never stopped that violence. Being Black and making sense in an anti-Black world hardly does. Even if my sexuality couldn't be changed, that wouldn't prevent anyone from forcing me to try to silence or deny it—any more than never naming my desires had prevented my parents from policing anything that might resemble queerness, even while I was presumably straight. Taylor could just pretend I hadn't claimed I was gay at all, until the opportunity arose to convincingly point out my demons. Our parents could wield their valid skepticism of Eurocentric science, the same science that had justified our enslavement, to disregard any proof I offered that I had always been this way, especially since the science is inconclusive at best—after all, studies with identical twins do strongly imply sexuality is not entirely genetic.[32] And while "Born This Way" couldn't save me from these attacks, it also didn't leave room for anyone whose journey to their sexuality was flexible, or just less cut and dried. Even if being born this way is the answer for some gay people, it could not be the answer for everyone. I wanted to wield it as if it were.

But what if you weren't born with any static sexuality? What if what I found so loud and impossible to ignore was just you wanting to be free to share intimacy with people you loved and not be told that this was unclean? Even today, only sometimes is my desire for the intimacy I need physical. Sometimes I have felt these desires for intimacy with women as well. It's just that the world prohibits me from asking it of men, and you kept asking for that intimacy anyway.

Your courage to ask for the intimacy you needed, despite the ways this intimacy was criminalized and punished, is what I think Richard was really asking about—almost as if he hoped to find that courage, too. Almost as if he hadn't even platonically touched another man in years, but his aunt had just died and he really could have used a fucking hug from any one of those of us he considered men who were standing around him. I was afraid giving one to him might risk me looking even softer than I already felt, might risk revealing that I don't consider myself a man, though I think I needed a hug, too. I can be a coward. Your courage is what I am starting to understand queerness really is, and it takes brave choices that I don't always make.

I wanted to tell Richard that I didn't have a choice in being queer, because if I did have one, I would have to answer for why I didn't choose queerness more often, why I didn't choose to embrace you and your freedoms, and why I don't choose that over and over again knowing that the alternative is a cage of abusing myself in order to conform to normative roles I will never completely fit. I would have to explain why I was in this button-down that you would have never worn without being forced. So instead of answering I fidgeted with the collar of the uncomfortably male shirt, took a sip of my uncomfortably empty drink.

"I mean," Richard clarified nervously, "I don't have a problem with you being gay. I just know you can get hella pussy. You're giving it all up!"

"I don't know if it works like that," I tried. He just gave me another puzzled look, so I made up an excuse to end the conversation and headed to the driveway, where a basketball hoop was set up.

"Three on three?" I offered the five cousins—all boys—shooting around. They accepted. I played in my dress clothes but had to take off my shoes. I left my socks on because my toenails were still painted black from the pedicure I got before my brother's wedding. When we were tied 10–10 with the game going to 11, I took off the button-down shirt, too, sweat forcing me to wrench it from my body. I hoped it ripped on the way off. It didn't. I did not choose to rip it.

But I could win this game, and at least that was certain. I could grunt and push just to score a point like the manliest man with the most pronounced Adam's apple. I could watch my feet bleed a plash against the concrete and say it's all worth it. I didn't give this up, even if you would have.

I could show my cousin: Here is my cleanliness. Here is a performance of toughness we were both taught as boys is the same thing as love. When I was knocked headfirst into the garage door, I shook it off. I knocked the next cousin who posted up against me into the garage door as payback. Two players had to leave the court due to injuries, but my team won. A conspicuously drunk uncle clapped approvingly from the back porch.

"That was a good game," he said, with more than a hint of surprise. "Don't tell your mother," he said, pouring me another drink. I put the button-down back on and walked inside Kadeem's house. I looked at the scars on my feet, thought of you and how far gone you were.

I try to avoid drawing attention to the scars on my body that remind me of how you were lost, because many of them I played a hand in creating. Many were caused by trying to prove something to the world, to my family, that never needed proving. Many were caused by trying to show I was man enough to defend myself, or gay enough never to have to question my sexuality at all, when to you, questions had been okay.

I am ashamed to admit that I do not always choose to be queer. I do not always choose to question how I police my own intimacy, even within the context of my gayness. I do not always ask what it means when I desire thin, light-skinned, able-bodied partners (and friends) in a fatphobic, white-supremacist, ableist society. I do not always consider that there have been times I was attracted to a person I initially assumed was male who turned out later to be a transgender woman or a genderqueer person, and whether that means I was ever really attracted to a "man" in the first place, or just to my rigid ideas of manhood.

There are so many other questions I should be asking, about how my limited ideas around what

I think real men look like limit how I define myself and my sexuality, and thus my ability to find the intimacy I need. Do my attractions change when I know what influences them? Do I want them to change?

As I become closer to you, I am increasingly aware of my attractions to other people who aren't men. I find myself noticing sexual attractions to queer women, to genderqueer people, and to other non-men who offer new ways for me to love them and live freely. I also find myself noticing a type of romance in relationships that would never be described as sexual. But none of this makes for an identity that is legible in this world, and being illegible here is terrifying—and life threatening. I am not always courageous enough to face my fears.

Hari-Gaura, I find myself back in the same churches in which our family has become a pillar despite the measures I take to avoid them, because the truth is that I am not always so different from cousins who don't seem to be able to wrap their minds around not wanting to "get hella pussy" or not wanting to run through all the girls in New York. As gay as my dating practices have proved me to be, sometimes I just want to fit into a normative role, just like I think they do.

I'm not so different from our parents, who shake their heads at the inflexibility of this carceral world—at the inflexibility of the church hosting their sister's funeral or of the wife who pressures their child not to use their left hand—while being complicit in its limitations in other ways. Sometimes I want life to be easy, but resistance never is. I do not always choose to be queer, even though I know that I have to choose it consistently in order to get back to you.

~

Toward the end of the night, my little cousin Justus and I really hit it off. You might have been gone by the time she was born. She stayed with us at the Cleveland Heights house for a summer when she was five, and she's seventeen now.

"You were a fucking terror!" I told her with a laugh, remembering a scene of her cackling while running around and spraying a fire extinguisher through our very dry and not-on-fire home.

"I wasn't bad!" she insisted. And she wasn't. What I've been trying to tell you is that children shouldn't be flattened into one-dimensional concepts like "bad." But she was a fucking terror.

"You gonna have to take me to a gay club when I come visit you in New York, Hari," she said.

"For sure," I replied, assuming this was her attempt at affirming me in the midst of a family she sees as not affirming enough. I appreciated it.

"You know I'm like you, right?" she pushed.

"What do you mean?" I said.

"What do you mean, what do I mean? I'm gay!"

"Oh my God! Finally, another one!"

We broke out in laughter together like two glasses shattering after meeting too hard at the end of an overeager toast.

As far as I know, no one else in the family openly identifies as anything other than straight, and it was a momentous relief to share this load.

"Yeah, my dad was trying me when he found out. Had me call Auntie Kṛṣṇanandini because she dealt with it already with you."

"What did my mother say?" I asked.

"She asked if I was sure it wasn't a phase." Justus rolled her eyes. "She said she can't judge me because she has a son like me. That she will be praying for both of us."

I spent so much time looking one way, at my own shame around my journey to understanding my sexuality, that hearing Justus talk about hers felt like being blindsided by a truck. I never knew that any kind of crash could feel like love. Ain't God funny indeed.

I don't know if I was born gay, but I know making space for the way you manifested queerness in my life is a choice. A difficult choice. An everyday choice. Sometimes, choosing queerness feels like digging and digging and digging so deep inside myself to try to find freedom from the restrictions of this violently normative world that I can no longer see the light above. One second, I'm stuck in the dark, all alone, looking up at others who refuse to dig with me. Who choose heteronormativity instead. I can't witness anything without being reminded of how everything in this world upholds oppression, and I just want a new world entirely, but no one outside this hole wants to hear that shit. And I'm stuck in the darkest of places with just my most horrible mistakes and unimaginable desires to reckon with.

Sometimes, I want to pop my head out of this hole and play the normative role, too, at least for a little, because I'm just so tired of being lonely and afraid of who I really am when I ask myself the difficult questions freedom requires. I'm afraid I'll be so stuck down here under all the piles and piles of trauma I unburied trying to find myself that I won't be able to breathe.

But there was Justus, illustrating the truth that I can't ever really be alone doing this self-work. That choosing queerness always provides more beneficial possibilities to meet our needs for intimacy, even when we ourselves have previously made the mistake of criminalizing that choice. That my very real fear of and sadness in facing my traumas don't have to preclude joy. That sometimes you need to feel the fear and the sadness deeply in order to feel all the joy. That there is always a better option than the ones this world provides. And if we choose it, despite how difficult it may be to do so, we can always be better people than this world dictates us to be.

Hari-Gaura, if we listen hard enough, there are others singing down in the dark with us, doing this self-work, too, even when we can't see them.

Others who exist as annotations and redactions. Others who are digging, or who have been buried. Perhaps knowing that you could never truly be alone in this space of queerness is why you chose not to conform in a world that would kill you for your refusal. Perhaps learning that I can never truly be alone in this space of queerness is how I overcome my anxiety, the colonization of my mind. Wholeness has never been a matter of stability. It's a matter of being able to lose your footing, to question and doubt and waver with enough balance to avoid tipping over. And maybe yours can be another one of those deaths that brings the family together, for good this time, if I keep at the questions you left behind.

I couldn't fully answer his question then, but I worked up the courage to hug Richard tighter than I ever have at the end of that night. There is a world where the disappointment I interpreted in his eyes was less about the fact that I didn't take advantage of getting "hella pussy," and more about how I could not demonstrate to him your courage, which he wants to have as well. It may not be this world, but it is a world that I can build. I want to build it for him, for me, for Justus. She and I have been in touch regularly since the funeral. I hate FaceTime, but she FaceTimes me almost every day, like the fucking terror she has always been. I don't tell her that I hate it, though. She asks about my fiancé and shows me her girlfriend over the phone.

"Isn't she cute?" she asks. She is.

Justus doesn't let me hide my scars, but with her I know I don't need to. There should be no shame in these marks. They remind me that you

are gone, but they also remind me how to recon-
nect with you. The scars of losing our childhoods
show us how we have failed at staying whole historically, and so they are the best place for us to
begin to repair the fracture caused by our carceral
dissonance in the present. I won't always follow
their lessons, but I can always choose to try harder
next time. I can always choose queerness.

CHAPTER ELEVEN

MY GENDER IS BLACK

A few weeks after Aunt Cheryl's funeral, I was back on the train in Brooklyn, once again struggling to stay on track with making the choices I'd been reassured I needed to make to feel whole again. My calls with Justus had already begun to taper off, and the anxiety was creeping back. By the time I reached my stop, the white faces had mostly seeped out of the subway. Nostrand Avenue acts as the Brooklyn-bound C Train's water purifier, and white folks are the residue extracted through distillation, but there's no one to change the filter when it stops working. When gentrification really comes for us.

I was exhausted from a day of meeting with agents about screenwriting representation, followed by a session of being grilled by my therapist. He said I beat myself up too much. That I was taking on a lot with this whole "I always have to choose queerness" thing. I tried explaining that there's a crucial difference between beating myself up and holding myself accountable, between shame and self-reflection. He asked me what that difference was, and the words melted into formlessness like warm butter in my mouth. I tasted them, though. They were there.

My dog couldn't have cared less about my exhaustion, hopping up and down in excitement as soon as I opened the door. I changed into something more appropriate for the weather as she followed me to every room I walked through, waiting patiently at each entrance, tail infused with a jolt of life whenever I happened to make even the briefest eye contact.

"Let's go, Khia," I said, throwing on her harness and thinking of Mother Bhūmi. She never did like dogs—they are considered unclean in the Vaiṣṇava religion—but once upon a time, I didn't like going for walks around the block. For Khia, I do it twice a day, and in return she never leaves me alone for too long.

"He maaaad nice!" Old Dude shouted at me from across the street, holding on to the *A* like if he lost it too soon, he'd lose himself. Or maybe he held on to it just so that he *could* lose himself in the expanse he created with it. I didn't know. But I knew that he was from Brooklyn.

The way you hold words means something here.

Something about loss and survival. It's not always easy to tell which of the two.

It's not always a binary. It's not just how long you hold words, but where you let them drop and where you pick them back up.

"What breed he is?"

"She's a pit bull," I responded, but my voice, being the light, bass-less thing that it is, abandoned its mission halfway across the street and never reached his ears.

"Huh?"

"Pit bull!" I said a little louder, the effort of speaking at grown-man decibel level taking the air out of me. He waved me over. I was walking the other way, but I didn't want to be rude, so I crossed the street, a little relieved that I wouldn't have to shout anymore. Khia was confused by the sudden departure from our regular walking routine and resisted, so I used the harness to pull her back. Google says if we deviate from the same route every day, she won't be so hardheaded about walking, but she's too fucking hardheaded to deviate. This world loves to give us answers to a problem that the problem itself prevents us from accessing.

"What breed?" Old Dude repeated.

"Pit bull."

"Whaaaa? He hella small. He full grown? He friendly?"

"She's mixed with a bull terrier, I think. This is as big as she gets. She's nice—to people, at least." I laughed. Old Dude laughed back and leaned down to scratch Khia behind her bat-like ears, courtesy of her possible bull terrier lineage. At this point she was happy to have been dragged across the street, but I knew she still wouldn't go without a struggle next time, her annoying ass. Google stays wrong.

Niggas around here love my dog. Niggas around here love pit bulls period, but there's something about Khia that really gets them. I imagine that they love pit bulls because the breed has been unfairly written off as monstrously violent and criminalized through breed-specific legislation, and niggas around here know what that feels like. But Khia specifically?

"It's his pure white coat, my nigga," Old Dude said. "Shit is dooope." He looked up while holding the *o*, and I was sure he would lose himself when his gaze stopped at my midriff. But his eyes eventually still made their way up to mine, and he still smiled. I could tell this was not a flirt, and still we survived.

Up until then I had forgotten I was wearing a crop top, although what the hell else would I be wearing? Certainly not that damn button-down. It was over ninety degrees that day. This was the only attire that made sense to me, and what I would have worn to my meetings if I'd had the choice, and maybe to my brother Syama's wedding, too. And for just that moment, it seemed to make perfect sense to Old Dude as well. For that moment, he could talk to queer old me without restraint. Without feeling a hatred toward his own relationship to manhood. Without taking that hatred out on me.

Khia does that to dudes around here. Or to me. I'm not sure whether it's that walking my dog makes cisgender straight Black men in this not-yet-fully-gentrified Brooklyn neighborhood more comfortable talking to me, or me more comfortable talking to them, figuring they won't wild out around a pit bull. It's not always easy to tell which of the two it is. It's not always a binary.

"What's his name?"

I had used female pronouns each time I referred to Khia, but to no avail. To dudes around here, she stays male and that's that. And it's not just dudes. Most people I come across seem to automatically assume Khia is a male dog because she's a pit bull. I'm not sure what they think all these male pit bulls mate with to procreate, but I guess they haven't thought that far. I can assume this has something to do with the breed's supposed physical strength and aggression, which patriarchy tells us cannot belong to women.

But why did I feel so inclined to correct Old Dude while calling him "Old Dude"—while gendering him, too—as if my assumptions about his gender didn't have far greater consequences than his about Khia's? Gender is so fucking weird.

"Have a good one, bro," he said with a final stiff pat on Khia's blocky head and left. I hate being called "bro." I have never felt like a "bro" or a "man" or a "mister" or a "sir," although "boy" and "brother" and "girl" and "sis" feel okay, for some reason. When I talk to customer service representatives over the phone with my bass-less voice, I sometimes get called "ma'am," and that doesn't feel right either, but I never correct them. What would the correction even be? All these words feel like cages to me, like I am being forced inside them against my will. Like I am being aligned to the world's conceptions of gender when my Black experience has so little to do with the world's.

But there, with Old Dude, with Khia, the words stopped feeling like a shove. It was about how long he held them, where he let them drop, and where he picked them back up—the Brooklyn way, the Black way, fried and buttered-like. Here is where you lose the violent limitations and find a place where you can truly survive. Here is where I find a god who can repair the fracture caused by my carceral dissonance.

For a second, Old Dude and I were able to lose ourselves beyond the way words like "straight," "dude," "bro," and "gay" defined us, even if those were the best we could formulate in the moment, because we weren't stuck in just that moment. For a second, we were able to lose ourselves beyond the way these words villainize and criminalize and cage us. Beyond the way these words might sometimes make us feel hatred toward ourselves, the way we might sometimes take that hatred out on one another. We were just two Black people in our still-not-completely-stolen Black Brooklyn hood, not being made to harm each other. I didn't really have the words for how freeing this was, but I tasted them, though. They were there.

There are no answers that Black folks' problems don't already preclude in this world, so we don't have to know all of them. We don't have to find a home in these words, because there never has been a home for us in anything this carceral world creates. We can and have always made homes elsewhere, like in the holds and drops and pickups and annotations and redactions. Like in gospel. In outdoing one another while dancing the Electric Slide, without making anyone feel shame. We can lose and have always lost or been denied everything the world says makes us who we are—this gender, this sexuality, this language. And when we refuse to use for harming one another the things we are told we are, like in that fleeting moment with Old Dude, I think that is what holding ourselves accountable without beating ourselves up looks like.

～

At thirteen, I was what my father called a "late bloomer," which sounded like an acknowledgment that I could be flowered with the sweet and tender petals of a blossom, but he still got upset at my delicacies. Back then I really had no way to tell if my penis was real or not. I knew it was supposed to be able to ejaculate, even if I had no idea what the stuff actually was that was supposed to come out of it, and at the time I couldn't make it do that. You could say that the burgeoning belief that my "boy parts" were fake was just me searching for someone to blame for what my parents seemed to simultaneously understand and deny about my gender: their idea of maleness did not fit me.

I discovered more evidence of my body's potential trickery when watching a *20/20*-type show with my parents one night that same year. I cherished these moments. Our family didn't watch a lot of TV together, didn't even have cable, and I didn't really mind that. Perhaps because of its rarity, when we did watch a show or movie together, it always seemed like a special occasion. Like a birthday. Or maybe a funeral. It seemed to me that Mata, whom I generally imagined as completely disinterested in secular concerns, became a new version of herself in front of the TV. More connected to everyone and everything that wasn't her god. But to the woman who had discovered Kṛṣṇa only as an adult, maybe this was just a return to an old self.

This episode of the show featured an investigation into the lives of intersex people who had gender reassignment surgery when they were babies. Their parents had decided, based on their doctors' recommendations, which of the two genders to force them into not long after they were born. The doctors' decisions were mostly determined by the size of the penis or clitoris, even though gender is far more than that. Or far less.

Many of these children grew into a deep confusion about their identities. A few later decided to transition from the gender they were assigned by their surgeons, some before anything was revealed to them about their past and the surgery.

Mata and my dad watched intently. I assumed they were trying to wrap their minds around the concept that gender isn't always so cut and dried, just as I was trying to do. That chromosomes and hormones and genitalia and feelings and doctors' orders are never enough to determine gender on their own. They looked concerned, my father's forehead becoming a more dangerous wave of wrinkles than the small ripples they usually were. Mata "mhmmm"-ing from all the way down in her throat with a grimace whenever more proof was presented that these childhood gender assignments were dangerous. And that's when I knew: my parents had made a mistake on me just like the parents in the show had made a mistake on their children.

At the time, it was the only explanation I could think of. It wasn't just my delayed puberty. In addition to my not-yet-there Adam's apple, I also had no idea what a *perineal raphe*, the ridge along the base of a penis, was, not to mention the fact that one could be more pronounced and slightly off-center, like mine. This was proof of the surgery. My gender battle scar. Proof that all this suffering and failing to become a man had a culprit.

I wanted to confront my parents about what I believed they had done to me, but I was certain they would feel compelled to come clean after the show. How could they watch all these people's lives be destroyed by being forced into gender cages against their will by their parents and doctors the world swears are experts, and not try to reverse course with their own child before it was too late? But when the episode concluded, my parents barely said a word. Though heavy with worry, their eyes were guiltless, and they simply told me to go to bed. Our special moment had come to an end.

I didn't have to erroneously appropriate the experiences of intersex children to understand that being forced into my parents' idea of maleness was wrong, or to heal from it, but at least I finally had something to blame. For why my voice was too soft—for why *I* was. For why I cried too much. For why I loved basketball only until I got into a fight over a game in high school just to prove my masculinity, and lost. For why I always lost at proving my masculinity, even when I got better at winning fights. For why treating girls like shit didn't feel right even when I got better at treating them the way boys around me did, the way I learned boys were supposed to. And though I could no longer hold this mistakenly imagined surgery responsible after puberty hit, the belief that I needed to blame someone for the destructive ways I learned and lived gender remained.

Blame comes too easy in a world built on prisons. Ours is a binary world, split between guilt and innocence, with no concern for healing. The inaccurate idea that my parents had surgically determined my gender without my consent provided me with someone to punish for the fact that all my boy friends were talking sex and girls and sex with girls, and I kept wanting to be the girl some of them had sex with, but couldn't. But blame never led to being able to be what I needed to be. More importantly, it never led to accountability for the ways I internalized my parents' harmful messages about what their children could or couldn't be either.

~

I grew up with little concept of half siblings, at least when it came to Mata's children. Because of this, it wasn't explicitly clear to me how the stepfather/stepchild dynamic contributed to the tension my older brother Mohan had with my father until recently.

"I don't want to tell your mother how to raise her children," it seemed my father would say whenever any of the kids did something he didn't like, although he didn't appear to hold back as much when it came to advising her how to raise Visnu, Kiss, and me. I don't assume he was lying about his wants, exactly, but I think now his more distant parenting of the others also might have come from the fact that he had a harder time seeing the children Mata had prior to marrying him as more than just "hers," even though he had been in their lives for most of them.

In some ways, I can imagine this left some of my siblings who weren't conceived by him feeling even more abandoned than they might have felt if they were missing only the presence of their biological father in their lives. My dad was there in the home, taking care of them, and certain to emphasize that the house was to be run by his rules, but Mohan, Ganga, and Ghanasyam were still not *his* children in important contexts, particularly when they broke those rules. In those contexts, they became my mother's problem alone—a consequence of how the world teaches us to blame Black single mothers for the faults of their children, to such a pathological degree that it doesn't even matter if they aren't single anymore or whether their children's actions are actually faults. To this day, my father often still blames my mother for taking the lead and denying him what he believes to be his rightful role as the head of the house—simply because he is a man—when something goes wrong in their home, even though he explicitly encouraged her to.

"A man should be able to deal with problems the way that men do," he argues, implying that the way of men lacks softness and care.

"I ain't afraid of no man," he insists, perhaps unintentionally illuminating that the issue stems from a need to defend his sense of masculinity from threats both real and imagined.

Naturally, when my older siblings started to become adults, they broke my father's conservative rules all the time. Mohan, the oldest, wasn't supposed to bring explicit CDs into the house. He wasn't supposed to have girls over. He wasn't supposed to use the family vehicle without asking my father first, even if he had asked my mother. My father didn't want to tell Mata what to do with her kids, but he also had to assert his dominance as the man of the house. So instead of working with her to establish solutions to my brother's rebellions (which probably would have involved being fully present as a father), he and Mohan clashed constantly.

Once, Mohan and my father had been yelling back and forth all day when Mata called all the children to the living room to have a frank discussion about house rules. I was in high school at the time, and Mohan had just come back to live with us after losing his job. He was in his late twenties then, and even more disaffected with my father's strict rules than he'd been as a teenager. I suppose that these rules operated as a stark reminder that Mohan still didn't belong in my father's house, in my father's family, even though belonging is what every child deserves.

Mata began by opening up the floor for the children to speak candidly.

"I just feel like you haven't been there for us like a father should be," Mohan admitted, his eyelids working furiously to mop up any hint of tears. I had never seen him speak so vulnerably about his feelings to my father. But my father responded by looking Mohan straight in his eyes, which had reluctantly become weirs, resolutely stone-faced.

"Why are you crying?" my father pried.

"He can cry," our sister Ganga chimed in defensively. "That's a horrible feeling to have."

"You boys need to man up," my dad responded, ignoring her, revulsion palpable in his words. "I don't want to tell her how to raise her children, but your mother needs to teach you that. This is why a woman can't raise no men."

It would take too much work for Mohan's eyelids to be successful now. I wanted to tell him that he didn't have to, that he could cry, but I knew that wasn't true. I knew he couldn't, at least within the confines of the world I still deferred to. We children had all been shown from a young age that men don't cry or apologize, that crying and apologizing were womanlike and weak, and I knew there were punishments for these actions. I knew that punishing women, and us for our proximity to them, was the way the world worked, and I believed it was too much to ask for more. So I did not comfort my brother. I did not defend my mother. I watched my father get up and walk away, and then I got up and walked away, too.

Despite all that Mother Bhūmi and Mata did to move the moon and stars to create space for our family, I grew up witnessing even the most powerful women being subjected to the whims and desires of the men around them. My father would make unfair comments about Mata's ability to mother her children, and few of the adults in the community she created seemed to bat an eye. Some of the men in my family would get drunk and count off women like conquests, their own daughters like trinkets. I would hear whispers of some of them beating their conquests and trinkets into submission, others of sexually assaulting them, but the whisperers lacked alarm, and I followed their warnings to bury mine, too.

Though these blatant displays of misogynoir never seemed right, they always seemed normal, and when you have to choose between the two, this world encourages you to pick the latter. So for a long time I did. Even when I understood that I would never be like my father or any of these other men in my life, even when I believed I wasn't born male, even when I loudly proclaimed myself to be gay, I still tried to operate within the confines of this sexist reality that placed men and their desires above women and theirs. Sometimes, I still do.

Blaming my parents for my failure to achieve manhood never stopped me from attacking women. It never stopped me from making degrading comments about women's appearances based on white-supremacist beauty standards. I still dismissed women's concerns as overly emotional because they were women. I touched women without their consent and waved it off as a joke, "because I am gay!" Blaming my parents, rather than attempting to hold myself accountable and heal from my conditioning, allowed me to convince myself that I couldn't possibly hurt women this way because I wasn't attracted to them, as if violence has ever been dependent on attraction. As if I got to dictate what should happen to women's bodies just because my intentions differed from the cisgender, heterosexual men who did the same before me. As if it didn't hurt when straight women did the same to me because they assumed I was a gay man. Intentions have never negated impact.

The carceral state cannot end the trauma that comes with carceral dissonance; it can only repurpose it. The same gendered violence that caused me to lose my childhood turns seamlessly into an excuse to commit gendered violence against others. Like the cisgender, heterosexual

Black men in my family I always knew I could never truly be like, I used my own powerlessness to legitimize asserting power over others in powerless positions. And I am no more innocent of this than my father.

The women I harmed through trying to claim some sort of normative gender coherence despite my failure at manhood have names and perspectives of their own. They are Mata, my sisters, my high school and college friends. I hope there are fewer of them in recent years, and I don't write this to erase their perspectives. There is no bravery in admitting any of this. It is necessary inasmuch as it demonstrates that finding healing for the very real gender violence I experienced, as someone who never fully identified with manhood, requires more than blaming and punishing others for my inability to identify with it—the only option the carceral state would have us believe exists.

~

Today, I consider myself nonbinary. But, at most, I look like a man who sometimes wears women's makeup and clothing, if you can look like such a thing. Neither of those things is *who* I am, however. Clothing is made of thread and dye, not gender, and a nonbinary gender identity is made when one knows they are neither man nor woman. I know that I am made of Black love and Black pain and Black hope and Black loss. I used to push back harder on being called a "man," remind whomever said it that I use "they/them" pronouns, and that is still true. Conversations about pronouns and the impossibility of determining gender based on what someone "looks like" are still important, especially in a world that targets and harms transgender, intersex, and genderqueer people in genocidal ways.

But too often my conversations stopped there, when the issue is deeper than that. I want to start conversations about my gender in a different place, at the beginning of all the gendered violence that has facilitated my carceral dissonance, and that comes long before I ever even thought about my *perineal raphe*.

I discovered one such starting place while reading the work of Black feminist scholar Hortense Spillers. In her essay "Mama's Baby, Papa's Maybe: An American Grammar Book," she argues that the social language of this country following the African slave trade requires "the dehumanizing, ungendering, and defacing project of African persons."[33] Black people were brought here as commodities, not people. Black babies were regularly torn away from their mothers' breasts, and Black families were denied kinship bonds because we weren't imagined as requiring the things that white people's idea of a human being required.

If Spillers is correct, then whatever terms we find to gender ourselves within a language that was created to describe Black folks as non-people will necessarily indicate our gender is done wrong, because a commodity cannot rightfully be man, woman, or child. To do gender in this world means we will always be able to be blamed for failing at it.

We see this in how Black women are blamed for taking leadership roles in their families, and thereby raising boys to be "too soft," even while Black men are blamed for their absence from the home (without regard to how this absence often is a result of state-sanctioned death or prison, or to the fact that Black men who aren't in prison or dead have actually been shown to be more involved with their children than white men).[34] I saw this personally in how my mother was punished by my father for being a woman and parenting her children and how Mohan was punished for being a man and attempting to find belonging as my father's child. We see this in how Black, queer folks are imagined to be the reason for the "destruction of the Black family," even though the Black family is always already being destroyed by the carceral state.

If this system of enslavement did not end but only evolved into other racialized state-sanctioned practices that undergird this country's justice system, then my gender was always in crisis. No amount of blaming one's constructed penis, one's queer children, one's conservative parents, or anything other than destroying and healing from the carceral system that evolved from enslavement itself can ultimately change that. And each Black person, across and outside of the gendered spectrum, has a responsibility in this.

~

Fri, Aug. 3, 2018, at 8:39 p.m.

Hari,

I have some things to say on our relationship. When I was younger I felt like you thought you had to go do your own thing, ya know find yourself and what not. And there was a period where you didn't really associate too much with us. I get that.

I just wish you would've been my big brother while you did that, ya know? Because as a kid I couldn't understand what you were going through, it just seemed like you were absent . . . when I would've needed you.

I had some resentment to you for what I saw as being a kind of absent older brother. I suppose I feel like you just went off and left me and didn't even see me.

It would've been nice to have you . . . Like so many times I wish you would've been there and you weren't. Like you were just somebody in New York, completely disconnected.

~

A few weeks ago, I received one of those texts where you have to press the ellipses to read the full thing. It was from my youngest brother, Visnu. I held my breath, clicked it, read this message, and cried. I cried because I wanted to say that I never knew what he was feeling when I left for New York, but that would mostly be a lie. I knew when I left home that he became a constant target of Mother Bhūmi's, when he was far too young to understand the root of the violence surrounding her mental illness. I knew that my mother and father didn't know how to protect him. I knew he was lonely in the patriarchal home that silenced his softness, just like I had been, but I called my loneliness different because of my gender. I called my loneliness "nonbinary," and this still might be the most succinct way to describe it, but sometimes I called it this just to excuse why I sought some escape from the loneliness without my baby brother. Why I blamed him and everything else I left, with no concern for anyone's healing, including my own. Why I abandoned home and Cleveland and my family and my Blackness, trying to be seen by white people in college. Why I so easily write off cisgender heterosexual Black people for any and all infractions. Because they don't experience gender like I do, none of them, including my little brother, could ever understand.

But my anxieties around my gender were never about whether I was nonbinary, or intersex, or gay or straight. They weren't about a need to be understood. They were about feeling that being imprisoned by these concepts, being forced to act or be or look a certain way because the carceral world needed a way to understand me, made it impossible for me to feel the freedom Mata had tried to safeguard in me as a child. And it made me an agent in stealing the freedoms from others, too.

My anxieties were about knowing that I would never truly be the man my mother or my father expected me to be, and I couldn't be any woman they would accept me being either, no matter how hard I tried, because their expectations were rooted in standards designed for me not to meet. They were about knowing that my gender would always be done wrong, would always feel like a mistake, would always be the reason the world would demand something be cut away from me, even if that severance did nothing to make me fit into the world any better. And both Visnu and Mohan, who are as cisgender and straight as any Black person can be, must have journeyed through these anxieties, too, even if we ended up at different places.

On a macro level, all my brothers and sisters went through the same violent conditioning I did. They grew up being told that men don't cry, touch, or apologize and that women are subject to the whims of those around them, too. They experienced the same castigations from our parents when they stepped out of our strictly defined roles. The same fear that they would never be enough and could not be anything else. And the same childlike desire to still be something else even when faced with this terror.

Visnu's letter reminded me to consider all the Black boys and girls—whether I know them to be queer or not—who are harmed or harm each other just to prove themselves men and women enough to no avail. Who are queer in the context of their "collective position relative to state and capitalist power," as political scientist Dr. Cathy Cohen puts it, rather than just in the context of their personal identification.[35] Girls whom we may not call "nonbinary" only because they haven't claimed it publicly but who are still struggling with their gender because it was never designed for them. Boys who, even if they don't have the same desires to express their gender as I do, deny themselves even the slightest touch with other men. Who deny it because they've heard "that's gay," and they either do not identify as gay or are afraid to, even though they desire and need intimate touch in their lives, like everyone does. Black boys who cannot bring themselves to express true care or sadness or fear because that's not what their interpretation of god allows them to do. Black girls who cannot assert themselves without being called aggressive. In this carceral state, all Black people battle through a lack of gender coherence, and so we all have the responsibility to refuse to comply with the state's gendered roles that ensure this battle remains.

My gender, if that's what it must be called, is not defined by how I dress, or what my bass-less voice sounds like, although those things may all play a part. If my gender is to be freeing, it must be defined by my destruction of and accountability for the carceral systems that hindered my parents' love for their Black children.

It must answer the question my therapist posed, must model the difference between holding a person accountable and beating them up, the difference between healing and punitive. The answer is in the holds and drops and pickups. The answer is not in any language this carceral state knows. Shame and punishment can address only transgressions that are visible, and we have no control over where the state directs its gaze. Shame can't address the harms we carry with us in the shadows, in our family secrets, in our beliefs and desires. It inherently creates one set of standards for people who can afford what it takes to avoid public scrutiny and another for those who can't. But as Old Dude on my block demonstrated, Blackness has always offered other tongues, if only we choose to listen.

CHAPTER TWELVE

A PRAYER FOR NEW LANGUAGE

Hari-Gaura,

I am engaged now. Can you believe it? I am engaged to a boy. The type of boy of your dreams. A Black boy with teeth that dig a cavern into his tongue, through which the cutest lisp spills out like a freshwater stream. A boy with teeth that are crooked, with teeth that are perfect. With teeth through which he whispers for me to grease his scalp on lazy Sunday afternoons. Or tries to whisper. He can't quite do it. It seems to be physiologically impossible for him. But I read somewhere that whispering requires the abduction of vocal cords. I know "abduction" can mean the way muscles pull away from each other, but I also know it can mean his voice is too vast to be kidnapped.

"I'm sorry, I'm too loud," he says repentantly after laughing so boomingly that I am commanded to listen to him instead of the television show we are lying down to watch, now that the roots of his locs have been properly moisturized. He must have noticed that I am tired and my head hurts. I just want to watch my show, and the cannonade annoys me. And though we are getting married soon, I am still afraid of these moments. I am still afraid of how I don't always know how to listen, even to those I love the most. Even when commanded to. Even when I know that I should.

I've been so preoccupied with talking at you and trying to raise you from the dead that I haven't fully grasped the beauty you offer in teaching me about how to listen. Something about how to let folks rest in peace, especially when their peace is different from mine. Louder than mine.

Society places familiarity at the root of care so much that I always see danger in anything with which I have less than a significant degree of similarity. So much so that I feel compelled to run from anything that doesn't rest inside my comfort zone, or to prove that it does despite reality. But perhaps learning to listen to Black children, both gone and still here, is a necessary model for how to be present for others even when our experiences diverge. Even amid the differences of our wants, needs, and desires. Even when forced to stay physically apart. Even when I don't fully know the other person's language. And isn't that all love really is?

When Timothy proposed after the opening night of his one-man show last year, I told him yes, but I don't think "Will you marry me?" was really the question. He doesn't even believe in state-sanctioned marriage. Neither of us believes that the state should have the power to legitimize our relationship, and we don't believe that the benefits marriage affords to people should be refused to those who don't or can't tie the knot. We don't believe in how the fight for "same-sex marriage" took up so much of last decade's "queer agenda," when so many Black, queer kids like you were living and dying on the streets, when so many Black transgender and intersex kids were fighting and dying in opposition to the idea that there is such a thing as a "same sex," and neither of us believes in re-creating a heteronormative family image in gay drag.

"Fuck marriage!" I told Tim when we discussed the possibility months before his proposal, something I certainly suggest everyone do before springing any life-changing decision on someone they claim to love. "But I do want a ceremony to celebrate our love, and I want to be in the best legal position to adopt our children," I conceded.

I explained my thought process to my best friend, Lisa, when we met up for the first time after my engagement, before asking her to be my maid of honor.

"Of course!" she replied in a squeak that can be produced only when you are as small as she is and the excitement for the good fortune of someone you care about tries and fails to abduct your vocal cords. Lisa is four feet ten with the thickest socks on her feet, but she always reminds me that

Black Virginian women have never let their size be the reason they disappear.

"Or will it be best woman?" she pondered aloud, her southern twang blanketing the words in a warmth only Black southern twangs can create. I told her yes, which wasn't an answer, but I don't think "Is it maid of honor or best woman?" was really the question.

"Fuck marriage and how gendered it is!" she conceded. But so often, we both admitted, this limited gendered language offers the only words we can think of to describe our relationships with other people.

Lisa and I were suddenly five drinks in, and our excitement had been sufficiently libated into a clumsy release of our demons, the liquor beaming a spotlight onto the darkest monsters in the gaps between us.

"Maybe you won't get it because you're not a woman and the pressure to be with someone is different for you," Lisa said, "but I get so lonely when my friends find serious partners."

I ordered both of us another round.

"But it's not just because I'm reminded that I'm single," she continued. "I am trying not to give too much energy to those pressures. But when my friends get serious partners, they forget about me. I just hate always coming second to everyone."

"You don't come second to me. You're my best friend," I assured her.

"But that's not the same," she told me, and I knew she was right. "Are you really ever going to choose me over Timothy?" We'd had this conversation before. We keep having it because we keep asking things that aren't really the questions. That aren't really what we need to ask but seem to be all we have the words for.

"And I'm not asking you to choose me," she said. "I would never ask that. That's why I know how this is going to go. Because that's how it has already gone. As a single woman, this is the labor I expect to do."

She pointed out all the time I spend at home in Brooklyn now. How, since I moved in with Timothy, I rarely come to Harlem, where she and most of the rest of our friends live.

"When you are in a relationship, that person comes first," she said. Her little hand is no bigger than yours ever became before you left this body to me, Hari-Gaura, but somehow it made its way fully around the giant glass of six-dollar house merlot.

I apologized. She told me I didn't have to. I told her I will do a better job of being there when she needs me in the future. Of listening when I know I should. That though I knew that lovers and friends aren't the same, I didn't believe that always prioritizing the former at the expense of the latter was the way things have to be. That her feeling sad about these priorities and me doing nothing to address her concerns shouldn't be the inevitable conclusion just because she's a woman. I tried to explain that love needn't be a competition, and we should be able to show up in different ways for different people without comparison. That it feels like we can't only because capitalism turns everything into a limited commodity, leaving us with a shortage of connection.

Then I reiterated that she is my best friend, as if that wasn't just its own type of prioritizing. As if I didn't know this wasn't really the answer either. As if I knew what was.

Hari-Gaura, you spoke a love language that still feels foreign to me.

People may laugh when I talk of your imaginary friends today, but there was something critical I can't quite master about how you allowed Kula's, Saia's, and India's love to be enough, even when they weren't "here" in the same way as you. It ensured that there never was a competition to put a favorite above the rest. It established freedom from the expectation for them to do more emotional labor simply because they were girls and freedom to not even expect them to always be girls, as imaginary friends don't require a static gender the way this society demands of us. I know that your love for these friends was liberating primarily because they weren't limited by this anti-Black realm. But what does that mean for me if I can't seem to secure an escape from this world?

If anyone can help me along my journey to mastering the tongue you spoke of love with, it's Timothy and his cute-ass lisp. We met at a Black queer picnic hosted by a mutual friend. We were both dating other people at the time. Me casually, him not so much. We'd been friends on social media for a while. We're both writers, and I could tell through his work that he loved Black folk, so I fucked with him. He was at the picnic with his boyfriend. I was there with my friends and roommates Ahmad and Charles.

I had never met Timothy in person and was struck when I saw him in real life. I mean I literally felt as if I'd been hit by something. More a comet than lightning. More "IthoughtIknewwhatlovewasbutwhatI knewisinadequatetodescribethisfeeling" than "love at first sight." I legit told Charles to keep me away from Timothy because he was just too damn fine and I didn't want to start any trouble. Charles said I was "sprung" and to this day jokingly throws my behavior at the picnic in my face whenever my fiancé comes up in conversation.

"You still sprung," Charles laughs, and I laugh, too. Can't deny the facts.

I could say that Timothy is the jealous type.

"I was actually mad that my ex kept talking about you after we all met," he tells me now. The picnic was also the first time I met his then partner, and I guess I had made a little too much of an impression.

When Timothy and his ex broke up, I was still seeing the person I had been dating, so we didn't connect on that level straightaway. After I was out of my situationship, Tim reached out to submit a piece he'd written analyzing what he'd learned about anti-Black state-sanctioned violence from living with HIV, a widely criminalized disease, to RaceBaitr. It was a brilliant piece, so I accepted it.

I told him it was brilliant, and he pretended he was surprised to hear it—"*OMG, thank you!*"

I think our past relationships had made both of us good at pretending, and though I was sprung from the get-go, I also stunted like reading the piece didn't make me want him even more. If you hear him tell it, I was the one who kept messaging after the piece was published. But I have receipts showing that he was the one digging me. He kept asking how I was doing and all that, like he really cared.

Eventually I told him about my problems. How my anxiety was starting to make it feel like everything was moving too fast, beating too fast, turning too fast, and I couldn't keep up. You know, things you tell somebody when they're used to you pretending and you're trying to see if the truth will scare them off. At some point, he asked me out. Took me to a restaurant. Lied and said his pants ripped on the way to the place when he knew they were torn before he put them on and just wanted me to notice his thighs. His gorgeous, former-state-tracklete thighs.

I could say the rest is history, and that's the familiar way of telling this story. But the familiar way is a lie. Love didn't just happen, and the story's not over yet. I no longer believe in falling in love— at least not the way the story's usually told. Tim showed me that love is not just a feeling you get, just lightning and you have no choice but to let the static run through you. When the comet hits, you don't always know what to let run through you.

Timothy and I don't always know where our friends fit into the picture. We don't always know when and where kids do. We don't always know where everyone else does either. We are still figuring out how to manage a serodiscordant relationship—where one partner has HIV, and one partner doesn't. How to deal with the trauma from past sexual violence that refuses to stop rearing its hideous head from time to time. We don't always know how to best address our boundaries around monogamy and whether they should stay.

Last week, Timothy and I were watching the Amazon show *Homecoming* in our living room. Stephan James's fine ass came on the screen, and I said something aloud about how Stephan James's fine ass had just come on-screen. I had begun to notice that I felt uncomfortable stating what to me were benign observations—like my natural attractions—in front of Timothy, and so I called myself making the conscious decision to challenge what I deemed an unfairly imposed restriction around my thoughts and feelings.

He paused the show. Admitted that he felt uncomfortable, and that he knew it wasn't fair for him to. I admitted that I don't want to be in a relationship where I don't feel free to witness beauty when I see it. He asked if I wanted an open relationship. I said I don't think we are at the point where we could even consider that yet, and right now I just want us to work through this step. He pushed. I admitted that my ideal relationship would allow casual flirting with mutual agreements, but I had no desire to have sex with anyone else right now. He wondered if I was already doing that. We fought.

In the familiar way of telling this story, I could say that I won. The familiar way makes me the good person again, always. It's the one I keep coming back to even when I say I am trying to be intentional about challenging it. It starts with "Timothy is the jealous type," as if I hadn't once flirted with my ex earlier in our relationship, as if Tim hadn't seen it when I thought I was being discreet, and as if that were the same as "casual flirting with mutual agreements." As if I weren't priming the listener to believe my side. As if there have to be sides.

The familiar story doesn't require me to admit that I hadn't acknowledged how what I did earlier in the relationship had hurt him deeply, before challenging what I deemed an unfairly imposed restriction on my thoughts and feelings. It makes it seem like repairing Tim's trust was simple. It doesn't require I tell you that I didn't apologize for my actions sincerely. I can pretend that I really thought him fighting me about this TV show was just about an actor neither of us will probably ever meet, and not about how I never expressed my relationship needs to someone who has been so willing to provide for them.

The truth is that Tim's honesty about his feelings was more than I have been able to give about my struggles with love. He has given me so much time and space to come to my own messy realizations because he knows better than I that messy realizations are okay, even when I have squandered that time and space with excuses and avoidance. He has cared for me still because he still believes in me. In us.

The day after our argument, Timothy and I sat down before the TV again. He said sorry for how he responded, reminded me that this was possible. Acknowledged it wasn't fair that he asked me a question he wasn't ready to hear the answer to. He conceded that we can take our relationship step by step. That our love can look different—that it won't always seem familiar, like what it's "supposed" to be, or even feel good in every given moment. Said that he knows he has insecurities, and that he is working on them. He asked if that was okay, but now I can understand that this wasn't really the question. Now I can understand that he was really asking if I was willing to keep working, too.

Timothy is always showing me how to love in better ways. How to love without needing to be the good guy, without needing to be the best friend, without needing to feel everything the other person feels. He reads my essays and holds me accountable when I'd rather write excuses for my behavior. He trusts that there is more to me than my failures, even when I still don't have all the words to prove him right. He believes when I say I am trying, even after all the mistakes I've made, because he sees what's inside me, even when I can't. I think he sees you.

"I know, I talk too loud," he says later, after he laughs through our show, and I whisper back to him that he is making up for my bass-less voice. That we make up for each other. He always cleans the bathroom because he knows I hate it, and I (almost) always do the dishes. We don't have to keep hashing it out. We just have to provide for what needs to be done, within the healthy boundaries we agree to, and commit to always getting better. He laughs loudly again and I am commanded to listen. I am still afraid to, but this time I do.

CHAPTER THIRTEEN

LOGGING OUT OF PASSPORT TWITTER

In 2017, Timothy and I went on our first out-of-state trip together to Puerto Rico. The country had just been thrust into the mayhem of Donald Trump's first term, and I had absorbed, without adequate critique, countless images proliferated by travel companies and bloggers promoting vacationing as self-care. At the time, I had bought what these vested interests were selling about the accessible foreignness of the island, and so the off-the-mainland colony seemed like the perfect reprieve from the politics of this anti-Black place.

It was early spring. As soon as I stepped off the plane, the tropical air seeped straight through the many layers I'd thrown on to keep the briskness of New York at bay before departing. Without waiting to reach the road, I peeled my sweaters away, racing to beat the perspiration uncorking underneath.

Already, I was enthusiastically bringing to life the exotic vision of this colony that the state had presented me with. But still I found myself acting surprised when the colonialist ideas around exotic lands I'd consumed sprang to life, too.

Outside the airport, taxi drivers competed with each other to wave us down in Spanish. We understood only enough to realize that the price they quoted was higher than what the Uber app displayed, so we retreated to the option that returned us to the language we knew: the language of on-demand, careless comfort—even when we were 1,600 miles away from home. A language that many people cling to for assurances of safety around the products and services they buy, however precarious that safety is. The language used to promote the gig economy, a system that helps employers avoid fundamental guarantees to workers like minimum wage, overtime, social security, and the right to sue for discrimination by treating them as contractors, with a particularly devastating effect on this island's workforce. It's not that ordering an Uber makes you a fundamentally bad person, but like many of the things we do for ease and comfort without considering larger implications, it isn't fundamentally harmless either. Still, it's undeniable that this new economy helps Black people enjoy services we might otherwise struggle to access, and as the travel blogs testify, what is vacation without enjoyment?

The Uber app pinged to alert us that Raul would be at the airport in ten minutes, and we waited in sweaty anticipation for this familiar way toward what we hoped to be new experiences, ignoring the paradox of it all. As soon as we piled into his car, we explained to Raul that we were new to the area, although this probably wasn't news to him. He must have seen many others like us before, who came to use his home as an escape from their lives.

As he drove us toward our hotel in San Juan, Raul pointed out in English all the places we should visit and, closer to our destination, the ones we should avoid.

"Down there is La Perla," he said, motioning toward a vibrant village at the bottom of a steep hill near the center of the city. Historically, La Perla had been a site for slaughterhouses and the homes of former slaves, which were legally prohibited from occupying the main community center, and today it is known as a hub of the local music industry. From what I could tell, most of the inhabitants were still Black, in stark juxtaposition to the whiter and wealthier tourists swarming the boundary of the city's downtown at the top of the hill. We wouldn't see until later the numerous Black and Indigenous people pushed into the background, those who still provide most of the labor to keep the center running for everyone else's entertainment.

"Don't go to La Perla," Raul explained.

"Why not?" I asked.

"Danger," he said. "Lots of drugs, gangs. You seem like good people. Good people don't go to La Perla."

I bristled at the implications, but I didn't believe I had adequate words to express why I was bothered by Raul's comment across our language barrier, so I didn't say anything. Timothy rolled his eyes at me and I rolled mine back, even as I bought into what I perceived to be Raul's warped worldview by embodying these same "good" people in so many other ways during our trip. People who cast aside the realities of Black folks with less proximity to power in a capitalistic pursuit of comfort.

At the time, Puerto Rico was in the midst of an economic disaster that already had helped propel eighty-seven thousand people to desert the island, even before Hurricane Maria's devastation. That number itself was just a small fraction of an ongoing exodus of economic refugees who'd been fleeing since the beginning of Operation Bootstrap, a series of government projects that began midcentury, designed to transform the local agricultural economy into a more industrial one.

As Bootstrap forced the labor market to shift from agriculture to tourism, it increased overall wages and, perhaps more importantly to its designers, company profits. It also spurred massive unemployment for the former agricultural workers. Now, the government claimed to need good tourists more than ever to restimulate its economy, as if tourism weren't part of the problem in the first place.

I hadn't gone to Puerto Rico under the impression that my presence alone would benefit anyone but tourism companies, but I hadn't any deeper understanding of the other effects of my presence either.

I had heard about the island's financial crisis before we came, but in my self-centered desire for escape, I hadn't looked into it as much as I easily could and should have to know its scale and implications and, more importantly, the scale and implications of how I might show up in the midst of it.

I was shocked to witness the extent of the economic ruin, which had been exacerbated by calamitous austerity measures ushered in by an unelected board put in charge of fiscal policy by the President Obama–backed Puerto Rico Oversight, Management, and Economic Stability Act. Schools were shuttered across the city. All kinds of businesses were struggling. And "good" people were spending their money anywhere but down in La Perla.

In Raul's defense, suggesting that tourists like me avoid places like La Perla may have been for the best, considering the ignorance and police presence that follow and protect moneyed travelers at the expense of local communities. But feeding money to corporations and governments that discard and exploit vulnerable people has never fixed any problem that needs fixing. Colonialism and capitalism exploiting the masses for the benefit of a few "good" people were the things that *led* to the island's financial crisis, and tourism is central to this exploitation.

It's not enough to know that tourism isn't inherently helpful to local communities, although it does take some work to reject prevailing propaganda. I also had a responsibility to know how my presence might have been harmful. I owe any belated understanding of this to Puerto Rican friends who challenged me on how this responsibility was upheld or abdicated, friends who ask me to consider that this responsibility requires a deeper connection to and embrace of a land's context than seeing travel as an "escape" allows. Anti-Blackness is global, and there is no avoidance of it. There is only pretending that someone else's experience of it is not your concern.

In my desperate bid for escape, I spent much of the four days we were in town trying to avoid engaging with the obvious strains on the island's communities. Just as Raul had warned we might, we found drugs when we journeyed to La Perla, which we'd done specifically to secure the weed necessary to assist in my substance-sustained avoidance of reality.

It was easy to find someone who spoke English and told us where to go, and I wasn't afraid to ask. I told myself that my willingness to interact with the townspeople of La Perla in this way, and this one person's welcome of me, was a challenge to Raul's insistence that they weren't "good" people, and that this challenge was something to be proud of. But I had seen self-righteous saviors of impoverished communities before. I knew that going to poor Black neighborhoods just to make oneself feel like their hero was just as inadequate as any other exploitative touristy thing I could do while more and more people were forced out of their homes. Trying to prove Raul wrong by buying weed was just as useless as trying to be his version of a "good" tourist. Even when I have properly located a problem, carceral logics make it easy to adopt the wrong solutions.

I spent the entire trip using inadequate words, having inherited a different colonizer's tongue from the one many people there could understand. The violence of English is somehow more blatant when it's carelessly lobbed like boulders at people who don't speak it back. At people struggling directly due to the actions of people who speak like me. I had taken Spanish for four years in high school, and at one point I was conversant in it. Now it was just another thing that I had lost and couldn't quite reclaim.

I was seeking out the foreignness of Taíno land stolen by the US government and all the while calling the island what its thieves had called it. I'd meant the trip to be an escape, but having relationships with people by whom I am held accountable reminds me that escape has never made Black people any freer. Escape, like any type of avoidance, offers us a brief facade of access to power, but it ultimately benefits only capitalism and colonizers. Boríken is a place, not an escape, and to treat it as such is to exoticize its people, commodifying them as tools of my leisure.

Among the "good" tourist dollars I spent, on our last night on the island, Tim and I went zip-lining in the Yunque rain forest, a fifty-minute Uber ride from San Juan. Along the way, our new driver explained how the forest was under constant threat by developers and the government looking for quick ways to rake in money. Despite these threats, the clouds above still pour all day.

El Yunque is more than twenty-eight thousand acres of tumbling green hills, and only after our cab dropped us at the entrance did we find out that the registration tent was much deeper inside. As we walked through the fog of insects, a small tan sedan passed us by, then quickly slowed to a stop in front of us. In the back seat, a Black woman with an asymmetrical afro and a voice that sounded as if it had known intimately its fair share of cigarettes rolled the window down.

"Y'all going zip-lining?" she shouted. She was seated beside a young girl, and there were two other Black women in the front. Based on their energy, it seemed as if the driver had stopped only because the woman with the fro in the back seat asked her to, but she didn't seem to mind.

"Yes, do you know how to get there?" Timothy responded.

"Hop in!" the woman with the fro said, which wasn't an answer, but somehow she knew how to listen for questions unasked.

Their car fit only five people, but she insisted.

"We lap up all the time, and it's just down the road."

She told us her name was Brenda, asked us where we were from, told us she'd lived in New York for a few years, too.

"But they are gentrifying the fuck out of it. Fuck gentrification," she said. I agreed, mentioning how we had just learned about the constant threats developers, the gentrifier's kin, made to the forest and how poetic it seemed that the clouds kept pouring nonetheless. I did not mention the part I might be playing in those threats.

I was searching for adequate words in a foreign town, but Brenda talked enough for all of us. She spoke at least two languages, the two official ones of the island that colonization had established to erase the Indigenous ones that came before. Three if you include Black—Black like "fuck gentrification." Like how we didn't know Brenda at all, but to her that didn't mean we didn't share a kinship, or that we existed only to exploit or be exploited. Like how our *stranger*ness didn't mean we couldn't forge a relationship of accountability, one that challenges us to better meet our responsibilities to one another, too. Like how our foreignness to each other did not prevent her from caring for us, the way I had taken it to mean that I did not have to show care for some of her fellow people on the island.

"Y'all see that?" she asked Timothy and me in giddy excitement as we came upon our first zip line. "I'm so fucking scared!" She cheesed, staring straight into my eyes as if she knew me. As if knowing I was Black and that we were under the same kind of constant threat was knowing me enough.

After a few hours of gliding among the giant ferns, laughing with us and her friends, Brenda again insisted on driving us back to the edge of the park, the young girl back on Brenda's lap to provide us room.

"Wait, how did y'all get here?" she asked when we made it back to the street, more concerned than curious.

"We took an Uber. We can order another one now that we're here. Thank you so much!" I said.

She looked incredulous, relaxing her neck to allow the unbalanced weight of her crooked afro to tip her head to the side in disbelief.

"How much did that cost you coming here?!"

"Oh, only like fifty dollars," I reassured her.

"We split it and it was fine," Timothy followed up, noticing the concern blossoming across her face.

"Oh no," she said. "No, no, no. We are headed toward San Juan— we'll take you!"

We told her again it was fine, but this "we'll take you" wasn't really a question either.

As we drove back toward the city, Brenda asked how we knew each other. I told her Tim was my partner, and her eyes lit up like mine must have when my cousin Justus showed me her girlfriend.

"We're gay too!" she said, explaining she was dating the driver. The woman in the passenger's seat was the driver's sister, and the girl in the back was the driver's daughter. They didn't speak English as well as Brenda, but that hadn't stopped us from laughing together in the trees, and they seemed to immediately understand the excitement we shared and joined in with laughter now, too.

Brenda had said they could drive us only to the edge of town— "Al menos then you'll be close enough for a more reasonably priced cab"—but the car kept rolling closer and closer to our hotel until we were within walking distance.

"Is this good enough?" Brenda asked when we were about a ten-minute walk from where we were staying. I still don't know how far out of their way they had actually come in order to bring us there.

"This is more than perfect, thank you so much!" I said.

Timothy took out thirty dollars to give to Brenda as we got out. "For gas, at least," he said.

She just laughed that smoker's laugh, patted her fro, and slammed the door thunderously in our faces.

"Pay it forward," she yelled out the window.

Brenda's generosity was so ordinary, and yet I still find it booming over the language of the escape that I went to Boriként to find. It wasn't necessarily what she said or did that struck me; it was how familiar she made her words and actions feel, even when I had spent so long keeping people like her at arm's length in my futile search for comfort. This ordinary Black generosity, which has the power to hold across distance and time, was the language I was searching for, and it was one I'd always had access to, but I had turned away from where it could be found. It was the same language Mother Bhūmi used to ask me, in all my queerness that she would never know in this lifetime, to go on those long walks with her, despite my being stuck in fear and resentment of her. It was the same language I used, despite the very real horrors of our shared history, to respond with a yes. And it was the same language my Black Puerto Rican friends asked me to speak with when talking about their home, a language where no one's home means "careless escape," because everyone's home is a place where care is given generously.

I spent so long trying to escape regular Black life and the struggles that come with it that the regular care that comes, too, felt almost spectacular. It had been years since I'd really sat in appreciation of the Black neighbors who would let my family borrow sugar when we had run out of it and my father's paycheck hadn't come yet, although they regularly helped save my life. It had been years since I understood why strangers in my community so often stopped police from harassing me even when I was doing something "wrong," and I still find it hard sometimes to understand why they always felt so compelled to step in. Relationships of accountability remind me that I can *be them*—can replicate their generosity—for my own neighbors, both next door and across the diaspora, despite our differences and struggles and traumas, if I don't use differences and struggles and traumas as a barrier necessary to escape. The extraordinary ordinary of Blackness is inaccessible when all you see in ordinary Black life is something to escape in pursuit of white acceptance. When all you see in the Black people who come from different backgrounds and places and families from you is distance, instead of an opportunity to build across it.

At the same time, if observing white people has taught me anything, it is that being too gracious can have terrible consequences. We invite Dylann Roof into our place of worship, and he guns us down. We invite Rachel Dolezal into our organizations working for liberation, and she steals our identity. We forgive them both, and still, justice does not follow. And so, on a certain level, you could interpret this individualistic way of life imposed by a capitalistic society—this push to separate your own life, and whatever enjoyment you can find in it, from the lives of others—as useful for Black people's safety. Healthy boundaries are important when exploitation is as common as carbon. But when we only create boundaries between ourselves and those most vulnerable to state violence—the Blackest, the poorest, the ones the state can most easily other and exoticize—in attempts to access the power of those who control the levers, there is nothing healthy about the boundaries we are forced to draw. When our boundaries are inflexible, they are no better than the walls built around the borders of the state. It's clear now that I held on to these unhealthy boundaries, delineating care for myself and care for other Black people, during my trip to Borikén. And rectifying the harm I caused must be more than just claiming to have learned a lesson. It must include reckoning with how I create boundaries around myself within relationships of accountability into the future.

~

I have one white friend left.

Five years ago, after Cloud supported me through a difficult breakup with the partner I'd been living with, we moved into an apartment in Bed-Stuy. Before Cloud and I officially moved in together, they had let me stay in their previous apartment for a couple of months because I'd had to move out of mine so suddenly, and the roommate arrangement seemed to work well enough that we decided to continue it.

Cloud was also from the Midwest—Flint, Michigan—and had been born into a family that followed the Bahá'í faith. We bonded over the apparent commonalities of our upbringings and our shared affinity for drunken debauchery through a period neither of us recognized then as being one in which we were both plagued with depression. I met them at a party during my junior year of college, where they convinced me—with a fake accent, to which they impressively committed the entire night—that they were British.

"I studied abroad in London!" I responded excitedly when they told me the lie, apologizing for spilling my drink on their shoes. "Where did you live?"

"Oh, you know," they said, running their hand through their short brown hair, not even bothering to flick the thick droplets of tequila from their loafers, "I moved around a lot!"

I later found out that they were an actor, and they were using the night to practice their craft.

"Was that like, a class assignment or something?" I asked, still incredulous as we reminisced on a random Tuesday night in the living room of our new apartment.

"No!" Cloud admitted, smile as wide as a Cheshire cat's, "I just wanted to see if I could convince people."

"You're so . . . interesting."

"Better that than boring!"

"If I was sober, I would have known you were lying, though."

"If we were sober, we would have done a lot of things differently!" they replied, a devilish twinkle in their eye as we each threw another Patrón shot back, Wednesday be damned.

Bed-Stuy is one of the Brooklyn neighborhoods that is most thoroughly gentrified today, and this process was clearly underway five years ago. Having already begun to radicalize in my politics, I was by then railing to anyone who would listen about the Black storefronts disappearing, the Black food and culture disappearing, the Black people disappearing. But I still moved in with Cloud as if this didn't make me part of the same violence scourging the neighborhood.

When they were sober, Cloud usually said all the things a white "ally" is supposed to say about how and what whiteness takes from Black people, too, like we hadn't both just become the replacements of the Black people who were being taken away. Poof. As if gentrification were just a thing that happens, without actual players to make it.

As was later the case with my touristic exploits in Borikén, my attempts to disengage from certain realities of anti-Blackness made it easy for me to recognize the problem of gentrification in theory but not to apply the theory to my own life. Cloud was my friend, a friend I'd gone through so much real and deep and dark shit with, and our friendship became an excuse to ignore the risks their presence presented to my community, risks that existed regardless of either of our "good" intentions.

If Cloud were to have had any type of conflict with any of our Black neighbors—who were an impediment in the eyes of a state waiting for any excuse to clear them away for the next wave of white people—there would have been no telling the consequences. Like Saheed Vassell, Akai Gurley, and Sergio Reyes, Black people had been killed by cops in gentrifying Brooklyn neighborhoods for less. Even though Cloud and I personally refused to engage the police, in any scenario where cops were present, they would always be more likely to read innocence onto Cloud's white body and criminality onto the Black ones surrounding them.

Even without the physical presence of police, this type of deadly protection proliferates around white people. It was present in how quickly our landlord catered to Cloud's concerns about noise levels and maintenance requests, even at the expense of the routines and needs of other Black tenants. It was in how the store down the block became a place Cloud could leave personal belongings to pick up later, even as Black customers who frequented these same places were regarded as rabid thieves to be put down.

By uncritically bringing Cloud into Black spaces, particularly at this precarious moment in our neighborhood, I was selfishly asking others to pay the costs I hadn't even reflected on paying myself. And I was letting Cloud know that it was okay to be uncritical and careless when it comes to the safety of Black people, too. Sometimes they did exactly that. Sometimes they showed up at events for Black people, spoke on Black issues, and demanded things from Black people that we shouldn't be required to give. And this harm was always exacerbated when we drank.

"*I've* had too much?! That was only my fifth tequila!" Cloud tried in an Israeli accent after we'd just been kicked out of another bar. "You had at least seven. Anyway, where should we go next? Therapy Lounge?"

"No."

Cloud wasn't lying. I was even drunker than they were, and I understood the desire to keep the party going; we were both running away from demons. But not long before that night, I'd been sexually assaulted—again—at a different gay club mostly frequented by white men, and I had decided to avoid these cesspools of anti-Blackness and fetishization as much as possible in the wake. That decision was as clear to me seven drinks in as it would have been sober. There is only so far Black people can run, even when we are committed to escape.

"Why not?"

"I don't want to be around white gays right now."

Cloud screwed up their face. "You can't go just this one time?"

"No."

"Oh my fucking god, you are so fucking unreasonable!"

They screamed and stormed off, leaving me to deal with their whiteness, to deal with their belief that I had unreasonable anger toward it for wanting to protect myself. And I don't think Cloud would have said that my anger at whiteness was unreasonable this explicitly or yelled it like this if they were sober, but without healthy boundaries between us I would have always been left to deal with their whiteness. White people can run away from things that we can't. They can run away from facing the violence they enact upon us, even when they claim to love us, just to try and escape their demons. And if their demons frighten them enough, they will always choose to run, always choose their own violent protection over what is required to save us, and that is saying enough.

As someone who has struggled with substances myself, who has seen and loved so many family members and friends while they struggled and lost valiant battles to addiction all my life, I know that no one chooses alcoholism. But some of us do choose an escape from reality that an addiction to substances might help facilitate. I knew that Cloud's reality was difficult in ways that are theirs to detail, and so I understood deeply why they might want to leave it behind. The problem was, as a white person in a white-supremacist world, the reality they wanted to escape also included their responsibilities to me and my safety as a Black person. That reality also included a responsibility to respect my saying no, even if the reason I offered or refused it seemed unreasonable to them. And the very real difficulties Cloud experienced that drinking helped them forget—and forgetting was paramount, even if it meant attacking me for when I offered and refused to give consent—do not take away from the anti-Black abuses I experienced as a result. Do not take away from the fact that there were choices. Cloud's very real difficulties do not take away from how they would force me to compromise my safety for their own destructive desires throughout our relationship and do not take away from the fact that my community's safety was sacrificed, too. They abused alcohol in ways that harmed me as a Black person, that forced Black people in general into traumatizing situations for the sake of their escape, *because* of their anti-Blackness, not the other way around.

We didn't talk about this incident again, but we began going to more Black venues after that, even though we did not lessen our drinking—either of us. Cloud did not stop running away from the anti-Black violence they enacted. And I did not stop running away from my responsibility to distance myself and other Black people from it.

"I don't know what their problem is," Cloud said, asking for a cigarette after a security guard at the mostly Black nightclub we'd turned into our watering hole against its will told them to go outside and get some air. "I don't like this place anyway."

I loved it, but I didn't say anything. I didn't know what to say. I could say, *Cloud, you have to drink less*, but that wouldn't make them listen to the things and the places I loved. And neither would drinking less, really. And without enough distance between us to honor our unique experiences as a beneficiary of anti-Black violence and a victim of it, they could always just point to the fact of me drinking the same amount to explain that they were just as okay as I was. We were friends who did the same things, and so either we both had the same drinking problem or neither of us did. That is what happens when you don't draw healthy boundaries between people with whom you share a relationship.

Another friend of mine—Black—came to check on us outside the club and asked for a cigarette, too. He inhaled it with something about god being good. Cloud was an atheist, and in my experience, drunk white atheists have lots of questions when you talk about Black gods. So Cloud asked their questions. And Cloud didn't listen to the answers. "I just think it's so stupid to believe in some all-powerful being in the sky," Cloud said finally, voicing the thing they'd already decided to say, even before launching any of these invasive questions at this unsuspecting Black man, who told me, with his eyes, to come get my drunk white atheist friend. Told me to remember that Cloud would never understand the gods we find to liberate us. So Cloud and I left, but we came back, and back, and back, always to this same space where I needed to get my drunk white friend and stop them from enacting anti-Blackness, because I was still trying to use alcohol myself to escape responsibility for our relationship rather than putting the necessary distance between us. *Cloud is locked in the bathroom at this Black lounge, and no one else can use it, but I just shrug and keep on dancing. Cloud is cussing out the bartender at this Black bar, and no one else can place an order, but at least I sneaked in my own flask. Cloud is ogling some Black boy who is just trying not to be fetishized by white gays, exactly like I was the night Cloud cussed me out for saying no.* Until finally, a few years later, Cloud accepted that they had a drinking problem. Which, like I said, meant that I had one, too. Which, like I said, was never the problem to begin with.

A year ago, Cloud, who had been sober for a few months then, invited me to join them at an Alcoholics Anonymous meeting.

"Okay," I said, intending this to be a polite little lie. By that time, I knew that their problem with avoidance was bigger than alcohol, and mine was bigger, too, and different from theirs. But I did not want to have a conversation trying to explain all this. I did not have the language then, and Cloud could not speak history into existence just by talking through it with me like other Black people could. Cloud did not share what I shared with the Black boy in the club who was trying to avoid their gaze. There is so much exhaustion in detailing what no one else is able to do while white people and their problems are attended to, and that exhaustion is taking a thing, too. But I guess that just comes with the territory of calling a white person my friend. I guess, for as long as I do call Cloud that, refusing to address all these things was just another feature of my problem with avoidance in the first place.

"I'd really, really like you to come," Cloud insisted, flashing that bright smile of theirs and struggling commendably to walk the line between nagging and stern encouragement.

"I said I will!" I repeated, punching them playfully on the shoulder.

But I didn't. I couldn't, not before I'd explained to them how difficult those years had been for me. How beautiful and terrible it was to see someone I cared for falling apart like I was, but in a way I could not understand or excuse. In a way that demanded my obliteration, too. How beautiful and terrible it was that they wanted the way I fell apart to be the same as the way they did. How beautiful and terrible and terrible and terrible.

After the AA meeting, Cloud asked me to dinner to talk. When I arrived, I was surprised to see their eyes straining so much that the veins in each reddened from the effort of trying to stop them from filling with tears. They explained that the meeting had been to commemorate a significant step they'd completed in their sobriety and that they had wanted me there to celebrate with them. That it would have meant a lot to them. That sometimes it feels like I don't support them enough, even as they try to support me. That sometimes it still seems to them like my anger at white people is so unreasonable that I can't make exceptions for them.

"Of course I support your sobriety," I said. But I think perhaps, at least for a long time, Cloud wanted me to *feel* their anguish, to reflect it back, to understand on the deepest level how monumental this moment in their journey toward healing was for them, and I no longer wanted to do that. Feeling what Cloud felt would always mean feeling all of whiteness and the violence it has wrought upon me and so many others. I didn't want to feel what they felt, even if I didn't want them to feel it either. And their belief that this was unreasonable would not make it true, just like it hadn't on that drunken night all those years before. The belief that it is unreasonable to honor the experiences we have that are unique from white people's, and the sanctity of those experiences, can, in fact, only make more harm come true.

I apologized, but I still didn't confirm the reality that I won't always understand how they feel. That we won't always feel the same. I didn't say that it wasn't my anger getting in the way, that it was their whiteness and my continued avoidance of acknowledging the necessity of finding distance from it. And though I told them that I genuinely regretted things working out this way around the AA meeting, and I was being honest, I didn't explain why I couldn't find myself feeling sad about it the way they seemed to want me to. I knew that there were a lot of things Cloud didn't support me in, sometimes through no fault of their own. There were a lot of things Cloud *couldn't* support me in, because that is just an aspect of a relationship where one party has "something to save" and the other never had "anything to lose," as Wilderson reminded me that James Baldwin wrote on his relationship with Norman Mailer. I didn't tell Cloud that it's okay if we experience the world differently, emotions differently, our relationships to substances differently, that we never should have tried to pretend otherwise, and I should have told them.

Cloud cried some more. I apologized again and went home. It took a long time for our relationship to recover, in part because it has taken this long for me to be able to fully articulate that empathy and care not only can be two different things but sometimes have to be. In part because I wasn't always sure it was worth articulating when the articulation of this takes so much out of a Black person. And it will take even longer for me to be able to figure out how to show this type of care to Cloud after choosing to continue a friendship with them in the face of my very real failure to empathize, a failure that I can now embrace.

All our relationships shape and are shaped by anti-Black conditioning. For my friendship with Cloud to work, there must be space for my Blackness that I keep protected, part of my home that is not open for others to travel to without a fruitful connection. Things I say that they cannot say. Things I want for myself that they will not ever know to want for themselves, like to no longer feel the weight of this anti-Black world squeezing the air from my body with every step I make. For this to be a relationship of accountability, there must be responsibilities that they have, like to find a way to rid themselves of whiteness, that I don't. Responsibilities I have, like to keep them from spilling white violence everywhere while holding them to finding a way to rid themselves of it. For this friendship to work, and we shouldn't feel compelled by society or anyone other than ourselves to make it, we have to find care despite the distance between us—even if that care looks a lot different from what care between friends is "supposed" to look like.

And I don't completely know what care between us *does* look like all the time. It will probably take more than either of us can fathom. But Cloud's willingness to accept and apologize and make amends for the anti-Black harms they created, to interrogate their relationship to Black spaces and Black relationships even when it doesn't seem they might ever discover the right answers, feels closer. Their willingness to understand and deal with the pain they felt from me avoiding these conversations without resorting to blame does, too. As does both of our refusals to use alcoholism as an excuse to run away from the harms they have caused and I have encouraged against other Black people, a refusal that is a recognizable component of their sobriety, and so does their encouraging me to see a Black, queer therapist so that I can better understand myself, even if they might not be able to understand me themself. Alongside me being clear about my needs and what I can offer, without us expecting to always be on the same page, our relationship consists more of those things now.

And I think we are both much healthier than when we tried to ignore the question of how and when the distance between us is necessary. If I am to have white friends, I have to hold them to account for the harms they cause because of my own accountability to Black people. Our relationship can't be limited to what I can do for Cloud personally, although everyone's health, including Cloud's, depends on refusing to limit the parameters of a relationship in this way in the first place.

The way I express care for Cloud will never look like the way I express care for another Black person. Refusing to create unhealthy boundaries between my own and other Black people's experiences demands that I have healthier boundaries in my relationships with white (and all non-Black) people, too. Similar to the way that a man's relationship to women is always shaped by patriarchy and misogyny, Cloud's relationship to me will be forever tangled up with their relationship to white supremacy and anti-Blackness, and it's always my responsibility to keep that anti-Blackness from harming my communities—and from harming me, because I am a part of my communities. It's always my responsibility to refuse to allow others who might carry anti-Blackness into Black spaces around me. It's my responsibility to acknowledge when I carry it, like I carried it in Borikén, like I carried it during that time in Bed-Stuy, without making excuses. To find a way to relinquish it, even if that means discomfort, even if that means giving up the parts of my relationships that this society has tried so hard to convince me are always to be desired.

I have to give up the parts of my relationships that, when writing this, made me want to provide Cloud with more space to commit anti-Blackness, just because of their demons and their addictions. The parts that made me want to reduce the fact that they ignored consent and attacked me for saying no to just a misunderstanding, especially if I didn't have the capacity to explicitly describe the full backstory of the sexual trauma that made me say it—as if any white person will ever have the full backstory of Black traumas. I have to give up the parts that provide space for always allowing white people the benefit of the doubt, even when they admit to hurting Black people, and the parts that provide space for the dangerous idea that requiring any other person to be accountable for their anti-Blackness is somehow ever unfair or one-sided or not enough to fulfill a relationship. Because dismantling anti-Blackness is always enough to fulfill a relationship.

CANTO III

Free

CHAPTER FOURTEEN

A PRAYER FOR HEALING

Hari-Gaura,

No one really dies of old age, science says. It's true that a body's cells have finite life spans, but it's ultimately diseases, which take advantage of a cell's increasing ineffectiveness at protecting against them, that kill. Time is only death's excuse. It isn't actually how I lost Mother Bhūmi. It isn't actually how I lost you, any more than it will be how I lose my mother. This country's history is full of viruses and cancers both wrought and exacerbated by colonization, and they have been murdering Black people for a long time now.

We are in the midst of a global health pandemic. As of today, COVID-19 has killed hundreds of thousands of people globally and more than one hundred thousand across this country, a greatly outsize proportion of them Black. Black people are more likely to be poor; to have inadequate access to hygiene and health care; to have underlying health issues; to have our concerns ignored by doctors;

and to be locked in prisons, where all these realities are exponentially more present.[36] For those of us who are not incarcerated, the state has instructed us to practice what they call "social distancing"— to stay inside our homes as much as possible, to wear a mask on our essential errands, and to stay six feet away from others and never gather in groups— so as to slow the spread of the disease. Most of these things are possible only for those who are not essential workers—people employed in food, delivery, and health-care industries primarily—or, of course, homeless, and a greatly outsize proportion of these groups are Black, too. And if we break social-distancing guidelines, we are threatened with being thrown *into* prisons. All this is because our carceral government ignored warnings, did not prepare our already overburdened, capitalistic health-care system, and refuses to make up the ground by properly investing in testing measures. It seems like this death and isolation will go on until the end of time.

But what is time, really? What is death? What is isolation when you are here, too? I've been trying to figure out exactly when your story ended and mine began, exactly when this carceral dissonance became irreconcilable. Now I know that there were many beginnings. But there *is* one moment I keep returning to.

I can't recall your precise age. You may have been ten. A few years ago I confessed to murkiness around this memory in an essay I wrote about the incident. A more established writer advised me, unsolicited, that the story was difficult to believe because I couldn't pin down how old you were when it happened.

It seemed a heartless response to one of my most vulnerable pieces of writing, but I know he was only repeating this world's greatest truth: An inability to define a person's age makes it impossible to believe in the validity of their suffering. Which is to say, Black people can never truly be victims in a society that doesn't afford us the freedoms of childhood or the agency of being adults. And for as long as I abided by this world's rules, the validity of my suffering was so difficult for even me to consider that I often mistook it for only a figment of my imagination.

Sometimes I want to believe that the only real part of this memory is the beginning, when you were sent to the room of the youngest son of one of Mata's friends for the night. We would frequently stay in Mata's friends' homes while traveling to different states for Hare Krṣṇa festivals and holidays, though I can't remember which holiday this one was. The girls were sent to another room and Mata's friend's oldest son, who would have been around fifteen at the time, to his own.

I remember clearly how, late one night, when we were all supposed to be asleep, the teenager came into the younger boys' room on the pretense of sharing some urgently hilarious joke. You must have been the only one awake. The older boy had always been a prankster, insatiable for laughter that seemed never to be enough to replace the sadness in his eyes, and one joke was insufficient. He kept joking and joking, then paused to see whether you would continue snickering when he asked if you wanted to come back to his room. But you didn't laugh.

Instead, you followed him down a pitch-black corridor into his bedroom. There he had erected a tent made of white sheets, as if he knew you were destined to find shelter among ghosts. When you entered, he proposed a game of Dare, and you agreed. It started off simple.

"I dare you to eat that old cracker off the ground."

"I dare you to hold your hand to the surface of that scalding heater for three seconds."

"I dare you to pull down your pants."

After both of you had your clothes off, he graduated to challenging you to touch parts of his body, but I don't remember the specifics. When I dream about it, I always wake up before that part, sometimes shamefully wetted in my body's desperate bid to desiccate this memory before I drown in the pool it has made as thick as raw honey.

My body has perfected how to make pleasure from pain. In order to find legibility in a world where you must be the villain, it needs me to forget about how you have been victimized.

I used to blame you for what happened. For your selflessness. For agreeing to relinquish yourself so that you might replace this other boy's sadness the way laughter was never able to. For being so trusting. For foolishly believing any Black child could fulfill their most frightening desires in this world and still claim safety. For why I can't escape these dangerously queer desires even now. And there was no resolving your existence with my commitment to punishing you for what, to this world submerged in misafropedia, are irreparable crimes.

You could say that this was the first moment I allowed a boy inside this body, but it would be more accurate to call it the first excavation of a boy—of you—from it. Underneath that tent, the touch of the oldest son of my mother's friend felt right to want but not right to receive, and my lack of faith in the sanctity of this contradiction would kill whatever innocence I still granted myself, just as Mata had always warned me a lack of faith would do.

You had been the only sacred thing I knew for sure, and so I believed your naive longing for illicit intimacies had created me queer in your image. I hated this body you bequeathed to me, and so I came up with countless ways to have no body at all as long as my knees still refused to be scrubbed clean of the dirt and crumbs from that boy's unswept floor thousands of showers later.

Creation stories have always confused me. No one ever really talks about who created the Creator. His advent just sort of happens, while the rest of us are made of clay and ribs and rape. But there must be a genesis before the Genesis. I know that you were queer before the tent. You were queer enough for this older boy to know, and for him to exploit the fact that you didn't know how to name it. Not all Black children who participate in their own harm in this way are queer. But if queerness is defined by questions about the kind of intimacy that lies outside of this world's scripts, questions that Black children like you—gendered or otherwise—are brave enough to ask, then all of them are queer enough. All of them experience a time before censoring their stainless desires for freedom and intimacy, which this misafropedic world will always abuse. And instead of exalting your desire for freedom, your trust, your vulnerability, I took to blaming you, yet another act of abuse in itself.

There was another sexual encounter later on with that same boy, I think. Or it was with the other family friend around his age who asked me to suck his dick behind our garage at the yellow house with chipping paint—in that always trash-riddled area between it and the fence blocking off the next house—around the same time. I can't remember clearly. But I know that each of these foggy memories would end with you saying yes, if I let them.

I know that I can only conceive of my existence without you after a time when you had been drowned in a pool of pleasure that another boy's body had created from pain inside our mouth. I know that I punished you out of existence for this, even though you would have never been given the chance to finish off the sexual encounter yourself. You weren't even able to yet, not that these older boys asked or would have waited.

And this unwillingness for anyone in the world, including me, to ask what you wanted, or to believe in the validity of protecting you in your journey to finding it, is what killed you, not anything you did. And this unwillingness to ask what Black children need or to believe in the necessity of protecting them, instead turning to carceral measures to punish the already punished, has always been the deadliest crisis we face. Black children should always be supported, not exploited or blamed. I know that now.

I'm sorry it took me so long to get here.

CHAPTER FIFTEEN
TRIGGER WARNING

A cursory study of feminism revealed to me a long time ago that I needn't say no to be sexually assaulted. But I would require a deeper understanding of power, coercion, and abuse to accept that I could say yes and still be. "Yes" comes with critical caveats. A child's consent for a sex act with an adult, for example, is impossible. It is dependent upon the manipulation and exploitation of the child's trust that their best interests are in the hearts of those tasked by society with protecting them—as they should be.

The terms of our existence include that adults are to prioritize children's well-being, but those terms are broken whenever an adult's selfish pleasures are prioritized instead. An agreement whose terms are disregarded is not an agreement at all.

But what are the terms children have for the agreements they make with one another?

As thick as the fog around the memory of my first sexual experience is, it has always been clear to me that whatever happened inside that tent of sheets at the home of my mother's friend was not rooted in the older boy's concern for my well-being. I could understand that I didn't deserve for anyone to get off on my body before my body could get off on itself. I knew I didn't deserve for someone who *did* get off on my body prematurely to then leave me to suffer through the devastating confusion of being used for pleasure and discarded without concern, support, or guidance. But it took me years to call what happened "assault."

I couldn't reconcile my concept of assault with the reality that this boy, though significantly older than I was, was still a child, too. He certainly had a far better grasp of the consequences of what he was doing. But knowing that I had agreed to and enjoyed what happened, and was not much younger than he was, wouldn't allow me to direct blame in any logical way.

Who is guilty when the innocent harm one another?

I always wonder whether that boy had older boys of his own lurking in the homes of his family's friends, his own insatiable pranksters who made him choose between facing their sadness or sharing in a liberating euphoria—which is never really a choice at all. To my knowledge, both he and the other boy, the one who asked me to perform fellatio on him behind my garage, grew up to identify as straight.

Were these moments born from curiosities they'd been denied exploring in safe and healthy ways? What is curiosity without safety measures if not a hunt? Were either of them asked during *their* first time, and like me, did they say yes? Like me, did they not fully know what they were agreeing to, which would necessarily encourage their loss of faith that childhoods could be protected in the first place?

I'll never know their answers to these questions, though not for lack of wanting. But in my writing and speaking about the topic, I have had the opportunity to hear many other experiences with childhood sexual violence. Sometimes, it seems as if I don't know a single person who hasn't experienced this trauma. In fact, the US Centers for Disease Control and Prevention estimates that 20 percent of all adults experience rape or sexual abuse by the age of eighteen. Because of their vulnerability in a society that does not support them, queer and gender-nonconforming children may be at even greater risk.[37]

A 2011 study found that over 50 percent of transgender people had experienced sexual violence at some point in their lives, and of those, 72 percent had also survived childhood sexual abuse. Relatedly, an ongoing survey by the organization Black Women's Blueprint has found that 60 percent of Black women are sexually assaulted by age eighteen, which falls between the 34.1 percent in a Boston community sample and the 65 percent in a Chicago sample who have reported childhood sexual abuse.[38]

The number of us who have endured this devastation in one form or another is astounding, proof of an undeniable epidemic of misafropedia and childhoods stolen. But numbers are the best secret keepers, and there are some stories even they can never fully tell.

My experience defied the scripts through which the state generally reads and quantifies sexual violence. My harm-doers and I were all Black boys. The state primarily defines sexual violence through specific lenses of gender, race, and age, which is why assaults on white women (and particularly at the hands of Black men) cause the most institutional outrage, concern, and punishment.[39] My harm-doers and I were children, when the state views childhood sexual violence through a punitive lens designed for adults, which is why child-pornography laws in many states have punished children who consensually send explicit pictures of themselves to other children. This is also why, combined with the racial element, the childhoods of Emmett Till and the Central Park Five were hardly considered by these same institutions of "justice."[40] So even though what I went through shaped debilitating anxieties around sex and an overwhelming shame about my sexuality—which will probably affect me for the rest of my life—"assault" still never rolls easily off my tongue.

I can only imagine how many other Black boys and girls and gender-nonconforming children have withstood assaults they couldn't or wouldn't name because the carceral state's language wasn't created to name them, and are therefore left out of these already breathtaking statistics. It's apparent that healing from the epidemic of sexual violence requires a fuller picture, and that itself requires a lens on Blackness and the new language it affords.

~

Just before the COVID-19 crisis struck, I was sitting with my friend George at a busy café in Brooklyn. George was writing a book about his experiences as a Black, queer person as well, and we often met there to write together. This time, I found myself stuck while writing about my experience with childhood sexual violence. I was still struggling with understanding the love language I used to speak with before the violation. I still didn't know how to write about the harm the state conditions Black people to do to one another, and I didn't know how to write about it with the proper amount of care for everyone involved.

George asked to use the charger that we were sharing between us, and I was almost relieved that he did. I handed it over, closing my not-yet-fully-charged MacBook.

"This is hard," I admitted. "I'm trying to describe my first sexual experience, but I don't know if I have the vocabulary for what actually happened."

He perked up, setting one henna-like tattooed hand on top of the other on the small table between us. "Oh, who was it with?"

I hated to disappoint his eagerness for what should be a cute gay coming-of-age story.

"A family friend," I said apologetically. "An older one."

I was equal parts relieved and disheartened that he immediately got it. He placed his hands back on his lap, sucked one corner of his mouth toward his full sideburns, and gave a knowing nod. I explained what happened to me at nine or ten, the things I could and couldn't remember, and how I learned that my Black body was both queer and not fully mine at all, and he cut me off.

At first, I was resistant to the interruption. George can be talkative, and though I love him for how easily communication comes to him, this can be disorienting when I'm really crunching to get through a piece of writing or in the middle of telling a story. But even when I have the strictest deadlines, I always ask him to join me at the café. Even if every moment went uninterrupted, it still would never feel like enough time to write everything that needs writing, and sharing the time I do have with someone who is also trying to combat the violence that shapes these stories makes it feel far more productive.

However, in this moment I quickly realized that George was simply talking through my story for me, picking up right where he interjected and filling in the details I couldn't or wouldn't recall with his own recollections. George's story and mine were so similar that for once I forgot that mine is covered in haze. His memory was my memory, and my memory became that of my childhood self again, too.

"I've also always been afraid to call it assault," George said, his large brown eyes betraying a gravity his excited voice countered, "because I don't think my harm-doer was evil."

"I guess that's what I am trying to get at. How we might have healed more if we could address this without our harm-doers having to be evil . . . if addressing harms wasn't the same as punishment."

I still wasn't entirely sure what the alternative looked like, I admitted to George. The carceral state requires us to be divided into good/evil binaries, and sometimes that feels like all I know. When I name the violence that happens to me, the carceral state tries to force me to punish and blame someone for it. If I refuse to punish and blame, it pressures me to give up naming my trauma. Healing from an assault when my harm-doer, emboldened by a culture swimming in rape, is not evil nonetheless requires a complete rejection of the carceral thinking that conditions me, and a refusal to strictly adhere to its language when that's the language I've been given.

I used to think prison abolition was just a question of the utility of physical human cages. Abolition was just about whether prison ends abuses or only concentrates them within its walls (and concentrates them among the marginalized incarcerated populations especially). It was just about how prisons have no concern for rehabilitation, which is why almost half of criminal offenders in the United States reoffend.[41]

But it was finally becoming clear that prison abolition was also about the way the punitive victim/perpetrator binary that undergirds prisons prevents us from having room to heal. Abolition is a rejection of a world in which punishment takes the place of that room to heal, a world in which blame takes the place of accountability.

This world doesn't give us words for alternatives, which makes abolition the Blackest language. Abolition asks us to consider not-yet-named realities, like one where we would rather lessen further wrongs than just harm the people who have wronged us. It asks us to look beyond good/evil binaries to truly reckon with the more complicated scripts Black lives actually follow.

If prison isn't the solution to social ills, then I have to consider my own role in solving them and rededicate myself to upholding the terms of a social agreement to prioritize the well-being of others—especially Black children—over punitive measures.

Prison abolition is intrinsically linked to Black liberation, as both require us to think of harm as existing not just within the singular moment it occurs. Prison abolition requires me to fully interrogate both American history and its notions of justice that target and incarcerate Black people specifically. A history of five-year-old Kodi Gaines being shot by agents of the state in his mother's arms. Of seven-year-old Aiyana Stanley-Jones being shot dead by agents of the state in her grandmother's home. Of twelve-year-old Tamir Rice being shot dead by agents of the state while playing in a park.

To heal from these harms would require I not be confined to believing that when these harms stop happening, the effects of them are done. Harm lasts. What happened to me and George and too many Black children is always happening. And it is happening to children everywhere. I cannot fix it by punishing individual people for individual actions in an individual past.

$\sim$

I violated my ex-partner. It happened five years ago. "Assault" doesn't roll easily off the tongue in this case either. He was drunk, a too-common state for both of us then, and though I had been drinking, too, I was more or less aware of what was going on. We had just come back from a party, and as soon as we got home, he went to bed while I took a shower. When I came to join him, he was lying still, looking as beautiful as anything that has ever belonged to me. I went to tell him so, whispered it in his ear as I kissed his neck, and then I went to show him. I want for that to mean I went to show him that he was beautiful, but in truth I went to show him that he belonged to me.

Because my ex was generally the initiator, I don't remember ever being turned down for sex with him, and I didn't assume this time would be any different. It was. In this moment, his consent also came with a critical caveat, his "yes" slurred and busy with extra consonants because of the alcohol still working its way through his body. His consent was dependent upon the trust that I had his best interests at heart, but I had made room for only my desires. His consent was dependent on my willingness to step back and safely assess his level of consciousness, and I broke the terms of the agreement we had made in committing to each other when I did not.

I usually start this story off with how I eventually stopped. With how my ex and I talked about it later and he insisted what happened was fine. Rather than a trigger warning, this is how I jam the gun. This is how I try to ensure that no one gets killed here, even though refusing to honestly acknowledge fully the dynamics of situations like this is exactly why I haven't healed from my own sexual trauma, is exactly what stole away the child I used to be. I want readers to know that my ex laughed about me even bringing these concerns up, because a part of me still wants to summon enough laughter into yet another thing filled with sadness to make everything all right.

I once told this story to a group of sexual assault survivors, and they pushed back against calling it the same thing that they had experienced.

"Making your ex a victim when he said he wasn't is razing his consent all over again," a white woman told me dismissively. She had a point. This language is never adequate enough, and if my ex says "victim" didn't describe him in that moment, then maybe it didn't. And I wonder if she was pushing back against the patriarchal idea that, simply by virtue of my admission, I might be celebrated as one of the "good ones" without doing anything more tangible to rectify the harm I caused. But she didn't acknowledge the ways people who experience sexual violence in a patriarchal society, especially Black people, are conditioned not to name the harms we endure.

Even if my ex doesn't claim to have been the victim of sexual violence in that exact moment, it shouldn't mean violence didn't occur or that my actions weren't harmful, though the carceral state might determine otherwise. The lack of victim cooperation is a common excuse for prosecutors to not pursue sexual assault cases. And regardless of whether a conviction in court results in healing, it is telling that this lack of cooperation is a primary factor in why just 2 percent of rapes are estimated to lead to one.[42]

Almost all the survivors of serial child abuser and former USA Gymnastics team doctor Larry Nassar admit that they did not at first consider the sexual abuse he enacted to be wrong, because he wrapped up his assaults in the jargon of medical justifications. Just because a survivor doesn't consciously know it or want their harm-doer to be punished doesn't mean there is no harm to a pattern of exploiting others that must be addressed. What I did to my ex was just one example of behaviors I learned and affirmed over time, behaviors that don't just affect a single person in a single moment but inform how I harmed others throughout my life—and how I allowed myself to be harmed.

Exploiting a body that does not belong to us is never just about making someone else a victim in a point in time; it is also about claiming the right to use power and control however we wish throughout our lives, a right the carceral state upholds. I say I assaulted my partner not just to make him a victim but because I failed to prioritize his well-being, despite the way his words slurred away any possible consent, and because I know that I made myself just like the older boy who assaulted me in that tent of sheets.

When I call what I did five years ago a violation, I mean to say that I was creating myself in my harm-doers' image. I was finishing off the job I'd started long ago of grave-robbing the little boy from inside me and replacing him with someone who knew no tenderness at all. Robbing Black childhoods is a job the carceral state has entrusted to me, entrusted to that older boy in the tent, and entrusted to all of us who accept living under the anti-Black project of misafropedia.

My ex saying that what I did was okay is an old beginning to this story, a beginning I must work to reject if I am ever to help put a stop to this cycle of abuse. If I am ever to heal from my debilitating anxieties around sex and an overwhelming shame about my sexuality.

Exploiting my ex's body for my own pleasure was a culmination of the ideas I had internalized through years of carceral logics. Through binary ideas about guilt and innocence, good and bad, punishment and injustice. Ideas about who owns Black bodies, how the bodies of Black people, particularly of Black queer and femme and women folk, never belong to themselves and are always commodities.

It was these carceral ideas that allowed me, as a drunk, gay college kid, to grab the bodies of female friends to whom I wasn't attracted as a "joke" or to push up on people at bars just because I *was* attracted to them. There will always be an excuse for harm in a carceral state when we pretend the harms of a moment are about only that moment and not about the history of a state that intentionally targets certain communities. For a long time, I pretended that punishment was the only answer to individuals acting out a culture of violence, a culture that has been well established by the state. And if I go on pretending, I can never destabilize that violent establishment. I can never know better answers.

CHAPTER SIXTEEN
A PRAYER FOR FREEDOM

Hari-Gaura,

I'm beginning to feel incredibly lonely after weeks of social distancing, but I find some comfort thinking about you. I've been remembering how you would sometimes ask Daddy to accompany you to the bathroom because you were afraid of being alone for too long. According to him, you would talk his ear off for minutes on end while sitting on the toilet.

"My father would do the same thing when he was getting older," Daddy says with nostalgic amusement. "The reddish tinge of your hair when you were young, calling me to talk to you like that while you were on the toilet—I said, you have just got to be my dad reincarnated."

Our grandfather, Reuben Hubbard, passed before we were born, and this story is the closest thing we've ever had to knowing him. I think what Daddy is trying to say when he brings it up is that he wishes he had gotten to know his father more intimately and that, in a way, you offered an answer to his prayers.

Asking Daddy to accompany you to the bathroom went on until you were about five years old, longer than many would likely deem appropriate, and certainly longer than you physically needed him to help. But it was a tenderness. A love language passed from a Black father to his child. It's probably clear that I don't remember everything from that time. But I remember that these bathroom sessions ended the same year you first dreamed of losing Daddy and the same year Mata cut your long hair, which had become much darker than your grandfather's reddish brown over the years.

I plan on raising children someday. As a queer person, I worry myself constantly about the boundaries between anything that could possibly be read as too intimate around kids, given how easy society makes it to project predation onto us. When I spent a summer babysitting my friend Nikkee's toddler, Martin, this fear led me to become overly conscious of how queer I appeared in public, reinforcing those carceral logics around myself. I was afraid of the judgment that infiltrated the faces we passed together when I was more visibly myself.

I imagined the people who witnessed me with Martin immediately assumed me dangerous, and so I tried to silence my queerness whenever I was with him to avoid their judgment. It's the same reason I suspected my mother imagined me some type of monster when I called her that one time and she heard Martin crying in the background. She asked about an essay I'd written on the sexual abuse I experienced as a child—out of the blue after never before asking about my writing without prompting—and immediately I assumed she was calling me a child-hazard. I know it was unfair, but I believed it anyway. "We will talk about it," I told her. We still haven't.

Daddy never seemed to worry about how spending time in the bathroom with you would appear, though. And for that brief moment in his own life, his father didn't either. All three of you were free in a way I struggle to be. I wonder if Daddy would have had more intimate stories to share of his father if that had been the case for longer. I wonder if I would have more intimate stories to share of our father if that had been the case longer with him and us, too.

Daddy swears he would have never hit you. "Except for that one time . . . ," he says, telling a story that I don't recollect. Mata says she doesn't remember anything like what I remember of that day you spent with your friend Mark either. But it makes sense that they wouldn't. It happened to me . . . or to you?

Is what I remember my past or yours? Or no one's?

Can a thing really have happened if no other living person says it did?

Tell me you remember sleeping over at Mark's house, him catching you up on all the cartoons you hadn't seen since you'd been away from his home and its cable. Doug canceled his birthday because he was tired of everything changing with age. Tommy, Chuckie, and the gang went on a vacation in Vegas, likely without considering the effects of tourism on the local people either. Helga created a new student newspaper to challenge Arnold's. And the following morning, you and Mark took a shower together like you sometimes did when you were that age.

Tell me you remember how, fresh off a recap of the show, something struck Mark to begin singing the *Rugrats* theme song in the tub, doot-dooting in place of the xylophone melody. How you joined in and, in the excitement, got a little too into the music. It wasn't grabbing a sponge and pretending it was a microphone while dramatically lathering your body with soap that I'm referring to. It was how, as you did those things, you pushed up onto Mark, grinding your naked body on his to the beat of the song.

Tell me you remember that, at the time, Mark only laughed and pushed you away, although he had every right to be uncomfortable. This was a prime opportunity to learn about the importance of respecting other people's bodies. Instead, when Mark told his mother, and his mother told Daddy, our father whipped you harder than you'd ever been whipped before.

He swears he didn't, but I remember it so clearly. I could never forget how Daddy kept repeating that this wasn't what boys were sup-posed to do as he beat it into you. I could never forget how Daddy told you this whupping was "for your own good," even as it seemed to last forever. Even as it scarred my relationship with our body and the bodies of others for just as long. Instead of teaching you that you should not deny people agency over their bodies, over who can claim their bodies, he beat you for the queerness he thought your body betrayed.

I find myself needing to believe in the certainty of my version of the past just as much as my father needs to believe in a history in which he would never have hit me—except for that one time. When I let him know I was including this story here, Daddy and I spent two hours arguing, with as much softness as we could muster, about whether he really hit me, instead of discussing how I still don't always regard other people's bodies with the respect they deserve, or how he still blames my queerness on something wrong with the food I eat.

"You can't blame the person," he says, his version of "hate the sin but not the sinner." "You gotta blame the food, all the GMOs—that's what's making everyone gay today. It's not your fault." But something is always to blame.

What would it mean for both Daddy and me to spend less energy fighting to justify our perception of the past and more energy figuring out why we hold these perceptions? What would it mean for Daddy to have never hit me, in the face of his continued insistence that I am fundamentally fucked up? Regardless of whose fault it is, what does it mean that I cannot be fully myself in front of my own father? That I can hardly be myself, period, since you were here with me? What would it mean if this incident was never just about Daddy and me and our perceptions of the past at all?

You never should have danced on Mark without his approval. I know as much as anyone how a disregard for a child's wants and needs can lead to monstrosities. I know as much as anyone the importance of addressing this tendency before it continues to harm more and more people.

Carceral thinking was never going to teach you this. Punishment cannot teach us what healthy interactions with one another look like. It never will lead to healing for those harmed. Punishment only ever taught me to adopt the same punitive gaze for myself that follows me on the streets when I am caring for Martin and to run away from accountability in my interactions like the one with Mark. It only ever taught me to turn that gaze outward at my father to avoid looking at myself.

Whether Daddy really hit you that day is important. But what is also important is his refusal to believe that he might have, and my inability to engage with that refusal because I only needed him to believe in my version of the past. The details of our sexual assault as a child are critical, but what is also critical is admitting my discomfort around my mother asking about those details when she did, and talking with her about it. It matters how my father came from sitting freely with you in the bathroom, from sitting freely with his dying father in the bathroom, to considering my queerness a problem. Retracing how he got there without a focus on blame and guilt and punitiveness is how he can find freedom again.

And if it's true that we will all someday die just like my grandfather, then how I get there without a focus on blame and guilt and punitiveness matters for my freedom, too. It has always mattered for freeing you, Hari-Gaura. Knowing this truth is what's most comforting in these lonely times.

CHAPTER SEVENTEEN

IF WE MUST DIE

"If we must die, let it not be like hogs, hunted and . . . and . . ." and the next word disappeared into the air like smoke floating off a candle, although it had been right there not a moment before. I stifled a curse, returning my attention to the book of poetry lying on the dining room table in front of me.

"Penned! Hunted and penned in an inglorious spot."

I closed the book gently, keeping my index finger wedged between its lightly worn pages as a placeholder in case I lost track of what I was attempting to commit to memory again. Or rather, for when I lost track. I looked up at the ceiling and closed my eyes as if they were two holes in a chalice that the words would inevitably leak out from if left level and unplugged.

"If we must die . . ."

I don't recall exactly when I stopped celebrating Kwanzaa, or why. Perhaps it had something to do with the dubious legacy left behind by Maulana Karenga, the holiday's founder, and his abusive treatment of women. Or maybe the custom of celebrating pan-Africanism had been just another thing that would have to be discarded along with my childhood in my quest for belonging in a misafropedic world.

But during the years that I observed the weeklong holiday with my family, Mata would task her children with memorizing a poem that spoke to the principle of the final day—*Imani*, or faith—which was also when we invited outside guests to celebrate with us. This time, one of the last times, I had chosen "If We Must Die" by Jamaican-born Harlem Renaissance writer Claude McKay.

"If we must die, oh let us nobly die . . ."

I'm not completely sure what drew me to the poem. It was short, and I could clearly use any such feature that functioned as an aid to memorizing that I could get. But I fell deeply in love with the piece on a more profound level quickly after I discovered it. McKay, who was born just twenty-four years after Paul Bogle had been hanged for leading a deadly revolt against Jamaica's British colonizers, had written the poem as a response to the Red Summer of 1919, in which a string of white-supremacist mob attacks left hundreds of Black people slaughtered across the United States.

There was something about the way McKay framed the inevitability of death against an oppressive onslaught, not as a reality to ceaselessly and futilely attempt to avoid, but as something sacred. Death didn't have to just be. It could also *do* something for the dead and the dying, if honored rightly. This felt like a god I could believe in again in the face of my steady trek toward losing my religion. It had been no more than a year since my first sexual assault, and I'd felt the air of death hovering around me ever since. I'd also just completed a history lesson on Emmett Till, and the image of his teenage face resting in the casket after being brutalized by white supremacists was still branded into my brain. If only these words could be branded there instead . . .

"Though far outnumbered, let us show us brave . . ."

Auntie Grace, a few other Black Hare Kṛṣṇa devotees, and some of my father's fellow congregants from his mosque began arriving at our home just after sundown, dressed in kente cloth and greeting us with the traditional shout of "Habari Gani." The greeting is Swahili for

"What's the news?" and the news was that I hadn't yet finished memorizing my poem, but Mata was still cooking up the feast in the kitchen, and so at least there was time.

"Habari Gani," I replied without looking up. But the rancorous noise that Black gatherings tend to breathe into life made it nearly impossible to concentrate. I shouldn't have waited until the last minute.

"Hari, help your auntie with this here!" Auntie Grace requested as she burst onto the scene through the front door of our Heights home. I obediently went to grab an aluminum pan from her arms. Through its lid I could smell that it was brimming with macaroni and cheese with an aroma besting even my aunt's sweet perfume, which stuck to me as she squeezed me tight in an embrace. I dropped the pan off in the kitchen with Mata, but before I could get back to the table and my book, my cousin Rachelle, Auntie Grace's only daughter, barreled toward me.

"Let me show you something," Rachelle said as she ran up without even taking off her coat. Since I'd grown apart from Mark, Rachelle had become the main conduit to my understanding of popular culture during my homeschooling and years without cable, and I'm certain she had some hilarious jokes to relay from the latest Bernie Mac comedy special. She embraced this role much more proudly than Mark had, relishing the little taste of glory she could elicit through embodying the famed figures she introduced to me.

"I can't. I have to finish this."

"What's that?"

"Memorizing a poem."

Rachelle frowned, stretching out the scar I had left on the right cheek of her doll-like face from clawing at it in a catfight when we were both toddlers. She had left a nearly identical one on my opposite cheek in the same skirmish. A few more inches, and both scratches would have threatened our eyesight, but our parents only ever laughed about it.

"Hari, you was fighting like a little girl," Auntie Grace would say with a chuckle, nudging me in the ribs. So Rachelle and I both learned to laugh about it, too. That's what makes fighting among people you love different.

"Auntie Kṛṣṇanandini is making y'all do that?" Rachelle asked, wrinkling up her nose.

I made an annoyed face back at her, and Rachelle shrugged before leaving me to the poem.

By the time Mata began laying the traditional straw mat on the table, surrounding the kinara candleholder with an ear of dried corn for each child in the house, a bowl of fruits, and a giant wooden cup representing unity—or Umoja—I felt more confident that I'd retained McKay's words. The confidence stuck to me even in the midst of the circus our house had become, as more and more revelers trickled in. But before I could catch up with Rachelle and join the excitement, my mother caught me by the arm.

"Place these in the kinara."

She handed me a bundle of three red and three green candles to be set in the candleholder on either side of a black one, representing the African blood, land, and people that made us who we were. As soon as I had finished, I made a play back to the staircase to meet my cousin again, but Mata stuck a grill lighter out in my path before I could make it up the steps. She had never let me light the candles before. She gave that weighty look parents sometimes give when you've crossed some unofficial boundary into a new stage of life, which I now understood to also mean one step closer to death, but if we must die . . .

Once I lit the Mishumaa Saba candles, everyone encircled the table, and my father led a short prayer.

"Today, we are gathered here to celebrate the things that make us who we are," Mata said. "We wouldn't be here without Kṛṣṇa, first and foremost, but also without the ancestors who came before us. I invite everyone to shout out the name of someone who has left this plane behind for us to recognize collectively."

"Aunt Leen," Auntie Grace submitted.

"Asé!" everyone chanted in response as Mata poured a libation from the unity cup into a potted plant near the table, an offering to my great aunt.

"Helen Hubbard."

"Asé!"

"Andy Cunningham."

"Reuben Hubbard."

"Topsy Cunningham."

"Asé! Asé! Asé!"

"We are also here to celebrate the final principle of Kwanzaa: Imani, or faith," Mata continued when all the ancestors had received their offerings. "It's our faith that has brought our people through history, and it's our faith that will keep us going. So the children have memorized some poems that they chose for the way they help us understand what that means. But I will go first."

It was the first time Mata had joined us in this tradition. She placed the unity cup down and stood by the table, a shine in her rose-petal eyes that found itself there whenever she began to tell a story she thought to be powerful. She had chosen the poem "Mother to Son" by Langston Hughes.

"Well, son, I'll tell you: Life for me ain't been no crystal stair," Mata began. She went on describing the steps she knew too well: rough, without comforts, in disrepair.

Everyone seemed to be enraptured by my mother's full commitment to this surprise performance, even Rachelle. But I could hardly pay attention over the accelerating beating of my heart as the anxiety about my upcoming turn blossomed. I bounced back and forth on the balls of my feet while I replayed the poem back again in my head, letting

Mata's voice wash over me as she practically sang of places on her stairs *"where there ain't been no light . . ."*

~

I feel myself standing and shaking under the stress, as if watching my mother at Kwanzaa again, while browsing YouTube to find the video I'm looking for. I see it and click "Play," and twenty-three-year-old Korryn Gaines is suddenly yelling into the camera, my fingers smashing imprecisely at the keyboard for the volume button as her voice blares through my earphones. When I finally get the sound at a manageable level, I notice that her face looks as old as it does young, like you can tell it has gone through tacks and splinters and upturned boards but has somehow still come out unscathed. Black doesn't always show its cracks, but that doesn't mean they aren't there.

Korryn is light skinned with bright hazel eyes that kind of remind me of my sister Ganga's. That kind of remind me that the blood in my own light-skinned body isn't all mine, isn't represented fully by the Black candles, is evidence of the systematic rape of Black mothers on plantations.

Korryn is small, but her voice isn't.

"You will have to murder me," Korryn tells an off-camera police officer, the first of many prophecies that would prove her a seer.

In the video, Korryn is parked on the side of a quiet street with her two young children in the back. Halfway through the recording, Korryn hands the camera to her then five-year-old son, Kodi. He looks a little like I did when I was his age. Today, he has a jagged scar from a wound on his cheek, too, this one left behind by an officer's bullet some weeks later while his mother held him in her arms during her murder, but I don't imagine he ever laughs about it.

In the video, Kodi sits in the back seat beside his one-year-old sister. They are crying, clearly aware of the danger their mother is in, but

Korryn just tells him to keep recording, to make sure we witness this. To make sure I do, though I can hardly pay attention over the rapid beating of my heart as Korryn's rage bleeds out the screen over me.

"You stop crying, okay? And you let them know that (the police) stole your mother."

Right before she began filming, Korryn had been pulled over for missing car tags, but she refused to give up her car.

"They're not going to steal my vehicle, and they're not going to kidnap me the way they think that they are. They are going to have to kill me today," she says to no one in particular, but it feels like she is talking to me.

It felt the same way when I saw Sandra Bland say almost the same thing just a year earlier, while filming her own arrest, before dying in a jail cell under "mysterious" conditions following a minor traffic stop in Texas. It was hard for me to listen then, too.

"You see these fucking rebels back here?" Korryn tells the officer, referencing the children behind her. That's when she says the words I am trying to commit to memory this time: "I'll live on forever, my nigga. Forever!"

~

When I was five and woke up screaming after a nightmare that she and my father had died, Mata sat me down gently and wiped my tears.

"We will all leave this material world someday," she said, the same sad smile on her face she puts on now when she's talking about her diagnosis, about COVID-19, about Aunt Cheryl and Mother Bhūmi and all the family we've already lost. The same twinkle in her eye when she begins telling a story she finds powerful.

"The good news is, Kṛṣṇa tells us that we are not this body. The soul lives on forever."

But by the time I first saw the video of Korryn Gaines, I had long stopped believing in Kṛṣṇa. I couldn't reconcile images of lost souls dancing happily in the heavens with our communities burning beneath them, with me burning beneath them, and so I gave up faith in what had started to feel like nothing more than the silly superstition that death could be sacred. And I replaced it with the ceaselessly futile avoidance of reality that fuels my anxiety today.

But here was another mother telling her five-year-old about that faith again. She wasn't telling him to forget that our communities are burning, to forget about what causes our deaths. She was telling him about how refusing the carceral logic of those who pour the gasoline is more important than living by that logic. She was telling him that death doesn't have to be ceaselessly and futilely avoided, that it can also *do* something for the dead and the dying, if honored rightly. She was saying, as my friend Kevin Rigby Jr. put it once, that "we must find ways of reading and writing that register the ways Black people reorient their relationships to toxicity, in/sanity, death, and what it means to be alive."

"You fight them," Korryn says, referencing the aggressing police.

"Okay," Kodi replies as his crying eases.

"They are not for us. They want to kill us. And you never, ever back down from them."

At the end of the video, the officers drag Gaines from her car, stealing her daughter from her arms. They do not kill her that day. Sometimes the carceral state murders Black people more slowly. Years of neglecting a serious medical issue, which is one reason why uterine cancer is deadlier for Black women like my mother. A lifetime of exacerbating a person's mental health crises, like with Mother Bhūmi. Different variations of Black loss caused by the same carceral state's pillaging. For Gaines, her murder culminated a few weeks later while police served the warrant for the same traffic stop she recorded.

When officers showed up then at her home with the warrant, Korryn refused again. Again, she tried to allow us to witness, tried to record what happened to her, but this time the police reached out to Facebook and asked them to cut off her streaming privileges. The social media company quickly did so, a powerful case for considering how surveillance might ultimately be no more than an anti-Black, carceral tool of the state, even when we try and repurpose it to save ourselves, and police sent in a SWAT team after five hours of "negotiating"—for an incident that began with missing car tags. Korryn didn't open the door. Her boyfriend ran away with their one-year-old daughter, but she and Kodi stayed behind.

"You see what they do to us, right?" she tells her son in the video of the earlier incident in the car. During the raid on her home, the police received the key to her apartment from a building super, who immediately complied with their request for it. The cops broke in. Korryn was armed. They shot her and her son. Kodi was lucky enough to survive, if you call this surviving. Asé, Asé, Asé.

~

"I'se still climbin' and life for me ain't been no crystal stair."

When Mata ended the poem, it was my turn to go next. The anxiety overcame me, and I stumbled over the ending. I never completed it, though everyone clapped anyway.

I think maybe it has been my turn ever since. I think maybe the poem still calls for completion, and I have just been drowning under the anxiety of trying to live in a world that would strip me of my childhood. What would it mean to honor death as sacred? How would we fight for our lives in the midst of generational trauma, in the midst of a pandemic, in the midst of relentless state violence that is hell-bent on killing us?

In 2012, George Zimmerman, a white Florida neighborhood watchman, shot and killed seventeen-year-old Trayvon Martin as the Black teenager walked back to his father's home after running to the store to buy a drink and a pack of Skittles. Zimmerman claimed he feared for his life, even though he followed the unarmed, much smaller boy with a gun, even after being advised not to by police.

In a time where our communities were organizing in new ways given the rise of social media, the case became a bona fide spectacle. More than 10 million people tuned in to watch, many with bated breath as, just after 10:00 p.m. on a Saturday in July, jurors returned with their verdict. I was one of those millions of people watching anxiously, having not yet fully given up hope in this justice system; having deluded myself into thinking that justice can, at least sometimes, still come from it; having clung to the belief that putting our trauma on TV on such a scale, making it visible and impossible to turn away from, would somehow bring restitution. I was wrong once again.

At "not guilty," I said nothing. I looked at my partner, surprised to see that many tears were able to make it down his face so quickly. Surprised to feel my cheeks wet, too, without even having the time to feel the sadness erupt from my body. Surprised to hear the words, even though I shouldn't have been. Even though I'd heard them in cases like these so many times before.

I don't remember walking outside, but a few minutes later my partner and I were on the street, drunk and angry and directionless. We uprooted plants from in front of the stores in our Crown Heights neighborhood and overturned trash cans. We screamed and prayed and even laughed maniacally. Maybe it was pointless, and our actions may have even harmed people who shouldn't have been harmed, but we didn't know what else to do. Those storefronts, which brought so much white money into our gentrifying neighborhood—the same gentrifying neighborhood where police stayed prowling for children like Trayvon who threatened capital with their mere presence—felt complicit, too. We didn't know what else could be done, because the only answer we were given had, once again, not been an answer at all.

This sociopolitical era can't be discussed without reckoning with Black Lives Matter, a movement formed out of the ashes of George Zimmerman's acquittal. Organizations led primarily by Black women channeled some of the grassroots energy that had long been simmering in response to lynchings like this under a hashtag that took off following the police killing of eighteen-year-old Mike Brown in Ferguson, Missouri, two years later. Today, that energy has been transformed into numerous demonstrations, activist organizations, and policy proposals across the globe.

The deaths of Trayvon Martin and Mike Brown are understandably cited by many Black writers and organizers of this era as moments that define their politicization. These moments certainly had a huge impact on my activism as well—I attended my first political rally after Zimmerman was acquitted, and was arrested for the first time protesting after Brown's death. But as undeniably important as these stories and the stories of other Black cisgender heterosexual men killed by the state and its agents for no apparent reason are, they draw a sharp contrast with the relative silence in activism around Korryn's death.

This particular YouTube video of Korryn's traffic stop was taken from her Instagram account and uploaded by a Black man who uses it as proof Korryn was delusional and deserved her punishment of murder.

"I'm giving you all these chances," the officer says in the video, his voice dripping with condescension and the carceral state's idea of reason. And the Black man who uploaded it seems to find it reasonable. If she gets out of the car, the cop tells Korryn, she can walk home with her kids right now. The carceral state is always so sensible. She should have wanted to live above all else. All she had to do was not resist. Comply. Put her hands up, and she would have.

It makes sense that the man who uploaded this video didn't understand Korryn. The stories of Black liberation movements that the state permits are almost always filled with the blood and faces of men. Are almost always filled with us dying with our hands up, begging them not to shoot. That's the way the carceral world works. To refuse this narrative for one of violent resistance—or any resistance that can be modeled by the revolutionary ways Black women and queer folks fight back against the state—is insanity.

Revolution is easy to speak, but when someone like Gaines comes along and commits to it, when it comes time to actually put McKay's words into action, to sacrifice, to consistently choose to hold ourselves accountable to our beliefs, we often run away. When Assata Shakur and Joy James and Mariame Kaba and the numerous Black women and gender-nonconforming people who have never experienced or wanted popular recognition remind us that this carceral state cannot be reformed, only abolished, the popular stories that systematically exclude their perspectives beckon us away. And in so turning away, we leave our future, our children, our childhoods behind. We give them none of the honor they deserve, just like we do for all the other ancestors who made us who we are.

Black life under the carceral state may be taken at any time by "reasonable" police error, or by lead contamination consolidating specifically in Black neighborhoods, or by doctors who don't acknowledge Black patients' claims as legitimate, or by food deserts sprouting in Black communities, or by a callously managed global health crisis that primarily affects the poorest and those structurally denied health care, or by innumerable other ways Black people's health outcomes are specifically diminished. And the gaps between these outcomes and white people's have never closed in any significant way, despite liberal progress narratives that often celebrate the increased visibility of our traumas.[43]

But when Korryn spoke of "living on forever," she offered another way to do Black life. It would force us to acknowledge all the ways we are already constantly dying when we'd rather lean on avoidance. It might even actually spur the most material versions of these deaths. But the only life where Black people can ever be truly whole must be found in refusing carceral thinking, behaviors, and institutions. I never want to lose that understanding again. I never want to lose who I was before I subscribed to an abolitionist framework again. I never want to lose, again, the words that struck me during that celebration of our ancestors:

> What though before us lies the open grave?
> Like men we'll face the murderous, cowardly pack
> Pressed to the wall, dying, but fighting back!

CHAPTER EIGHTEEN
A PRAYER FOR COURAGE

Hari-Gaura,

I think what's at the core of my anxiety is that I'm afraid of the suddenness of death. I left you behind in a selfish attempt to survive the state's rampage, but the threat never ceases for too long. Cancer here. A trigger-happy cop there. A deadly contagion. I know that death is inevitable, but that's no more than a small hurdle in the face of my urge to run from it. I keep running further and further away from you, but the fear of meeting your same fate only subsides briefly—if that. And when it comes back, it comes roaring with a vengeance. Carceral dissonance is nothing more than a cycle of panic, centered upon attempts to minimize the terror of death's constant specter in a carceral state.

Today is one of those days when the anxiety blankets everything and the idea of death won't stop haunting me. I'm FaceTiming one of my closest friends, Jahvaris, while trying to walk my dog, who still doesn't want to be walked. I still hate

FaceTime, but since it isn't healthy to meet in person now, it's the only way we can see each other. I think he notices my morbid preoccupations. I wish he'd notice you, too—maybe that would make it easier for me to do the same—but he just looks on through the screen in concern as I take another pull of the cigarette I bummed a moment ago. I chuckle as his scruffy, worried face becomes what happens when you push in the nose of a teddy bear.

"You have to imagine—all substances were completely off the table growing up," I tell him, a plume of smoke and burning tar masking my face, "so even just seeing my sister smoking a cigarette felt like the world had been turned upside down."

I'm telling Jahvaris the story of that moment during the summer when you were about ten and stayed with our sister Bhakti for a few weeks. It's the only way I can think to explain my ambivalent relationship with smoking after Jahvaris encouraged me to give it up. It's a story about why I always bum and never buy. Why I always quit and come back. Why I keep repeating patterns of avoidance that do nothing to stave off mortality and in fact invite death to return with a vengeance—in this particular instance by destroying my lungs.

Bhakti had just gotten married to her second husband, and I haven't seen her so giddy since—although I don't see her as much as I'd like, her being a police officer in Chicago and all. Or was that perceived giddiness just an expression of her own anxieties about another marriage that would prove not to last? Funny how easily only grasping the edges of a memory can transform it into something other than what it originally was.

I remember the scene as more Hitchcockian than you probably experienced it. Bhakti had again without question taken you with her to pick up something you'd asked for from the convenience store. She's still one of the most openhanded people I know, comparable only to our oldest sister, Rani, despite our profound disagreements over what her job allows her to give, over how much space policing provides the fingers to bloom as any hand unfurls. It was pitch black, pouring rain. In my memory, the night was filled with dark figures with long trench coats and top hats, a frighteningly gritty crime occurring right around every corner.

I explain to Jahvaris how you stayed in the car as Bhakti walked inside the store, and after a few minutes, she stepped back out with someone it seemed like she knew. How you couldn't hear what they were talking about, but you saw our second-eldest sister's friend offer her a cigarette, and you saw her take it. How your heart stopped. I don't think you judged her at all, but Mata had never missed a chance to warn about how deadly cigarettes were, and so it would make sense if you were sure Bhakti would someday pay with her life. It would make sense if that was why you began to cry.

"That sounds ridiculous now," I tell Jahvaris, still laughing and taking another drag of the Newport. I consider tossing it into a puddle of sandy water on the side of the road but don't. I briefly wonder how sand made it this far away from the beach and into the middle of Brooklyn. Since Mata's diagnosis, I had been drinking more, smoking more, and pulling away from Timothy more because I didn't want to face his concern over my increasing turn to substances, only to find myself now facing Jahvaris, and the coronavirus pandemic had exacerbated it all.

"I mean, it was only a cigarette, but I was sobbing. I don't even think she smoked regularly or anything," I say with a hollow laugh. "As I got older I realized, it's only a cigarette," I continue, taking another drag. "We're all going to die anyway."

A few weeks after I found out about Mata's cancer, Timothy was invited to do a poetry reading at the Brooklyn Museum. There were a few hours between the end of the workday and the show, so I asked Jahvaris to get a drink with me to kill the time. A few drinks, if I'm being honest. I'm not always. Once Jahvaris and I arrived at the museum, I tried to hide my tipsiness from Timothy because he was starting to believe I had a drinking problem, and I didn't want to add fuel to the fire. He greeted me with a kiss, and I held my gasoline breath for fear of exploding.

After Mata's diagnosis, everything already felt like a hand about to strike a match in a gaseous place, and COVID-19 was the flame. Every second feels like it could be the one in which I lose everything, and drinking and smoking my worries away often seems more plausible than preparing.

Embracing the slow death often seems more realistic than facing any other, so I hide behind numbing drugs and nicotine words that offered relief in the moment, without concerning myself with when the dying comes roaring back.

Jahvaris has always wanted the best for his friends. "I just want you to be happy," he repeats so often that the phrase has become a running joke in our circle. Right now, the drinking and smoking are making me happy. If there is anyone who would understand my need to escape, I thought, it would be Jahvaris. His brother Trayvon Martin's murder at the hands of a neighborhood watchman in 2012 had become a rallying cry for an entire Black liberation movement, so he must have been struggling to avoid the imminent shadow of death now, too.

"You have to imagine," I tell him, taking another drag, "how this could be a comfort. Don't you just want me to be happy?" I ask, even though I know we're all going to die anyway.

I laugh again, but his expression does not change.

"Real happiness isn't so fleeting," Jahvaris replies. And somehow I know he isn't judging me at all. "Yes, we're all going to die, but you don't have to die that way."

And in this moment, Hari-Gaura, I realize that I dismissed your fear of our sister dying, just to replace it with my own fear of death. With a fear that seemed quieter and calmer, more mature. Capitalism and its cult of productivity encourage individuals to want to seem above it all, to seem unbothered, to have their shit together no matter what is going on around them. To not let the danger of the world get to them, because then they won't do anything about the danger. Because then they'll take the fleeting happiness and slow death over the sudden risks and lasting joys that children know. Because then I'd stay running from you.

But there is another way. There has always been another way.

I don't know if Jahvaris sees you in me, but I see you more clearly around friends who hold me accountable for my health and well-being, even through the phone. I see you more clearly now. I finally throw away the rest of the cigarette—at least this time. The fear, it is still here, but I feel some real happiness, too. Not comfort—joy. And I just want to make it last this time. There are many more terrors I'll have to face.

CHAPTER NINETEEN

ABOLITION

At her worst, Mother Bhūmi was as terrifying as anything I'd ever seen. There was no telling what could set her off, and when something did, her anger would erupt like a volcano in her throat. As she yelled, saliva would foam to fill her mouth and have to be dodged like cascading lava. The turmeric-colored jaundice of her eyes would be eclipsed by molten crimson as they no longer dared to close, not even for a blink.

Nothing could interrupt her furor but Kṛṣṇa or the man she still loved who no longer lived, both of whom she called upon in desperation when spouting off about whatever had prompted this episode proved insufficient. Father Rupchand never showed up, but sometimes her shouts of "Kṛṣṇa" were enough to calm her. When they weren't, I was afraid Mother Bhūmi would wind up attacking me, even though she never did. Sometimes, she would strike out at Mata, though. Sometimes, I didn't know if she would ever stop striking out. Sometimes, it seemed as if she didn't. There are nights I still see my grandmother's face in my nightmares.

For the most part, Mata held her own during these natural disasters. Daddy helped out as best any relief worker could, when even

Kanye West could once see clearly how the state withholds relief from Black people. Mata's calm in the storm of her mother fraying apart was too depressing to envy but was a quality I revered nonetheless.

I understood that our mother didn't want to call the police on hers, and though still quite young, I understood why.

I had seen cops slamming Mother Bhūmi's frail body to the ground with my own eyes, and I'd seen Mata watching it happen. I'd seen how something inside Mata broke each time she watched her mother break down, and how each time Mother Bhūmi had a break-down, Mata tried something a little different, chanted "Hare Kṛṣṇa" a little louder, until she could hardly speak another name of her god.

Mata's near-tireless desire for an alternative to police in these impossible moments was fueled by a monumental love for her mother. A love that acknowledged both that Mother Bhūmi could harm and be harmed, and that she shouldn't be limited to being understood as exclusively committing or at the mercy of abuse. A complicated love. A Black love. The same love I know now that, despite our strained history, Mata has for me. The same love I have been using this whole book to try and find my way back to knowing how to give.

Mata understood that her mother didn't deserve to be punished for the harm her mental illness exacerbated, and yet punishment was all that the carceral state offered. Still, Mata prayed and prayed for something else, for a world outside of this one, and never stopped believing in a god who could make that a reality.

I am my mother's child, for better and for worse. Maybe it was inevitable that I would wind up on what also feels like an endless spiritual quest for the means to manage the harms done by the people I love without furthering those harms. Maybe it was inevitable that I would also end up failing so often.

I am more convinced than ever that the work to abolish prisons and police and to repair the fracture caused by carceral dissonance is that chant—the one birthday gift Mata has always asked for. The one thing that would allow my mother, like Korryn Gaines, to live on forever, by destroying the most fundamental tool with which this world has attempted to steal her children, her legacy, her lifeblood away.

~

Every time I visited the zoo as a child, I thought about how cruel it seemed that anyone would confine animals to cages and call it just, say it was for their own good, when I could see so clearly these animals were yearning for freedom. I always preferred the roaming cows of Gita Nagari and could never even fathom keeping my dog in a kennel for more than a brief moment.

And so the idea of humans in cages never sat well with me, even when I'd learned all the justifications. When Michelle Alexander outlined in *The New Jim Crow* how today's prisons are an extension of segregationist policies in this country, which themselves were an extension of chattel slavery, I knew—like Korryn wanted Kodi to know—that the enforcers of the carceral state's justice "are not for us. They want to kill us." I knew that they never were, and always have. I knew that there was something wrong with how the state could both murder Amadou Diallo, Oscar Grant, Sandra Bland, and Rekia Boyd and then present itself as the arbiter of justice in their murder cases. There was something unjustifiable in how the state could use carceral violence to confine and kill Black people, whom I could feel so clearly yearning for freedom, and call it just, say it was for our own good.

I knew all this, just like I knew why Mata didn't call the police on Mother Bhūmi—even as a boy. But when I grew up, I also learned how to disregard my childhood understandings, conditioned by misafropedia to believe that Black children don't really know anything. Instead of embracing what I understood early on about the fundamental wrongness of prisons, I learned to ask myself the kinds of questions about prison abolition that I heard other rational adults asking around me: "Without prisons, where do all the rapists and murderers go? What do we replace prisons with?"

My cousin Eric has been in prison for most of my life. When I was in middle school, he got out after his first extended stint for robbery, which he'd started when he was a teenager. I was so excited to finally see him free again. But maybe he never really was.

I don't mean that the state threw him right back into the cage, although like many of those who are raked through the carceral system, he didn't escape that fate either. He did return to prison when he was convicted of raping and murdering fifty-seven-year-old Susan Blockson just a few years later and sentenced to life—after the prosecutor argued that he was "the worst offender and this is the worst offense." What I mean is that at trial Eric's lawyers explained in explicit detail how Auntie Cheryl's drug abuse had deprived my cousin of his childhood—how her child had often become the drug she abused the worst—and how his first prison sentence, and the frequent and accepted violence of all types he endured throughout it, only reinforced that loss. I mean that his mother was described as foaming at the mouth, her eyes turning crimson red while she struck him with whatever she could get her hands on, all for being a child.

"I was subjected to countless forms of abuse," Eric tells me. "No one cared if I lived or died. There was brainwashing, turning siblings against siblings. I was very much alone, (literally) locked in a pitch-black dungeon, starving. I was just a kid . . . I was just a kid."

Auntie Cheryl was her mother's child, for better and for worse, and this legacy Eric inherited of Black childhoods stolen away meant that he had known a type of prison his entire life. Even before his first conviction. A prison created, as all prisons are, based on the false idea that carceral punishment befalls only those who are deserving.

This is the same idea that led a small group of my cousins to gossip in front of me when I was just a child—a queer child—about their unconfirmed assumptions that Eric had switched over to "that life," imagining for him experiences with sexual violence the first time he was incarcerated, without any proof other than knowing prison to be a breeding ground for sexual violence. The same idea led them to show more worry, at least it seemed to me as a repressed queer child, that "that life" could be gay than that it could have involved rape.

I had known certain aspects of this type of prison, too, a prison that is built on allowing, even endorsing, certain abuses in the name of punishing a person for transgressing the rules of an anti-Black, anti-queer, misafropedic society. And when some abuses are endorsed, as they always are in a carceral system that uses abuse to punish people, the vulnerable are always collateral, because they, by definition, are the most likely to have their abuse justified.

At her worst Mother Bhūmi was as terrifying as anything I'd ever seen, but this was also when she most needed healing. It's this need for healing that is always lost when we demand punishment for all crimes. A punitive world flattens us. It makes us think of each other within the suffocating limits of either good or bad, deserving of punishment or innocent, instead of seeing each other as the complex beings we are. But Mother Bhūmi, like all of us, contained multitudes and histories and context. None of us are mindless monsters, no matter if our mouths foam up when we attack those who do not deserve it. None of us are *just* murderers or rapists, even if we have committed murder or rape. Even if we must be taken out of a space to ensure the safety of others.

I do not mean to imply that Susan Blockson's family had no right to rage or to wish violence on her murderer (although Eric insists on his innocence to this day, and he certainly did not have the resources to mount a convincing defense). And I don't mean to ask that we have more empathy for those who enact abuse, nor to deny that there should be consequences when a person harms someone else. I would never ask Blockson's family to forgive her killer or to put themselves in his shoes. I am jaded about "merciful" gods forever compelling Black people to forgive and empathize with our abusers while the abuse continues without accountability. It was Mata, in all her valiant work toward an alternative to punishment, who showed me the ultimate failure of this kind of mercy. It was she who sometimes chose only to keep chanting in response to Mother Bhūmi physically attacking her in front of her children, only to keep chanting in response to my grandmother spending months terrorizing Visnu and Kiss when they were just babies, calling them sinful demons who were damned to hell. To me, this type of forgiveness is little better than punishment. Both refuse the question of redress: this forgiveness does so out of a too-flattened sense of kindness, and punishment does it out of resentment. Mata may not have always fully realized what I've come to understand in my attempt to live my name, which is that the best parts of her chanting—the abolitionist parts—were always more than the words and the beads.

Abolition posits that redress is possible when we are allowed to hold resentment and kindness simultaneously, without these sentiments being forced into binary opposition. It posits that people who do bad things can do better, in this life or the next, if acknowledged as being part of a community to which they are accountable, a community that cares for and supports them without letting them off the hook. And I know this to be true, because I talk with my big cuz all the time, and he shares inspiring stories and beautiful dreams and compassionate words and loving thoughts. Ours would be a better world if he could share those things with more people, and he can't share them within the confines of prison any more than he could if he stayed committed to the carceral logics that lead people to rape and murder. The same carceral logics that make prisons petri dishes for the sexual violence and abuse and unnatural deaths that the most vulnerable communities will endure both within and outside of prisons for as long as prisons exist.

It may not be possible to compose stories and dreams and words powerful enough to make up for the lack of beauty and compassion and love a person feels when their family member is murdered and that they might feel when crossing paths with the person who presumably committed that act. To say that prison is no place for harm-doers is not to say that living in proximity with those they've harmed is the place for them either.

There is no single, simple answer to what a healing response might look like in the absence of prisons. But there are simple questions we can ask ourselves and our communities to find the answer for us in a given moment: Am I taking this action against a perpetrator of harm to perpetrate more harm against them? Or will it truly help me (and/or others) not just to feel better momentarily but to carry less harm and hurt into the world? And what can I learn from my ancestors and other Indigenous people about healing without reinforcing carceral systems?

Sometimes, many times, our response to harms might contain conflicting motivations because they were never meant to fall neatly within a binary either. Ethicist Jill Stauffer confronts this possibility in *Ethical Loneliness*, analyzing Jean Améry's writings on his desire for violent retribution in response to the horrors he experienced during the Holocaust. Stauffer argues that Améry is an example of someone who wanted payback "not (or not only) out of a will to harm others but in order to regain a moral equivalence stolen from him by abuse."[44] Healing cannot come out of punishment because punishment's only purpose is to create more harm. But healing can sometimes entail limited harm, in order to lessen harm ultimately. And when this is the case, the desire to commit an act that entails some harm can't be dismissed as purely punitive. But we can truly know whether our desire for harm can be measured as part of a healing practice only when we are in tune with our whole selves and with our communities. The carceral state can never answer these questions for us.

Auntie Cheryl is Mother Bhūmi's daughter, and Eric and I are both the sons of Mother Bhūmi's daughters. The history and context of what we have done in our lives certainly doesn't excuse any abuse we've enacted. Acknowledging the fullness of my experiences not only forces me to rethink how I respond to others' harmful actions but also demands I acknowledge my own harmful actions, even when I have deluded myself into thinking I am one of the "good ones."

Fully acknowledging my reality would mean rejecting all that I have learned about punishing myself and others in my vain attempt to find comfort in this world, at the expense of their freedom and mine. At the expense of their childhood and mine.

My friend and fellow writer Darnell L. Moore once told me that there is no story worth telling that isn't self-reflective, and that is the beating heart of abolition. This is why abolition requires repairing the fracture caused by the carceral dissonance within ourselves.

Yes, prisons are cruel structures, but abolition forces us to also reckon with cruelty as a feature of a world that is divided into binaries of good and evil. These binaries keep that world turning by signifying who gets punished for crimes and when.

As I stopped trusting what I'd known about the cruelty of incarceration in childhood, I could hear inarguable statements like "there are people locked in prisons who don't belong there" and still support the prison system. I could even acknowledge that prison doesn't lead to rehabilitation for the murderers or rapists that I had convinced myself *do* belong there. I could understand that the institution of prison evolved from slavery, transforming into convict leasing and chain gangs to the monstrosity it is today. I could read all the articles and books about how prisons, by design, function as a way to continue the legacy of capture for Black people. But because I had adopted misafropedic thinking and dismissed a prison-free world as the naive idealism of a Black child, I could still defend the necessity of prisons.

Carceral dissonance means being okay with someone else paying the price of the undeniable horrors that come with prison culture. I claimed to be concerned about murder and rape, but murder and rape happen in prison to the most marginalized—to queer folk, to women, to disabled people, to transgender folk, and of course to Black people—at even greater degrees than they do on the outside. To truly care about murder and rape, I would also have to truly care about the conditions for murder and rape that are inherent to the way prisons have been designed.

The self-reflective question isn't where the murderers and rapists go in a world without prisons. It's how we fill the lack that drives people to take what isn't theirs in a world that responds to lack *with* prisons. If we continue to uphold the practices of this world, some of these people may go to prison, but they won't stop murdering and raping while there, or once released. Many of them go easily instead into the highest offices, which is why both Presidents Donald Trump and Bill Clinton have been credibly accused of rape with little effect on their public support. Murderers and rapists also go easily into the police force and prison administrations.[45] And as long as we are okay with someone else paying these prices, rapists and murderers go easily into the psyches of all of us who grow up in a world built by murder and rape. They convince us that any other world is impossible to create, just so that they will always exist.

~

In 2011, Cherán, a small Central Mexican town, had finally had enough. Faced with increased aggression by exploitative loggers who conspired with cartels and state politicians to exploit and destroy forests and water sources, a women-led group of the area's Indigenous Purépecha community began an uprising against what they began calling "the narco government." This uprising eventually returned the town to a form of self-governance they claimed was based on the town's practices before political parties and institutions infiltrated the community decades earlier. Along with the loggers, state politicians and state police were also banned from the town.

Afterward, three hundred campfire barricades were erected across Cherán for security purposes, including one in each of the city's four neighborhoods. They became known collectively as the fogatas and doubled as nightly meeting places for the town to discuss governance. According to international watchdog against state repression El Enemigo Común, "Each fogata would send proposals and a representative to neighborhood assemblies and then to community assemblies. The fogata element of the communal government in Cherán was the only new element" to be added to its historical stateless form of governance.

BBC reporter Linda Pressly writes that Michoacán, the state in which the Purépecha community of Cherán resides, has one of the highest rates of violent crime in the country. But this violence, of course, is facilitated by centuries of colonialism and exploitation, which cannot be removed from the state government the people of Cherán rebelled against. And in the town's previous year, as Pressly writes with palpable surprise, without state police and the politicians who use them to punish their opposition, there have been no recorded murders, kidnappings, or disappearances. These acts would still be referred to the attorney general if they were to occur, but the town deals with other transgressions—which have mostly been alcohol related since the uprising—primarily through alternatives such as fines and service.

I don't want to romanticize Cherán, where I have not been and whose people I do not know. These exact strategies cannot possibly work for every community, and certainly anti-Blackness would throw another wrench into any plans for a Black community liberated from police and prisons. Even some other Mexican towns that have tried to follow Cherán's revolutionary model have failed. But the city is just one example among many others showing that what we are told is impossible is not.

No one would be surprised by this story if we did not operate under colonized understandings and carceral thinking. A police state has never been inevitable. Of course it is possible to trust each other more than we trust our oppressors. Across the globe, there are histories of Indigenous communities without police and prisons, and if I have realized anything through therapy and ancestor communication, it's that our past is never gone forever.

Repairing the fracture caused by carceral dissonance and becoming whole with our childhoods requires abolition because it means trusting ourselves to be more than mindless monsters who would violate each other as soon as police are no longer there to keep us in our place.

Abolition doesn't propose that once prisons are gone, all society's ills will disappear. It proposes that illness is meant to be treated in the first place, not locked away. It proposes that we commit to finding ways to treat our ills now, together, no matter how impossible or dangerous or childish the world might make it seem.

～

"It's just impossible," my sister Ganga said when she called me a few years ago to talk about her on-again-off-again husband, Śiva. At the time, they were off.

"I've been trying to make it work, but I think we would both be healthier apart. I don't think he's ready to heal."

"I mean, are any of us?" I asked, not completely serious. I love Śiva and was sorry to see things end up this way. But I had witnessed the fraying of their relationship enough times to know beforehand that this was coming, and each time it came closer to finality. And each time I knew Ganga was right.

"He's just so emotionally immature. I want to believe I can work with him, but I can't," she said. "And now he refuses to send my belongings to school, so I was going to go pick them up. Will you come with me?"

Ganga couched the request in her need for someone to drive the U-Haul because she had to drive her SUV, but I interpreted that to mean she was also worried. I knew from Mata what an expert at hiding their worry looks like, and Ganga is the most like our mother of all of us. Maybe she was also looking for alternatives to a situation with impossible answers. Maybe she didn't feel completely comfortable to confront Śiva on her own. Maybe she didn't want Śiva harmed by potential police violence if she turned to them for help instead, even if he would not take responsibility for his own harms against her yet.

Ganga said Śiva had never been physically violent with her, and he doesn't seem to me like that type of person, but they never do. Her ex-boyfriend Andrew didn't seem like that type of person either, but he was. I once said to her that I wished she would have told me about Andrew when that happened, that I would have killed him, even though I was still a teenager at the time. That I was sad and angry at everything that got in the way of us having the type of relationship where she could tell me those things. I was doing that thing I sometimes still do where I make a woman's problems all about how I should be able to save them. The offer to accompany her was, I guess, her way of offering healing into that relationship, of reclaiming it for a new future. *If you want to be there for me, here is your chance.* And so, even though I had lost my glasses and couldn't really see well enough to drive, I told her yes. *Of course I will go. We will get your belongings. I will be there for you.*

When we got to the door, my heart was pounding. Śiva is a big man. I hadn't gotten into a fight in years, and though I didn't think it would come to that, I didn't even want to consider the possibility of breaking that streak with someone I loved, and still do. A part of me wanted to just have Ganga call the police and have them deal with it. That would have been easier. So much easier.

When you find yourself facing real conflict, what it means to want alternatives to police and prisons comes into clearer, more damning focus, even if you are missing your glasses. When you're up against someone who is not ready to heal, coming to them with an approach based on healing is not always easy. Getting involved in these situations can cause oneself physical harm or exacerbate the situation for the more vulnerable party later. But it is these moments, where there is no easy answer, that matter most. It is in moments of crisis that Korryn Gaines's words really come into play.

Showing up for my sisters has always been difficult, which is probably why Ganga and I didn't have the kind of relationship where she could tell me everything before I started to get back in touch with my childhood, and therefore my courage. It's also probably why I could tell Śiva didn't expect to see me there. When he did, his voice softened. He addressed me calmly, aimed all his aggression at Ganga, his wife, the most vulnerable. He protested to her when I went in to take what she said she needed. No physical altercation ever occurred, but I felt the exhaustion of showing up for my sister in my body all the same.

The police would later tell Ganga that, because she and Śiva were married, the law said that she could not take anything from their home. The law said nothing she owned was hers. This was the solution she was supposed to turn to.

A few months ago, a friend experienced a mental health crisis and announced their intentions for suicide on Facebook. Charleena Lyles had recently been killed by Seattle police after having her own mental breakdown, and I knew bringing police into this situation would be inviting the very entity that had just demonstrated the propensity to worsen all my friend's problems. I immediately threw on a coat and called a car to get to my friend's apartment as soon as possible. But still I turned hesitantly to my fiancé, feeling in my anxious body the same exhaustion I'd felt at Ganga's house, and asked, "Should we call the police?"

What do Black people who want to commit to abolition do when we have a crisis and cannot put out the fire on our own? What do we do when we are under threat? Violated? Attacked? Living through a global health pandemic? When our loved ones are killed? The state presents us with one answer on purpose. The state makes police and prisons seem inevitable on purpose. Without the state enforcing laws to keep our lives in order, no one would ever be safe, we are told.

But I have never been safe.

Ganga and her belongings were never safe. My friend was never safe. The only options the state gives are meant to create the illusion of safety. Are meant to make sure we can go on living without a connection to our childhoods, and call that living. If the police don't immediately kill our loved ones in a crisis, they are here only to make sure that our loved ones can go on living without wanting to.

"Let's just get there first," Timothy said as I shook with the possibility of my friend suffering, a caring reminder of what was at stake. "We're only ten minutes away," he reasoned, giving off a calm that resembled my mother and that I did not envy but needed nonetheless.

Sure enough, when we got to our friend's apartment, the police had just broken down the door. As someone who has experienced my own home being smashed into, I can imagine that this was its own compounding trauma. But our friend was still conscious and would be okay—as okay as anyone can be when they decide not to be here anymore and others decide otherwise for them and call that love. I still don't know the answer to the question my friend and colleague Amber Butts poses in an essay for RaceBaitr: "Are the ones we love able to choose death, or is our relationship with them about ownership, possession, and obligation? If it is, we are not allowed living *or* dying as our full selves."[46]

I'm not sure whether refusing to call the police in that specific instance, or even wanting to stop my friend from taking their own life in the first place, was a more legitimate love, but I'm sure that building a world that my friend wants to live in is. And I'm sure that *this* world, with all its prisons, both physical and otherwise and made of our own carceral ideologies, is not that one.

I'm sure that I have work to do to create the new world my friend deserved. That I deserved as a child. That Susan Blockson and Eric and Auntie Cheryl and Mother Bhūmi deserved. I'm sure that I can try harder to heal from my own abusive ways that contribute to making this world so punitive. I'm sure that I can try harder to ensure that all my responses to crises, both my own and those of others, are based in healing, which would require them not to involve an abusive police force, even when it's scary or dangerous or exhausting.

I can better prepare for another situation like my friend's crisis by laying out in advance the conditions for whom to call and when. I can better help others prepare for other crises, like by assisting my sister and friends who might need help in buying weapons for self-defense, and by committing to learning skills myself so that none of us have to rely on the state's claim to defend us. I can do a better job at being ready to challenge anyone who might abuse others in my presence, including myself. I can do a better job of not turning every challenge into a power play of punishment. I can let my neighbors know that in the middle of a public health crisis, they can rely on me to pick up groceries when they aren't able to do so themselves. I can do a better job of letting my loved ones know that I will always be there if they need me, and I can do a better job at actually showing up.

I know better is possible because when I was a child and looked in Mother Bhūmi's face at her worst, I still saw my grandmother. I know better is possible because it wasn't until later that I started seeing the face of my own grandma as nothing more than a nightmare. I know better is possible because I saw Mata searching for better, and I am still her son. I am still her son after all we've been through.

There is no void that prisons and punishment leave behind that is imperative to fill. Prisons and punishment *are* the void. Over centuries they have ripped my family away from each other. Anything else that I ask for, everything else that I ask for, is at least a step closer to our childhoods. Anything other than prisons and punishment brings me at least a little closer back to a sense of wholeness.

"It makes me want to cry remembering that day," Margarita Elvira Romero, one of the women who conspired against the Cherán loggers, told Pressly about the day of the uprising. "It was like a horror movie—but it was the best thing we could have done."

Abolition in practice sometimes feels like a colonizer's idea of a horror movie, especially in the midst of a pandemic, and it matters that this is what Romero told Pressly and how Pressly translated it. Truly healing from this monstrous violence means acknowledging the monsters everywhere, which includes those in ourselves. And I'd be a damn liar if I said that didn't make me want to cry sometimes. I'd be a damn liar if I said it isn't hard when I see Mother Bhūmi's face in my mother. In the mirror. In Eric and Śiva, too. But the carceral state wants us to be afraid of these difficult feelings for a reason. We owe it to ourselves to refuse how they condition fear and horror. We owe it to our children. I owe it to myself.

Because those walks with Mother Bhūmi around the block are still the best things I could have ever done. Because I couldn't have done them without beginning to understand again that alternatives to this carceral world exist. Without beginning to understand again the kind of love I used to know. I used to wish every day since she died that I could have gone on one last walk around the block with my grandma. I wished and wished that my childhood self could have seen her the way I came to know her when I started facing my nightmares, convinced that the childhood version of me had run out of time. But where he had run was never the end of the story.

A PRAYER FOR MY GRANDMOTHER

Hari-Gaura,

There was one walk I took with Mother Bhūmi where she barely spoke a word the entire time. This had never happened before, at least not the whole way through. Even during the strolls where I zoned out as she prattled on—and this was most of them— Grandma hardly skipped two beats of her monologues, requiring less that I show I was listening than that I allow her room to speak, just like Daddy.

Not this time. This time, I helped our grandmother slide her small feet into her beaded flats, held her arm gently as she glided down the front steps from the foyer of the Beechwood house, and waited for her lecture to begin as I assisted her to the sidewalk, but it never did.

"Is something wrong?" I asked, zipping up my jacket in the brisk wind and double-checking to make sure hers was fastened, too.

"No," she replied calmly, tightening her head wrap before it came loose.

I waited impatiently as we slowly made our way to the first cross street, and then to the main street, Taylor Road, where we took a right turn, and then to the next corner, where we turned right again to circle back home, but an elaboration never came. Mother Bhūmi looked fine enough. Much sturdier physically than the final time we would go on one of our walks. In fact, there would come a few years yet until that fateful day.

But on that day, the silence worried me more than her trembling voice ever could. I couldn't seem to find any suitable resting place for my hands, so I improvised something of an odd dance with my arms as my palms leaked sweat. My jaw clenched and unclenched just for the sake of the noise the pressure created in my head, killing my teeth in the process. I wasn't used to having to sit in the silence with our grandmother, and purely in order to keep the comfort of familiarity, I would welcome even a loud and dying thing before something quietly alive.

I'll never know for sure what was going through Grandma's mind then, but this time it wasn't room to speak that she was asking for. I believe now that she was reminding me that some things don't have to make noise to be present, and that it's important to listen to those things, too.

I think Mother Bhūmi was showing me that, like you, I might not one day hear her—I may not even see her—but that wouldn't mean she wasn't always there. That wouldn't mean she wasn't always okay. That wouldn't mean I couldn't always be okay in my relationship to her, even though so much had gone unsaid. I think now that she was preparing me to face the anxiety of the social isolation wreaked by this global pandemic. I think she was preparing me how to love and receive love when people don't or can't always show up the way I'm used to them showing up. How to love when *I* can't show up the way that the other person and I are used to.

"Is this working for you?" my therapist asked at the end of our last session. "Are you able to recognize when your Inner Child is communicating with you outside of this room, and to care for them?"

"I think I am getting better at it," I reply. "But that's for Hari-Gaura to say, isn't it?"

My therapist just smiled and checked for the time. "Well, you look to be managing, and I'm proud of you. But we have to end here."

I don't know if I will always recognize you, but I notice you with me so much more now. A few days ago, as our father barreled on about attempts at his emasculation, I could feel you here. I could hear you asking me to reject my complacency in the familiarity of this monologue for your sake. And I finally worked up a courage I hadn't really found before to actually challenge him to be accountable. And when I asked, as lovingly as I could, why he and Mata never warned their children of the known child predators in the Hare Kṛṣṇa community—a question you deserved someone demand an answer to—he interrupted his defensiveness to offer a sincere apology, albeit a very brief one.

"Son," he said with a weighty sigh, "I should have protected you better. I really should have protected you better."

And Mata still vigorously holds on to the belief that these same communities are the best protection one can offer their children, even with their child predators and without addressing their entrenched misafropedia. Sometimes I think this still means she can't always see the violence against children that occurs in the name of her faith. But it was through knowing that you were here, needing me to, that I managed to overcome my fear of rejection to ask her to read this book and to address what I'd learned about the horrors in the history of New Vrindaban. And she did.

"It was hard," she said quietly, "but this is a chapter in history that we should learn from, Hari-Gaura."

These small moments of healing still don't come easy. They still come with sweaty palms and clenched jaws and nightmares. They still come with tears and resistance and rage and frustration, and death is always on the horizon. But they also come with brilliant spurts of a love I am only now beginning to know again. A love that I always needed. A love that you so generously bring but that you always needed, too.

These moments of healing come with the laughter my father bequeathed to me, laughter I can now easily conjure just thinking about how the hair sprouting all over my body, which once made me feel so beastly, might be the same hair that Mata made us cut off in that failed attempt to force us into manhood all those years ago, the same hair I've missed for so long. These moments come with laughter just thinking about how I've now learned to embrace all the scars on this body that show me how to get back to you. Scars I have filled with ink and stories, stories I can return to only now that I have a deeper understanding.

And this laughter sometimes fills my whole belly until there is no room for anxiety to turn it, just as the tattoo depicting another of Mother Bhūmi's pastimes fills the largest of these scars. It illustrates the pastime about the four enlightened souls who decided to stay in the bodies of young boys so as not to be burdened with the distractions and false ego of adulthood. The four boys were turned away from the gates of heaven because the gatekeepers couldn't believe anyone so young could be enlightened enough to be in the presence of god. After the boys cursed the gatekeepers for their ignorance, condemning them to spend either three lifetimes as demons or seven as saintly people, the gatekeepers chose three just to get back home faster. They were sent down to this world to struggle with their god, knowing they could not beat him, not needing to, and they chose this timeline that others may not have chosen because they loved him. My back tattoo fills the scar with an image from the moment after one of the gatekeepers, in his first demon life, performed sacrifices even more powerful than Dhruva's. After the gods blessed the demon for his sacrifices with any benediction other than immortality, he thought he could outsmart them by asking for the boon not to be killed inside a building or out, during daytime or at night, on the ground or in the sky, by human or by beast. He did not know that some gods, like those my ancestors call me to, cannot be outsmarted.

The tattoo fills this largest scar with a depiction of Narasiṃha, Kṛṣṇa's incarnation as a half man, half lion—a body he chose in order to kill the demon on a veranda, during dusk, on his lap, just to protect the demon's son. A reminder that some violence is righteous, that binary thinking creates foolish shields, that children always deserve the truer protection of the gods I now pray to. The tattoo evoked Mata's laughter, too, when my cousin came to her with concern after seeing it, so frightened by my demons and the reasons I chose to face them instead of continuing to run away. We laugh, but I understand why this is such a frightening thing to so many.

And now our mother asks about Timothy whenever you and I speak to her, which is whenever she has the energy, as she battles through the latest round of cancer treatment, having returned back to the States.

Now our father has cried many times to us about how much he loves our mother and how afraid he is to lose her. Before this year I had seen him cry only one or two times in my entire life because of what always seemed to be an inflexible commitment to a stoic ideal of manhood.

Now both of our parents have agreed to come to our queer wedding, even though they are honest about their own anxieties around doing so. Now keeping our parents safe and healthy is more important, and having them at the wedding isn't all that matters. Now we can apologize sincerely to our parents for the harms we've brought them, too.

Now Mother Bhūmi is still here in the silence, walking with us everywhere that we go. Because now I can feel you here walking, too.

∼

I know that there is still a long, long journey left to truly heal from all this, but I also know that the destination is where you came from. I know that it is not a destination at all in the colonial sense of the word—it is not located in a single space and time in the form of some unchanging, inflexible tome of knowledge that you capture when you have found the end. You did not come from an unchanging world of capture. I know that the end is out of time as I thought I knew it, and into time as my ancestors do. Some parts of these relationships will never be mended in this life—but I can, and I will.

I swear to you: I will.

ACKNOWLEDGMENTS

While writing this book and reckoning with all the ghosts that were excavated in the process, I cried often, laughed maniacally just as much, questioned my sanity and my skills and my motives, learned to trust myself even with those questions still hanging thick in the air, then forgot and learned and forgot and learned to trust again. I lost friends and loved ones and gained a much deeper relationship with so many others.

Those others, the ones who showed me love through it all—through the stress of writing the first terrible draft, and the second terrible draft, and the third and fourth and fifth, up until all my conflicting thoughts and beliefs and stories finally began to come together in a readable way (even though some will debate whether this final product is not a terrible draft itself)—are owed so much from me. Writing this memoir was way more work than I thought it would be, was way more about the community I wrote it with and for than about me writing at all, and that community is owed so much greater appreciation than any acknowledgments can express. There are too many to name, and if you aren't mentioned due to some oversight, I hope you are able to forgive me, but this is only the start of the rest of a life I promise to spend in gratitude to all of you.

Mata, thank you for modeling healing and what it means to always strive to be a better, more caring person every day. Thank you for encouraging me to tell my truth, even in the moments it didn't line up with yours. I couldn't have written this, or anything worthwhile that I have ever written, without you teaching me what loving words can do.

Daddy, I'll always remember the importance of living my name, inshallah, and that is because of you. I hope you always remember how much I appreciate you for that.

Thank you, Rani, for your boundless generosity and for always being there for the rest of us; Bhakti, for showing up even when it's hard and trusting me to show up even when neither of us quite knows what showing up might look like; Kṛṣṇa-Kumari, for protecting me in the same beautiful way you have always protected your own children; Syama, for being so dope and cool and my model in so many ways without even trying; Mohan, for caring about the world so much it hurts, so much it heals, too. It's clear to me that you are all central to the most beautiful parts of this book, even in the places you're not named.

Thank you, Ganga, for reading drafts and holding me accountable when I needed that, for never being afraid to call out what is wrong and fight for what's right, for holding Mata's spirit so close to your own. So much of my capacity to deal with her illness is because I see her in you. Thank you, Ghanasyam, for being kind and generous and dope yourself, for somehow personifying all the best parts of this family.

Thank you, Kiss, for always operating out of love. I can't recall the last time I noticed it seeming like you didn't, and I'm sorry if there were moments when you couldn't say the same about me. Thank you, Visnu, for being so brilliant and passionate and unconditionally yourself, and for trusting me to guide you through the fire that such things cause. So much of this book I wrote so that you two can come out the other side of the flame stronger than I did, and so many parts of both of you are already more powerful than I could ever fathom.

Thank you, Nigel, Khadijah, Makedah, Vidah, Rasheed, Tauheedah, and David for adding a whole 'nother layer of love to this family.

Thank you, Zara, Rafe, Noah, Kira, Marlon, Jacob, Kirk Jr., Monique, Keval, Nimai, Peyton, Syama Jr., Prahlad, and Dominique for being the kindest and smartest nieces and nephews I could ever ask for. I hope when you are each old enough to read it, this book inspires you to continue the wonderful work you are already doing of taking care of each other and of your newest siblings/cousins, Toshani, Malani, and Aja.

Thank you to my agent, Rayhané, for always being in my corner and having so much patience as I learned my way through this field, and to Hafizah and Camille for giving me space to get my thoughts down clearly and helping make everything better through your careful editing. Thank you, Carmen, Emma, and everyone else on the Little A team for seeing me through this process, and Faceout Studio for designing and David for illustrating this gorgeous cover (I am still in awe!).

Thank you, Lisa, for taking care of the things and the people you love in awesome ways, and Phillip for believing in and supporting me even while maintaining the highest standards (which is only suitable to your being a master of this craft).

Thank you, Eric, Omar, and Shanika for healing me and showing me how to heal myself.

Thank you, George Johnson, Alex, and Aman for being the best writing partners, for watching me smash buttons into the keyboard and being generous enough to sometimes read what came out (then pointing me in the right direction even when the words didn't make sense), and Darnell, Kiese, Robert, Blair, and Steven, for loving us as you do and always offering guidance and support at every stage of my career.

Thank you, George Arnett, Leon, Jahvaris, Shikeith, Jon, and Gerry, for being ever-present and consistently encouraging and for keeping those group chats buzzing when we've been stuck so far away for so long and all needed this friend group more than ever. And thank you, Kevin, Ahmad, Daniel, Henry, and Sevonna for keeping me on track and always being there, too. Thank you, Darrius, for all those sad nights that you let me come over for a beer and a cigarette after writing through trauma, Johania and Nathanie for showing that you really meant it when you said we would always be there for each other (even though we still don't see each other enough!), and Q for all the times you wouldn't let me pay for hookah even when I only vented about how hard this book was the whole time we smoked it.

Thank you, Preston, Myesha, Hess, Brittney, and Chelsea for teaching me so many things about Black spirituality when I didn't even know our interactions to be lessons, and Delia and Tabias for keeping the invitation open for me to be a part of a community that learns and grows together. Thank you, Raquel, Bree, and Ro, whom I have still never met in person (I hope we can fix that soon!), but who have contributed more to my understandings of Blackness as my first real group of online friends than the majority of people with whom I have IRL relationships.

Thank you, Amber, Rachael, and Arielle for contributing so much to a Black AF, loving space as part of the RaceBaitr team, and for showing me over and over again what ethical work looks like.

Thank you, Cathy, Jenn, and the Black Youth Project team for offering me my first professional writing home and for having faith that I could steer it.

Thank you, Shanita and Da'Shaun, for helping me to be a better writer and abolitionist.

Thank you, Zen, for trusting me to care for you, even when it was hard, and for always trying to return care back.

Thank you, Michael Stout, Betty and Sasha, for giving me the space to dive deeper into our relationships and for demonstrating how to forgive without letting harm-doers off the hook. Thank you, Michael Hives and David, for proving there are no mistakes in love and for trusting me, too. Thank you, Justus, D'Aaron, and Ronald for reminding me that family is never lost, no matter how far they try to lock us away. Thank you, Bayna, for allowing me to be a part of your story and becoming a friend in the process.

Thank you to all my writing and scholarly influences, especially the Black feminist thinkers who laid the groundwork for this memoir.

And thank you to my best friend, my partner, my husband, Timothy, for reading everything I've ever written, even when you didn't have to, and always knowing what to say; for making sure I hear what needs to be said even when I don't want to hear it; for holding space for my anxiety and self-doubt without encouraging it; for fighting for a healthy version of us harder than I've ever seen anyone fight for anything; and for making fights feel so unlike the inherently harmful things I thought I knew them to be. I love you utterly and completely.

NOTES

Prologue: Misafropedia

1. When I reference Black people, I am speaking from my own experience as a descendant of enslaved people in America but referring to all people who descend from Africa. Experiences with colonization and carceral logics—beliefs rooted in policing, punishing, and incarcerating the socially undesirable—may manifest in different ways outside this country, but we all have had to fight those systems.

2. Kemi M. Doll, Cyndy R. Snyder, and Chandra L. Ford, "Endometrial Cancer Disparities: A Race-Conscious Critique of the Literature," *American Journal of Obstetrics and Gynecology* 218, no. 5 (May 2018): 474–482.e2, https://doi.org/10.1016/j.ajog.2017.09.016.

3. Ganga Bey, "Health Disparities at the Intersection of Gender and Race: Beyond Intersectionality Theory in Epidemiologic Research, " in *Quality of Life: Biopsychosocial Perspectives*, ed. G. S. Taukeni (London: IntechOpen Limited, forthcoming).

4. Roni Caryn Rabin, "Huge Racial Disparities Found in Deaths Linked to Pregnancy," *New York Times*, May 7, 2019, www.nytimes.com/2019/05/07/health/pregnancy-deaths-.html.

5. Todd M. Michney, "Beyond 'White Flight,'" *Belt Magazine*, May 31, 2017, https://beltmag.com/beyond-white-flight-history-one-cleveland-neighborhood-can-teach-us-race-housing-inequality/.

6. Trymaine Lee, "A Vast Wealth Gap, Driven by Segregation, Redlining, Evictions and Exclusion, Separates Black and White America," *New York Times Magazine*, August 14, 2019, www.nytimes.com/ interactive/2019/08/14/magazine/racial-wealth-gap.html; Alina Baciu, Yamrot Negussie, Amy Geller, and James N. Weinstein, eds., *Communities in Action: Pathways to Health Equity* (Washington, DC: National Academies Press, 2017), www.ncbi.nlm.nih.gov/books/NBK425844/; see Elizabeth Hinton, LeShae Henderson, and Cindy Reed, *An Unjust Burden: The Disparate Treatment of Black Americans in the Criminal Justice System*, Vera Evidence Brief (New York: Vera Institute of Justice, 2018), www.vera.org/downloads/publications/for-the-record-unjust-burden-racial-disparities.pdf.

7. Evelyn Brooks Higginbotham coined the term "respectability politics" in her book *Righteous Discontent: The Women's Movement in the Black Baptist Church, 1880–1920* (Cambridge, MA: Harvard University Press, 1993).

8. When I reference Indigenous people or cultures, I am including the original people of Africa. With the guidance of several practitioners of African traditional religions, particularly my friend Preston Anderson, I have come to a deeper understanding of Black diasporans as displaced Indigenous people. Read more in my article on this topic: "Why We Need to Stop Excluding Black Populations from Ideas of Who Is 'Indigenous,'" Black Youth Project, November 6, 2017, https://blackyouthproject.com/ need-stop-excluding-black-populations-ideas-indigenous/.

9. Moya Bailey and Trudy, "On Misogynoir: Citation, Erasure, and Plagiarism," *Feminist Media Studies* 18, no. 4 (March 13, 2018): 762–768, https://doi.org/10.1080/14680777.2018.1447395.

10. Luke Darby, "Florida Police Officer Arrested and Handcuffed a 6-Year-Old Black Girl for a Tantrum in Class," *GQ*, September 23, 2019, www. gq.com/story/six-year-old-black-girl-arrested-for-a-tantrum.

Chapter 1: Carceral Dissonance

11. See Michelle Kessel and Jessica Hopper, "Victims Speak Out about North Carolina Sterilization Program, Which Targeted Women, Young Girls and Blacks," Rocker Center, November 7, 2011, http://rockcenter. nbcnews.com/_news/2011/11/07/8640744-victims-speak-out-about-

north-carolina-sterilization-program-which-targeted-women-young-girls-and-blacks?lite.

12. See Dave Colon, "MTA Will Spend $249M on New Cops to Save $200M on Fare Evasion," *StreetsBlog NYC*, November 14, 2019, https://nyc.streetsblog.org/2019/11/14/mta-will-spend-249m-on-new-cops-to-save-200m-on-fare-evasion/.

13. See Terry Nguyen, "Fare Evasion Costs Cities Millions. But Will Cracking Down on It Solve Anything?," Vox, November 15, 2019, www.vox.com/the-goods/2019/11/12/20959914/fare-evasion-costs-cities-millions.

14. See Henry Grabar, "Andrew Cuomo and the Curious Case of the $81 Million Elevator," *Slate*, September 20, 2019, https://slate.com/business/2019/09/mta-elevators-are-the-perfect-example-of-new-yorks-cost-problems.html.

15. See Brian M. Rosenthal, "The Most Expensive Mile of Subway Track on Earth," *New York Times*, December 28, 2017, www.nytimes.com/2017/12/28/nyregion/new-york-subway-construction-costs.html.

16. See Kristopher S. Cunningham, Danna A. Spears, and Melanie Care, "Evaluation of Cardiac Hypertrophy in the Setting of Sudden Cardiac Death," *Forensic Sciences Research* 4, no. 3 (2019): 223–240, https://doi.org/10.1080/20961790.2019.1633761.

17. See Kevin Rashid Johnson, "Prison Labor Is Modern Slavery. I've Been Sent to Solitary for Speaking Out," *Guardian*, August 23, 2018, www.theguardian.com/commentisfree/2018/aug/23/prisoner-speak-out-american-slave-labor-strike; Peter Wagner and Bernadette Rabuy, "Following the Money of Mass Incarceration," Prison Policy Initiative, www.prisonpolicy.org/reports/money.html; and Alex Mayyasi, "How Does Prison Gerrymandering Work?," *Priceonomics*, October 20, 2015, https://priceonomics.com/how-does-prison-gerrymandering-work/.

18. Saidiya V. Hartman, *Scenes of Subjection: Terror, Slavery, and Self-Making in Nineteenth Century America* (Oxford: Oxford University Press, 1997), 19.

Chapter 3: Nowalaters

19. Although I want to stay faithful to how my mother's teaching job was described, I must acknowledge the dangers of the term "at-risk," which lets the systems that pose risks for Black children off the hook, thereby placing responsibility for avoiding such risks onto the children themselves. In place of this term, it is important to note what the risks actually are—in this case carceral punishment—and who actually causes them—in this case a carceral system that neglects and abuses Black children.

20. See Jessica Glenza, "'I Felt Like a Five-Year-Old Holding On to Hulk Hogan': Darren Wilson in His Own Words," *Guardian*, November 25, 2014, www.theguardian.com/us-news/2014/nov/25/darren-wilson-testimony-ferguson-michael-brown.

21. See Robert L. Smith, "Census Shows Cleveland Is the Second-Poorest City in the United States," Cleveland.com, January 12, 2019, www.cleveland.com/metro/2010/09/census_shows_cleveland_is_the.html.

22. See Rachel Dissell, "'An Uphill Battle': Lead Poisoning Stunts Students' Learning while Cleveland Leaders Fail to Tackle Lingering Problem," Cleveland.com, January 6, 2019, www.cleveland.com/metro/2019/01/an-uphill-battle-lead-poisoning-stunts-students-learning-while-cleveland-leaders-fail-to-tackle-lingering-problem.html.

Chapter 5: D*mb Smart

23. See Greg Toppo, "GAO Study: Segregation Worsening in U.S. Schools," *USA Today*, May 17, 2016, www.usatoday.com/story/news/2016/05/17/gao-study-segregation-worsening-us-schools/84508438/.

24. See Constance Grady, "I Tried to Write an Essay about Productivity in Quarantine. It Took Me a Month to Do It," Vox, April 17, 2020, www.vox.com/culture/2020/4/17/21201878/quarantine-productivity-social-distancing-coronavirus-pandemic-covid-19-capitalism-ep-thompson.

25. See "Black Children Five Times More Likely Than White Youth to Be Incarcerated," Equal Justice Initiative, September 14, 2017, https://eji.org/news/black-children-five-times-more-likely-than-whites-to-be-incarcerated/.

26. See Michael J. Dumas, "'Losing an Arm': Schooling as a Site of Black Suffering," *Race, Ethnicity and Education* 17, no. 1 (2014): 1–29, https://eric.ed.gov/?q=Dumas&pg=3&id=EJ1025418.

27. See Keeanga-Yamahtta Taylor, "Barack Obama's Original Sin: America's Post-Racial Illusion," *Guardian*, January 13, 2017, www.theguardian.com/us-news/2017/jan/13/barack-obama-legacy-racism-criminal-justice-system.

Chapter 6: A Prayer for Limitlessness

28. See J. Crocker, B. Cornwell, and B. Major, "The Stigma of Overweight: Affective Consequences of Attributional Ambiguity," *Journal of Personality and Social Psychology* 64, no. 1 (January 1993): 60–70, https://pubmed.ncbi.nlm.nih.gov/8421252/.

Chapter 9: Representation Matters?

29. See Delano R. Franklin and Samuel W. Zwickel, "Legacy Admit Rate Five Times That of Non-Legacies, Court Docs Show," *Harvard Crimson*, June 20, 2018, www.thecrimson.com/article/2018/6/20/admissions-docs-legacy/.

30. Frank B. Wilderson III, *Red, White & Black: Cinema and the Structure of U.S. Antagonisms* (Durham, NC: Duke University Press, 2010), 11–12.

31. Christina Sharpe, *In the Wake: On Blackness and Being* (Durham, NC: Duke University Press, 2016), 116–117.

Chapter 10: A Prayer for Choice

32. See Melissa Healy, "Scientists Find DNA Differences between Gay Men and Their Straight Twin Brothers," *Los Angeles Times*, October 8, 2015, www.latimes.com/science/sciencenow/la-sci-sn-genetic-homosexuality-nature-nurture-20151007-story.html.

Chapter 11: My Gender Is Black

33. Hortense J. Spillers, "Mama's Baby, Papa's Maybe: An American Grammar Book," in "Culture and Countermemory: The 'American' Connection," special issue, *Diacritics* 17, no. 2 (Summer 1987): 72.

34. See Jo Jones and William D. Mosher, *Fathers' Involvement with Their Children: United States, 2006–2010*, National Health Statistics Report No. 71 (Hyattsville, MD: National Center for Health Statistics, 2013), www.cdc.gov/nchs/data/nhsr/nhsr071.pdf.

35. See Cathy Cohen, "The Radical Potential of Queer? Twenty Years Later," *GLQ: A Journal of Lesbian and Gay Studies* 25, no. 1 (January 2019): 140–144.

Chapter 14: A Prayer for Healing

36. See Nina Misuraca Ignaczak and Michael Hobbes, "Black People Are Dying of COVID-19 at Alarming Rates. Here's Why," *Huffington Post*, April 8, 2020, www.huffpost.com/entry/black-people-are-dying-of-covid-19-at-alarming-rates-heres-why_n_5e8cdb76c5b62459a930512a.

Chapter 15: Trigger Warning

37. See Mirror Memoirs, https://mirrormemoirs.com/.

38. See Carolyn M. West and Kalimah Johnson, *Sexual Violence in the Lives of African American Women* (National Resource Center on Domestic Violence, March 2013), https://vawnet.org/sites/default/files/materials/files/2016-09/AR_SVAAWomenRevised.pdf.

39. See Chelsea Hale and Meghan Matt, "The Intersection of Race and Rape Viewed through the Prism of a Modern-Day Emmett Till," American Bar Association, July 16, 2019, www.americanbar.org/groups/litigation/committees/diversity-inclusion/articles/2019/summer2019-intersection-of-race-and-rape/.

40. See Julia Halloran McLaughlin, "Crime and Punishment: Teen Sexting in Context," *Penn State Law Review* 115, no. 1 (2010): 135–181, www.pennstatelawreview.org/115/1/115%20Penn%20St.%20L.%20Rev.%20135.pdf.

41. See Jeremiah Agenyi, "Recidivism in the United States—an Overview," Atlas Corps, May 31, 2017, https://atlascorps.org/recidivism-united-states-overview/.

42. See Christopher Coble, "How Often Do Rape Charges Lead to Sex Crime Convictions?," *FindLaw*, July 28, 2017, https://blogs.findlaw.com/blotter/2017/07/how-often-do-rape-charges-lead-to-sex-crime-convictions.html.

Chapter 17: If We Must Die

43. See David R. Williams and Selina A. Mohammed, "Racism and Health I: Pathways and Scientific Evidence," *American Behavioral Scientist* 57, no. 8 (August 2013): 1152–1173, https://journals.sagepub.com/doi/abs/10.1177/0002764213487340.

Chapter 19: Abolition

44. Jill Stauffer, *Ethical Loneliness: The Injustice of Not Being Heard* (New York: Columbia University Press, 2015), 125.

45. See Elliott C. McLaughlin, "Police Officers in the US Were Charged with More Than 400 Rapes over a 9-Year Period," CNN, October 19, 2018, www.cnn.com/2018/10/19/us/police-sexual-assaults-maryland-scope/index.html; Michael Arntfield, "The Preferred Jobs of Serial Killers: Aircraft Machinist, Arborist, General Labourer and Cop," *Maclean's*, May 9, 2018, www.macleans.ca/society/the-preferred-jobs-of-serial-killers-aircraft-machinist-arborist-general-labourer-and-cop/; and Matthew Spina, "When a Protector Becomes a Predator," November 22, 2015, https://s3.amazonaws.com/bncore/projects/abusing-the-law/index.html?fbclid=IwAR3JX9zOrThZTdr9CpBMwvrSJ6soVRLT_dj_9i7K99AbY5PVuyuagrGyu6o.

46. See Amber Butts, "No One Is Obligated to Remain: Consent, Agency and Supporting Loved Ones Who Want to Let Go," RaceBaitr, September 26, 2018, https://racebaitr.com/2018/09/26/no-one-is-obligated-to-remain-consent-agency-supporting-loved-ones-who-want-to-let-go/.

ABOUT THE AUTHOR

Photo © Brandon Nick

Hari Ziyad is a cultural critic, a screenwriter, and the editor in chief of RaceBaitr. They are a 2021 Lambda Literary Fellow, and their writing has been featured in BuzzFeed, *Out*, the *Guardian*, *Paste* magazine, and the academic journal *Critical Ethnic Studies*, among other publications. Previously they were the managing editor of the Black Youth Project and a script consultant on the television series *David Makes Man*. Hari spends their all-too-rare free time trying to get their friends to give the latest generation of R & B starlets a chance and attempting to entertain their always very unbothered pit bull mix, Khione. For more information about the author, visit www.hariziyad.com.